THE SOCIAL ECONOMY

THE SOCIAL ECONOMY

International Perspectives on Economic Solidarity

EDITED BY ASH AMIN

Zed Books

LONDON & NEW YORK

The Social Economy: International Perspectives on Economic Solidarity was first published in 2009 by Zed Books Ltd, 7 Cynthia Street, London N1 9JF, UK and Room 400, 175 Fifth Avenue, New York, NY 10010, USA

www.zedbooks.co.uk

Editorial copyright © Ash Amin 2009
Copyright in this collection © Zed Books 2009

The right of Ash Amin to be identified as the editor of this work has been asserted by him in accordance with the Copyright, Designs and Patents Act, 1988

Designed and typeset in Monotype Garamond by illuminati,

FSC
Mixed Sources
Product group from well-managed
forests and other controlled sources
Cert no. SGS-COC-2953
www.fsc.org
© 1996 Forest Stewardship Council

Grosmont, www.illuminatibooks.co.uk
Index by John Barker
Cover designed by Rogue Four Design
Printed and bound in Great Britain by CPI
Antony Rowe, Chippenham and Eastbourne

Distributed in the USA exclusively by Palgrave Macmillan, a division of St Martin's Press, LLC, 175 Fifth Avenue, New York, NY 10010, USA

A catalogue record for this book is available from the British Library
Library of Congress Cataloging in Publication Data available

ISBN 978 1 84813 281 8 hb
ISBN 978 1 84813 282 5 pb
ISBN 978 1 84813 283 2 eb

Contents

Figures, tables and boxes

Acknowledgements

This book is the product of an international symposium on the social economy held at Durham University in March 2008. The symposium was funded by the UK Economic and Social Research Council (ESRC) and OneNorthEast (ONE), the regional development agency for north-east England.

I am grateful to Pat Richie, then Director of Strategy at ONE, and to the ESRC for supporting the symposium. I am also grateful to Ray Hudson, my co-investigator on a two-year project on ethnographies of the UK social economy funded by the ESRC (RES-000–23–0987), which concluded with this symposium.

I also wish to thank participants at the March event for making it such a stimulating occasion, especially Roger Spear, Neil Stott, Jonathan Darling, Helen Wilson and José Vigil for offering written accounts of the discussion. My gratitude also to Lynn Barclay for helping to edit Chapter 7.

Finally, my sincerest thanks to Kimberly Armstrong for organizing the symposium and helping to put the book together; two ordeals that made considerable demands on her time.

PART I

Conceptual dilemmas

I

Locating the social economy

Ash Amin

As economic crisis continues to spread around the globe, questions are being asked about what will follow. Even mainstream opinion, so sure about the market economy, is asking whether capitalism can survive in its present form. There is increasing talk of stringent economic regulation and the need to temper greed and individualism, make the economy work for human and social development, return control of the economy to states and stakeholders, and harness economic progress to social and environmental sustainability. The search seems to be on for a kinder, greener, less unequal and more redistributive capitalism. No doubt the intensity of this search will depend upon how well market capitalism recovers from the crisis.

The critics of capitalism see the present time as an opportunity to move on, to alter radically the meaning and social status of the economy, so that the inequality, egotism and recurrent crises built in to capitalism can be overcome. For socialists, Greens, communitarians, and other anti-capitalists, the current finance-led meltdown is the symptom of a deeper systemic flaw, necessitating a different kind of economic system. They argue that a new system should allow diverse forms of social ownership, harness finance to productive use, mobilize local resources and capabilities, serve social and developmental needs, empower producers and consumers, and reinforce human solidarity and ethical care. It must do more than socialize the market economy, by making money, markets and the productive system work for human development, ecological preservation, spatial equality and collective fellowship.

This transitional moment, with its pointed questions about the economy to come, provides an opportunity to assess the role and potential of the 'social economy'. Until a decade ago, the term, if known, was used mainly by the fringe, to describe activity in the 'alternative economy' (e.g. practices of non-monetary exchange, micro-finance, ethical trade or community enterprise). In the developed economies, despite their legacies of unemployment, inequality and fiscal stress on the state to deliver comprehensive welfare, mainstream opinion held that responsibility for balancing economic prosperity and social well-being lay in the hands of states and markets. The same was true in the developing economies, notwithstanding their legacies of persistent poverty, inequality, economic inefficiency and state failure. Here, policy emphasis remained on making markets work, building state responsiveness, improving the terms of international economic integration, and dealing with corporatism. Even in discourse on transition towards a needs-driven, non-capitalist economy, the social economy barely featured.

The social economy then, as today, was understood as commercial and non-commercial activity largely in the hands of third-sector or community organizations that gives priority to meeting social (and environmental) needs before profit maximization. Typically, this would include community-based organizations employing young mothers to provide affordable crèche facilities to low-wage families in a poor neighbourhood or worker-owned enterprise or non-profit organization making goods from recycled materials for low-income households. This kind of engagement in the economy was considered to be residual or marginal, at best a temporary solution in communities and spaces bypassed or damaged by markets and states. The social economy was not expected to contribute in any significant way to job generation, market formation and wealth creation. Exceptions such as the thriving social co-operatives in parts of Spain and in Italy, or social enterprises in regions such as Quebec managing to combine market and welfare roles, were reviewed as examples of success against the grain of private-sector and state centrality.

In the last decade, the term 'social economy', or variants such as 'solidarity economy', have become more widely used in academic and policy discourse, within both developing and developed economies. Most significantly, the understanding of its status has changed in quite radical ways. The social economy is no longer seen as a histori-cal leftover or of marginal social and economic value. Mainstream opinion has begun to recognize the potential of the social economy to build socio-economic capability and tap latent economic potential based on welfare markets (Nicholls, 2006). This new interest joins traditional fringe interest in the social economy as real evidence of post-capitalist possibility based on social participation and an explicit ethic of care.

Governments around the world, supported by parties and institu-tions of varying political hue, have begun to introduce legislation and policies to stimulate and support the social economy, and increasingly on business grounds. Crèches, community farms, waste recycling projects, social housing schemes, neighbourhood regeneration projects, ethical trade and alternative finance ventures, community-based train-ing programmes, and so on, are being rebranded as generators of new work and new markets based on the trade of socially needed products and on the economic empowerment of disadvantaged communities. This shift in mainstream thinking is not entirely of a utilitarian nature. It also stems from a desire to make capitalism more 'caring', through markets and modes of delivery that are socially responsible, needs-based and stakeholder-oriented. It tends to view the economy as a heterogeneous entity composed of many kinds of market engage-ment, social coordination and ethical orientation.

It is precisely this emerging, but disputed, centrality of the social economy that makes this book so timely. The book examines the social economy from distinctive conceptual positions as well as on the basis of grounded evidence from a number of developed and developing countries. Uniquely, it brings together in English the work of leading scholars of the social economy who are also actively engaged in national and international policy formulation and advocacy. The book offers new thinking on three issues in particular. First, it positions the social economy in its wider context, especially in relation to state and market. Second, it shows how the dynamics, strengths, weaknesses and achievements of the social economy have to be understood in the context of local circumstances and legacies. Third, the book steers policy analysis towards differentiating general interventions from those that must remain context-specific (thereby rebalancing a discourse that has lost sight of the particularities of situated practice). These three aspects are developed in the rest of this chapter.

Market, state and social economy

While there may be some consensus on the growing role of the social economy in delivering welfare, jobs and economic prosperity, there seems less agreement on whether this should be distinct from the role played by market and state. In Chapter 2, John Pearce, a pioneer of the community business movement in Scotland, argues that the social economy must be seen as part of a distinctive third sector or system, marked by unique values and principles. Pearce defines the first sector as profit-oriented, organized around private interests, and exclusively sustained by commercial trade; the second sector as non-trading and involving planned provision of public services by the state; and the third sector as one engaged in both trading and non-trading activities, but characterized by community-based or social ownership and a clear commitment to principles of self-help, mutual obligation and social relevance.

Pearce is clear, therefore, that the social economy fulfils a specific function beyond market and state, one that would be compromised under pressure to adapt to the values and principles of the private or public sector. The application of market performance measures, for example, to evaluate eligibility for public funding (instead of measures consistent with the ethos of the social economy, such as social utility) risks diverting social enterprises from their core mission to meet social needs, build solidarity and regenerate local communities, by forcing them down the commercial route. Similarly, state use of the social economy to reduce its welfare obligations could undermine the often slow, personalized and multiple care that third-sector initiatives close to communities pride themselves in offering, under pressure to comply with standardized public-sector rules on efficiency, price and delivery.

This emphasis on the distinctiveness of the social economy is strongly echoed by other contributions in the book (see also Amin et al., 2002; Evers and Laville, 2003; Nyssens, 2006). For example, Julie Graham and Janelle Cornwell, the Community Economies Collective and Katherine Gibson, José Luis Coraggio and María Sol Arroyo, and Nöelle Lechat reveal that the social enterprises they have worked with (respectively in Massachusetts, the Philippines, Buenos Aires and South Brazil) consider market engagement and profit-making as a means to a different kind of economy; one that values social entrepreneurship, collective working, integrating work and family life, and social and environmental responsibility. The actors involved in the enterprises – and the researchers studying them – are clear that goals are different from those in the economic mainstream, regarding the meaning and purpose of economic activity, and its social and political role.

While clarity over goals might be unambiguous, their realization is far from straightforward. The above chapters, along with Jenny Cameron's chapter on social enterprise in Australia, acknowledge the very real tension that exists in balancing market/profit demands and social/ethical ambitions; a tension requiring constant vigilance and active management – sometimes at the expense of one or the other side of the balance, frequently testing the capabilities of ventures barely equipped to thrive economically. What is interesting, however – at least in the evidence presented in this book – is that these pressures are seen as a challenge to be addressed, rather than as a reason to abandon original goals. As Jean-Louis Laville observes in the final chapter, strong social and ethical motivations explain participation in the social economy, including the desire to see markets working for social and communal needs.

The contributions in the book also distinguish the social economy from the public sector. While they acknowledge the importance of links with the state in the form of appropriate legislation, market opportunities, support and recognition, they are also clear that the welfare role of the social economy is not to replicate or replace state provision. They caution against erosion of the welfare state through privatization or neglect to the degree that the third sector is forced to step in. They also insist that a qualitative difference exists between the state and the social economy in welfare provision. The latter is understood to offer more than a universal service, by working in non-standardized or non-bureaucratic ways, staying close to individual and community needs, and linking welfare provision to self-help, capacity-building and social integration. This distinction may rest on a certain caricature of the welfare state, by playing down reforms in recent years oriented towards responding to individual needs, working with other social agencies and building social capabilities, but significantly actors within the social economy – enterprises, volunteer organizations, representative bodies and intermediaries – continue to believe their welfare role to be distinctive.

That the social economy has its own specificity seems relatively uncontroversial. A more open question is whether the economy should be read as three separate systems (with the social economy unequivocally located in one of them) or as an entity differentiated along lines that blur the distinction between market, state and third sector, showing each domain to be highly variegated and possibly similar in some ways to activity in other domains. For example, it could be argued that a professionally run community crèche has more in common with a small state-run crèche that involves its clients or with a privately owned one that generates enough profit to offer free additional services to families than it has with a crèche that is managed by volunteers but lacks specialized skills, resources and experience. Similarly, a wood-recycling social enterprise employing people from disadvantaged backgrounds may be more similar in ethos and outcome to a profit-maximizing market leader with an active corporate social responsibility project in the same field than to a fair-trade company struggling to survive against cost-cutting competitors and forced to cut back on staff participation and empowerment.

Such examples suggest that while primary goals and legal status within the social economy may be distinctive, there may be more overlap with the private and public sectors in the areas of meeting needs, building capacity and social reintegration than is suggested by a three-system approach to the economy. Indeed, new thinking on the mainstream economy itself is revealing markets and regulating systems as highly variegated and hybrid. For example, work in behavioural economics, along with that in economic anthropology, socio-economics and cultural economy that is close to actors and outcomes on the ground, is showing how all economic activity must be thought of as an entanglement of material inputs, rules and routines, codes of conduct, norms and values, and varying desires, expectations, satisfactions and wants.

This work sees every domain of the economy as instituted, situated and socio-culturally inflected; calling for analysis of corporate practices, market dynamics, regulatory regimes, consumption patterns, and so on, as the hybrid of culture and political economy (Amin and Thrift, 2005; Sum and Jessop, 2008; du Gay and Pryke, 2002). It is thinking that draws on a long tradition of institutionalist and socio-cultural writing on the economy, including that of Polanyi, Veblen and Commons in the early twentieth century, and, in more recent years, that of heterodox economists such as Hodgson, Callon, Boltanski and Thevenot, Stark, Thrift, and Gibson-Graham. It shows that even the 'general' rules of the economy do not operate with iron-like certainty but as instituted habits. And, as such, they are as much habits of culture – conditioned preferences, settled consumption patterns, trading conventions, cultures of social interaction, traditions of learning and knowing – as they are the crystallizations of calculus, technology and operational formulas.

To read the economy along these lines is to be open to the assembled and evolving nature of every domain of the economy. Importantly, it is also to be prepared to rethink how the domains of the economy should be differentiated, in leaning towards distinctions of formative practice rather than conventional economic categories. For example, categorization based on economic conduct, as Gibson-Graham (2006) attempt in their typology of the 'diverse economy', might disassemble the social economy (and the third sector in general) as a coherent category. Gibson-Graham divide the economy by mode of entrepreneurial, transactional and labour conduct, to then identify variation in each of the three categories. Thus, transactions are divided between 'market', 'alternative market' and 'non-market' arrangements; labour between 'wage', 'alternative paid' and 'unpaid' forms; and enterprise between 'capitalist', 'alternative capitalist' and 'non-capitalist' organization.

In this typology, as Julie Graham and Janelle Cornwell reveal in Chapter 3, activities such as ethical trade and co-operative exchange belong to the 'alternative market' in terms of their transactional behaviour, as do also, however, activities such as barter, informal trade and the sale of public goods. In turn, the enterprise character-istics of these activities belong to the 'alternative capitalist' category, along with state enterprises, Green capitalists and socially responsible firms, while their labour practices appear in the 'alternative paid' or 'unpaid' segments of the labour typology, together with, but clearly also different from, indentured labour, housework and family care, or slave labour. Gibson-Graham's categorical descriptions and alloca-tions are not uncontroversial, but the salient point is that, depending on the mode of conduct considered (organizational, labour or trans-actional), the social economy can be placed in different segments of the economy, juxtaposed with other economic forms normally assumed to be categorically different. Such an expanded reading of the economy, treating non-capitalist forms as neither exceptional nor residual, and differentiating the economy by formative practices, invites a finer-grained reading of the social economy, able to recog-nize diverse practices that connect with markets and states in varying ways and to different degrees.

How the social economy is conceptualized in relation to the rest of the economy has a direct bearing on what is expected from it. In a three-system reading, the social economy can only play a distinc-tive role, in between or beyond state and market. It must address the limitations or failures of state welfare and private markets (by solving urgent social needs and preparing disadvantaged people and communities to return to paid work), or it must advance the cause of a different kind of economy – one that is more caring, needs-based, holistic and associative. Alternately, if conceptualized as a heterogeneous entity with varying degrees of proximity and overlap with an equally heterogeneous public and market economy, the social economy could be expected to work alongside, perhaps even in conjunction with, other actors including private businesses and state bodies, to deliver its commitment to economic engagement through social participation.

Situated practice

What the social economy can deliver ultimately depends on the economic, cultural and institutional context in which it develops. This shapes the characteristics, opportunities and room for manoeuvre of the social economy, which in turn affects local perceptions and expectations. For example, a barely developed social economy in a highly successful market economy might be seen to play no more than an adjunct or peripheral role, while an equally weak social economy situated in a context of extensive market and state failure might be expected to play a more active role in providing future work, economic opportunity and welfare. Similarly, a social economy showing signs of sustainable growth might be viewed as a remedy against capitalism in places where the latter is linked to extreme inequality and social rupture, but as a complementary field in places with reasonably well functioning markets and welfare states.

These powers of context are amply revealed by the international comparisons offered in this book, powers often ignored in academic and policy analysis. Thinking on the social economy remains fairly uniform, possibly because research internationally on the social economy is patchy and lacks qualitative detail, and possibly because policy interest in different countries has progressed in advance of the evidence. In contrast, the contributions here, which draw on qualitative evidence from a number of countries – Australasian, North and South American, and European – reveal important differences traced to local economic and institutional legacy, social and civic culture, and contemporary balances between market and state.

For example, Jerzy Hausner relates the limitations of the Polish social economy – still small, fragile, state-dependent, and focused on returning people into the mainstream economy – not only to the absence of an appropriate institutional framework, but also to the long-term erosion of social capital, especially under Communism. He argues that the development of an independent and vibrant social economy, for which there is ample economic opportunity and social need, has been hampered by a history of lack of public trust in the third sector and by low levels of community participation, social trust and co-operation within Polish society. In contrast, in her chapter on Quebec, Marguerite Mendell reveals how a long history of social activism and political leadership within the social economy, combined with progressive state recognition, has helped to build a robust social economy.

Quebec is frequently cited as a success story in terms of the contribution made by social enterprise – small and large – to employment generation, welfare provision and market innovation. This success, born out of grassroots response to severe economic downturn in the 1980s, has taken time to build, with institutional consolidation playing an important role in the process. Mendell shows how building a movement sustained by local activism, political campaigning and organizational consolidation initially helped to gather momentum behind the idea of 'solidarity economy' as a response to capitalist crisis, and later to secure an effective voice in mainstream regional economic and social planning. Gradually, official policy practice in Quebec has come to accept that the social economy has a significant role to play in the economy and that its representatives should be involved in decision-making.

Mendell and Hausner show how local success or failure cannot be understood without understanding local circumstances. However, such emphasis on situated practice is only in part a matter of geography – a question of national or regional institutional environment, economic climate, and social and civic culture. It must also recognize the micro-circumstances and development trajectories of individual social enterprises. These specificities of situated practice are undoubtedly affected by local context, but are not reducible to it, as shown by the case material discussed in the chapters on Australia, the Philippines, Massachusetts, Argentina and Brazil. The evidence shows how similarities or differences at the level of the individual venture can transcend contextual specificities.

A good illustration of the significance of enterprise-specific factors is the way in which the balance between ethical and business demands is handled. It is widely recognized by experts that reconciling market and welfare objectives remains a major challenge for social enterprises (Amin, 2009; Hudson, 2009). The commitment to social empowerment, meeting social needs and ethical practice is easily compromised by the pressure to compete in commercial markets, respond to stringent audits from funders, and constantly look for new income opportunities. And when a venture lacks business expertise or capacity to manage multiple and conflicting demands, it often faces collapse or is forced to compromise its social and ethical goals.

The ventures examined in the above-mentioned chapters have tended to reconcile such conflicting demands, even in quite inhospitable local circumstances. The United States, Australia, the Philippines and Argentina do not have developed social economies, robust third-sector policies or support structures, comprehensive or diversified welfare systems, or sufficient market endorsement of social enterprise. However, this has not prevented successful social enterprises from emerging, finely poised between operating in market niches of genuinely unfulfilled economic and social need, drawing on entrepreneurial and social vitality, and staying firm to the principles of social empowerment and collective obligation.

A recurrent theme in these chapters, explaining the survival and growth of social enterprises in affordable housing, food supply, gardening services, light manufacture and waste recycling, is that they remain community-oriented (responding to local needs as well as mobilizing local market potential and resources), rely centrally on social power (e.g. collective effort, social solidarity, moral energy), and grow incrementally and experimentally (e.g. building on success, learning from mistakes, using a profit-making arm to subsidize loss-making but socially useful activities).

Such elements of situated practice dig deep into the ethos of the single social enterprise, including individual motivation and expectation. Relatively little is known about why people get involved in the social economy – as entrepreneurs, employees or volunteers – and even less about how they perceive the experience or what they gain from it. Research on the ethnography of the social economy is only beginning to emerge (Amin, 2009). This absence has allowed sceptics of the very notion of the social economy or its role as a temporary labour market to claim that the sector is unable to offer more than modest goods and services or low-paid and often low-quality or precarious employment. They do not see the social economy as capable of providing stable, satisfying and empowering work.

The evidence here, in contrast, portrays a different picture. In Chapter 4, Carlo Borzaga and Sara Depedri draw on a comprehensive database on Italian social co-operatives to show that working conditions and job satisfaction compare favourably to equivalent work in the private and state sectors. Importantly, they also show that wages and job stability in the sectors have improved markedly since the mid-1990s, a change that increasingly allows people from varying backgrounds committed to public service and social solidarity to enter the social economy as a career. Borzaga and Depedri's findings show that in aggregate terms the experience of working in the social economy in Italy has been sufficiently positive to reinforce, rather than undermine, a desire to participate in an 'alternative', solidarity-based, economy.

Other chapters, interestingly, find evidence of similar commitment even in vulnerable social enterprises with margins and contractual circumstances preventing the offer of decent wages and working conditions. This commitment helps to sustain motivation and temper adversity, but importantly it also reflects a genuine desire to serve community and society, as well as to develop diverse capabilities. The awareness among social economy participants of being engaged in something different from mainstream work and its hierarchical rigidities and stark separation from community and home shines through the chapters on worker-run enterprises in Argentina, community businesses in Massachusetts and the Philippines, and social co-operatives in the rural areas of south Brazil.

These positive observations are not intended to gloss over or justify the frequently harsh and fragile working conditions in social enterprises. They are not meant to put social altruism and alterity before job security, decent pay and professional development. As already noted, social enterprises hampered by internal difficulties or external pressures do compromise their social and ethical commitments, at the expense of employees. However, the example of social enterprises with strong motivations, clear goals and collective ability to face challenges shows that applying standard measures of job satisfaction to the social economy tells only a partial story.

Building the social economy

The emphasis in this book simultaneously on situated practice and on the distinctiveness of the social economy compared to state and market raises an important policy question. This is whether common goals should be pursued through locally appropriate measures, or whether the goals should be changed to fit local circumstances. Currently, policy expectations in different parts of the world vary in quite substantial ways.

For example, in countries such as Britain and Denmark with established welfare states, but now pushing hard towards market reform, government interest in the social economy cannot be separated from the aim to roll back state provision by stimulating a 'social market' for welfare. Social enterprises are expected to provide a high-quality service at competitive prices as well as thrive as businesses in the open market in order to qualify for policy support. Critics argue, as already noted, that such a dual demand violates the distinctiveness of the social economy, along with threatening its very survival by forcing stretched ventures addressing tough social challenges to compete in the marketplace (Russell and Scott, 2007; Spear et al., 2008).

By contrast, in other advanced welfare states such as Canada, Italy and France, where the liberalization of the state has been less pronounced, and where an active social economy movement has succeeded in securing some public and policy influence, government response has been less instrumental. It is accepted that the third sector should operate in parallel to the private economy and the state, owing to its distinctive ethical and social ethos, despite connections between the three domains (e.g. large consumer co-operatives operating in the open market, or ventures subcontracting for the state or receiving public funding). Accordingly, business expectations, when tabled by policymakers, tend to be made with these principles in mind, which may partly explain why in France and Canada the social economy is called the 'solidarity economy'.

While in these developed market economies with strong welfare states the 'solidarity economy' is viewed as a parallel system, in left-leaning countries with weak market economies and weak welfare states, the term has begun to stand for post-capitalist possibility. With markets linked to continuing want and inequality, and states to suppressed social capacity and responsibility, the solidarity economy is perceived as a way forward to a fairer and more sustainable society based on popular mobilization to meet local needs. As the chapters on Brazil and Argentina show, governments and oppositions have begun to see worker co-operatives, micro-credit schemes, reciprocal trading networks, community-led initiatives, and social enterprises as more than experiments on the margin. Their survival and growth are read as a sign of real possibility in an alternative, non-capitalist, economy.

Such hopes for the social economy are far from common in the developing world. In most countries, the social economy languishes in obscurity, unsupported by the state, blending into the informal economy, frequently dependent on the energy of motivated individuals and third-sector organizations, and barely able to survive. It is a space of survival in the face of economic and social collapse, neither partner of nor alternative to the mainstream; only a glimmer of potential from grassroots organization in conditions of desperate abandonment (Appadurai, 2000; Chatterjee, 2004). Asserting this is not to dampen the success of examples such as those in the Philippines, discussed in Chapter 6, but to suggest – perhaps controversially – that conditions for the social economy to lead the way out of poverty and ill-being remain extremely weak in the developing world.

Ironically, public policy expectations in developed economies with highly privatized welfare systems such as the USA are not that different. Here, states understand their welfare role to be that of providing baseline support to the poorest and most disadvantaged people, leaving the rest to the private and third sectors. There is little official recognition of or support for the social economy either as a stepping stone into the mainstream or as an alternative mode of provision and social being. It is left to social enterprises and activists committed to the solidarity principles outlined above to interpret initiatives such as social housing, community gardens or neighbourhood improvement as steps towards an economy that values collective work, needs-based organization and care for the commons (Graham and Cornwell, Chapter 3 in this book).

Here, then, are four distinctly different policy expectations. Each one implies specific forms of intervention, ranging from minimal state support for the social economy (and increased burden on grassroots organizations and other intermediaries) and qualified state support for ventures able to demonstrate both welfare and market capability, to policies that recognize the social economy as a site of transformation towards a needs-based and solidarity-enhancing society. These situated differences cannot be ignored because, although they reflect changing political agendas and balances of power between stakeholders, they are also shaped by local legacies (e.g. the vitality and character of the economy, the traditions of state intervention in economy and society, and the history of the social economy/third sector itself). These legacies shape social economy perceptions and expectations.

This said, the policy steer in this book is decidedly against uses of the social economy to diminish state welfare commitment or to mimic the market economy. This is partly for conceptual reasons, with several chapters signing up to the 'third system' or 'solidarity economy' vision of the social economy. But it is also for practical reasons, based on the assessment that policies that value social enterprises for their market worth are likely to force practices that could compromise the core mission of the social economy to tackle social disadvantage and meet social needs.

The book does not suggest that markets and welfare goals are irreconcilable. Instead, it argues for explicit policy recognition of the tension between these goals, either by scaling back on market expectations or by helping to create slack by supporting the welfare functions of social enterprises. While John Pearce argues for new social audit measures that reflect the ethos and abilities of the third sector as the basis on which financial and non-financial support should be given, Jean-Louis Laville – drawing on EU experience – argues the case for sustained state support in the form of contracts, grants and incentives, and special credit or tax arrangements, so that the social value of the sector can be properly recognized and rewarded.

None of these arguments for financial support is a reason for creating state dependency or subsidizing inefficiency. In fact, actors in the social economy, as several chapters demonstrate, value their independence and the principle of self-determination. It is not state dependency or market protection that they seek, but a level playing field in which the social economy is able to realize its full potential. Constructing such a space requires financial support, but also other forms of support in keeping with the everyday dynamics of social enterprises, their ethos and their evolving needs. For example, as Lechat shows in the case of Brazil, state-sponsored research on the size, distribution and character of the sector has helped individual ventures to grow in confidence by knowing that they form part of a bigger entity, while the provision of shared space by local authorities has brought the ventures into contact with each other, helping them to share experience, learn from each other and explore joint opportunities.

Lechat also shows how incubation courses run by local universities have helped to provide vital training and advice to start-ups, as well as more specialized support later in the life of a venture, on matters such as managing the business portfolio or finances, or exploring new market opportunities. The opportunity to retain links with university academics who are also social economy activists is deemed to be of considerable significance, as it allows support to be tailored to individual trajectories at the same time as ensuring that originally agreed principles and values of solidarity are not compromised.

The need for policy intervention at different stages in the life of a venture – something that is barely recognized in current policy practice – is also confirmed by other chapters working with case evidence. In their four chapters, Graham and Cornwell, Cameron, the Community Economies Collective and Gibson, and Coraggio and Arroyo show how priorities and capabilities evolve gradually in a social enterprise, punctuated by certain critical turning points when appropriate policy interventions could make a crucial difference to survival. For example, many social enterprises that manage to survive the first few years through sheer force of ethical commitment and the enthusiasm of staff (aided by start-up funds, perhaps) find that continuity and growth rest upon the ability to make the right market choices and to manage the venture as a business to ensure that welfare commitments are not compromised as a result of insufficient demand or mismanagement. Access to bespoke public policy support at this make-or-break stage in areas such as product development, commercialization or business management would considerably ease the transition.

The contributions to the book also make it plain, however, that it is not only effective public policies that are needed to sustain a thriving social economy. State support has to become part of a wider field of advocacy and intervention involving other institutions. A social movement has to grow around social enterprises, acting on their behalf, commanding attention, facilitating contact between them, and providing varied channels of support. The success stories in this book are shown to be surrounded by ties involving local communities, public bodies, NGOs, activists, intermediaries, financial, political and legal organizations, and educational institutions. Frequently these collectives are joined together in elaborate networks of support, which include collaboration between them. Accordingly, several contributions prioritize the building of such relational assets as a policy goal, so that varied social economy needs can be addressed by a differentiated and sometimes overlapping set of institutions.

Constructing such a field is not simply about ensuring institutional variety. As Lechat, Mendell, Hausner and Laville argue in their chapters, it is also about building a mode of governance suited to the experimental, hybrid (e.g. combination of market and welfare functions), collaborative and democratic character of the social economy. The challenge is to develop a style of relational intervention beyond market and hierarchy, involving partnership between stakeholders and agile forms of response as needs and trajectories evolve, working closely with social enterprises, involving communities and respecting lay knowledge, knowing how to intervene strategically without instruction, and working together to generate a certain symbolism around the social economy (e.g. as transformative, ethical, empowering, and so on). This means, above all, committing to an open and collaborative approach – for example, willingness by the state, as shown in the chapters on Brazil, Canada and the EU, to involve the third sector in policymaking and to decentralize resource and initiative to its agencies. Within government itself, it means breaking down departmental barriers, perhaps with the help of transversal policymaking or a dedicated office of the third sector, to ensure that integrated policies for the social economy can be developed (and not at risk from being undermined by other government policies).

If a genuine desire exists internationally to lift the social economy out of the shadows so that it can play more than a marginal role in securing economic and social well-being, it is clear from this book that this task cannot be left to public policies alone, working in traditional ways. It requires constructing and valuing plural agency, and, above all, intervening in new ways that value heterarchy – multiple and relationally constituted governance for a new kind of economy (Stark, 2009). Whether a shift along these lines, harnessed to a vision of the social economy as a tool of socio-economic transformation, is possible in our times of economic retrenchment is another matter. The natural reflex may be to restore capitalism as we have known it, but past periods of transition have shown that new prosperity and well-being come out of radical innovation, structural change and new aspiration. Investing in the social economy on its own terms could form part of this bolder response to redefine, perhaps even transcend, capitalism.

References

Amin, A. (2009) 'Extraordinarily ordinary: Working in the social economy', *Journal of Social Enterprise* 5(1): 30–49.

Amin, A., A. Cameron and R. Hudson (2002) *Placing the Social Economy*, Routledge, London.

Amin, A., and N. Thrift (eds) (2005) *Cultural Economy: A Reader*, Blackwell, Oxford.

Appadurai, A. (2000) 'Grassroots globalisation and the research imagination', *Public Culture* 12(1): 1–19.

Chatterjee, P. (2004) *The Politics of the Governed: Reflections on Popular Politics in Most of the World*, Columbia University Press, New York.

Du Gay, P., and M. Pryke (2002) *Cultural Economy*, Sage, London.

Evers, A., and J.L. Laville (2003) *The Third Sector in Europe*, Edward Elgar, Cheltenham.

Gibson-Graham, J.K. (2006) *A Postcapitalist Politics*, University of Minnesota Press, Minneapolis.

Hudson, R. (2009) 'Life on the edge: Navigating the competitive tensions between the "social" and the "economic" in the social economy and in its relations to the mainstream', *Journal of Economic Geography* 9.

Nicholls, A. (ed.) (2006) *Social Enterprise: New Paradigms of Sustainable Social Change*, Oxford University Press, Oxford.

Nyssens, M. (2006) *Social Enterprise: At the Crossroads of Market, Public Policies and Civil Society*, Routledge, London.

Russell, L., and D. Scott (2007) *Social Enterprise in Practice*, Charities Aid Foundation, West Malling, Kent.

Spear, R., C. Cornforth and M. Aitken (2008) *For Love and Money: Governance in Social Enterprise*, Co-operatives Research Unit, Open University Press, Milton Keynes.

Stark, D. (2009) *The Sense of Dissonance: Accounts of Worth in Economic Life*, Princeton University Press, Princeton NJ.

Sum, N.-L., and B. Jessop (2008) *Towards a Cultural Political Economy*, Edward Elgar, Aldershot.

2

Social economy:

engaging as a third system?

John Pearce

In this chapter I aim, first, to identify the fundamental principles that underpin social economy organizations and that also distinguish them quite clearly from both private- and public-sector organizations. Second, I place the social economy in a wider context by describing how it can be viewed as a third, or alternative, *system* in the overall economy. Finally, I begin to explore some of the implications of the growing interest in and support for the social economy and what that means for social economy activists and for public policy.

The fundamental principles

It has in the UK become unfashionable to try to define social enterprise and social economy too tightly. Yet I believe it is essential, both to our understanding of and to the development of such organizations, that we are quite clear what we mean by the terms. There are a number of reasons for this. First, we need to know whether an organization is a bona fide social enterprise, especially if we are to develop programmes of positive discrimination (see later). There is growing concern about essentially private organizations masquerading as social enterprises. Second, society has a right to know if organizations that are recognized as part of the social economy are delivering the community benefit they claim; equally, social economy organizations surely share an ethical imperative to demonstrate that they are doing what they set out to do. Putting in place an effective social reporting method for all social economy organizations would begin to address this; and, in order to do that, we need first a means of identifying which are not social economy organizations. One of the principal recommendations of research undertaken by the Social Audit Network is that all social economy organizations should be required to prepare social accounts regularly and have them audited (see Kay and Pearce, 2008).

My starting point, therefore, is to ask, what are the fundamental principles which underpin social economy thinking and to which we should expect all bona fide social enterprises and social economy organizations to adhere?

First, of course, is the idea of *working for the common good*: seeking to have a beneficial impact on people and on the planet – and by definition ensuring that there is no, or at least minimal, damaging effect on people or on the planet from what social economy organizations do. It is common to talk about those impacts as the 'triple bottom line' – the impact on people, on the environment and on the (local) economy. In the field of social accounting and audit, we now expect organizations to ensure that their social accounts report on social, environmental and economic performance and impacts.[1]

In a sense there are two ideas lurking here. The first is the idea that the primary purpose of a social economy organization is to achieve a specific community benefit (or benefits), and the second is that in the process of achieving those benefits the organization operates in a way which is beneficial to people, planet and the local economy.

Social enterprises have taken some time to acknowledge that to be socially responsible in the twenty-first century they must be environmentally responsible, but there is now growing evidence that they are taking their environmental footprints more seriously and developing appropriate policies and practices which can be verified as part of their social audit. Similarly they are beginning to recognize much more clearly that they – even the most socially focused – have an economic impact which can be calculated and should be reported and that their economic practices such as trading fairly and ethically, buying locally, working with other social enterprises all make an important impact on the local economy and need to be considered and reported within social accounts.

Beyond this overarching, fundamental concept are other more specific principles:

- *Caring for human resources* Social economy organizations should care for, support and develop the people who are associated with it: paid employees and volunteers, management committee members and trustees, ordinary members and beneficiaries of the organization. This will cover not only terms and conditions for those who work but also the nature of the work itself – is it 'good work' undertaken in good conditions? It will also cover training and development such that individual as well as collective capacities of the organization's people are enhanced.
- *Good governance and accountability* It is axiomatic that a social economy organization should be independent of control and undue influence by outside interests and that its structure adopts effective democratic practices which ensure that key stakeholders and members are fully engaged. It is through making such practices work that the organization can be properly accountable to its identified constituency.[2]
- *Asset lock and use of profits* It is now generally accepted, first, that the assets of a social enterprise should be retained (or 'locked') for the benefit of the organization and its identified community or constituency of benefit; and, second, that profits should not be distributed for the private gain of members or directors – although of course people providing services (including essential capital) should be fairly rewarded.[3]

The Social Audit Network has recently published a research report that recommends that all social economy organizations should report using a common format in their social accounts on all the above fundamental principles, and has developed a draft format for this purpose (see Kay and Pearce, 2008).

Two further concepts are often associated with the social economy, which I personally would include in the 'fundamental' list, although this view has yet to achieve general consensus. These are:

- *Co-operation* Social economy organizations should work together collaboratively and build the sort of social capital which can serve to strengthen the sector, allow it to talk with one voice when needed and build on common values and aspirations. In theory many – maybe most – would agree with this, but when it comes down to day-to-day reality in a competitive world it becomes difficult to achieve.
- *Subsidiarity* This presumes that decisions and actions should always be taken at the lowest possible level in society, what Charles Handy (1994) has called 'reverse delegation', where power is only delegated upwards when there is a clear benefit from doing so and when the community is agreed it is for the best. This sense of local control and community strength has been at the heart of social economy thinking in the past but is now under considerable challenge from two directions. First, as some social enterprises grow they begin to operate well beyond their original boundary and that raises important questions about how they relate with those other communities (and competitors) where they provide services. Second, the changing relationship between the state and the social economy, when social enterprises contract with the state to provide services, brings with it some difficult challenges, to which I shall return later.

A modern mixed economy of three systems

The term 'social economy' has become increasingly accepted in the UK as a catch-all term for those organizations that may be distinguished from, on the one hand, the private sector and, on the other, the public or state sector. It is a good term, bringing together as it does the 'social' and the 'economic'. Figure 2.1, developed in 2003 by a colleague and me, seeks to illustrate a new way of understanding the role and importance of the social economy (aka the 'Third Sector') in relation to the public and private sectors.

FIGURE 2.1   Three systems of the economy

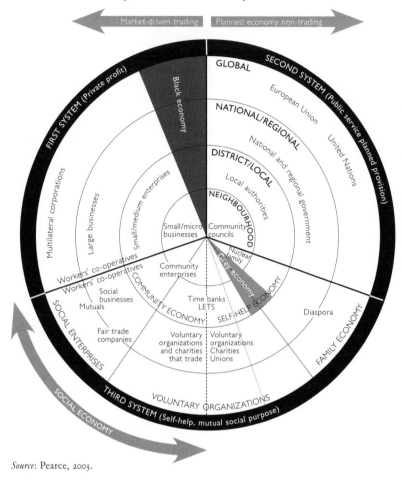

Source: Pearce, 2003.

The three sectors might be better described as 'systems' in that they represent quite different ways of managing economic – and social – affairs. The private sector is market-driven and private-profit-oriented, while the public sector is essentially non-trading and concerned with the planned provision of public services (although recent 'quasi privatizations' with public-sector regulators appear increasingly to be something of a hybrid model).

The third sector or system, which includes elements that are very market-driven as well as those that are wholly about public or community service, is characterized by the concept of our overarching fundamental principle: namely, working for the common good and with a general adherence to the other key principles outlined earlier. This sector, which we can refer to as the social economy, embraces a wide swathe of organizations from the worker co-operative movement, through the very commercially oriented social enterprises, to include voluntary organizations and charities, community organizations and neighbourhood groups. It embraces small and large organizations and stretches across (or down) to the domestic economy of families. It features especially strongly at neighbourhood level but is now a growing part in all levels of the economy, including internationally.[4]

It is now acknowledged that the social economy is a significant sector in the national economy – with all major political parties in the UK talking about its role and importance. In addition a number of 'mapping exercises' have been undertaken to try to establish just how big it is. That research almost certainly understates the reality. There will be many small community-based organizations, such as my local village hall enterprise, which slip under the radar; and there will be those, such as parts of the wider co-operative movement, the remaining mutual societies, housing associations, charities and other voluntary and community organizations, which rightly belong to the social economy sector – but which are not always counted and which do not always recognize themselves as part of a definable social economy.

It is increasingly hard to distinguish between a voluntary organization and a social enterprise. Indeed some describe themselves as both – or either – according to whom they are talking or according to the bit of their work they are describing. There are charities, large and small, which raise money, earn income and deliver services. The voluntary sector generally depends more and more on trading and commercially arranged contracts rather than on donated funds. Does there need to be a borderline between charities and voluntary organizations, on the one hand, and social enterprises, on the other? Or, as I believe, are they all part of a continuum? Are they not all social economy organizations with an identifiable common purpose to work for the common good and with a common set of fundamental principles?

It is interesting and important to reflect that not only has the Co-operative movement in the UK recently positioned itself quite firmly as part of the social economy but that its origins were as a small, volunteer-run community initiative in Rochdale in 1844 when some activists raised funds in order to provide good-quality and good-value food and household goods for local people. That volunteer shop, open only in the evenings in an upper room, grew to become a worldwide retailing, manufacturing and educational movement.

The concept of a continuum is dynamic and exciting because it means organizations can, and indeed do, change over time and shift position on the continuum but still remain part of the same sector. Indeed for some organizations different enterprises that they operate may be located at different positions along the continuum. The Co-op movement is the classic example of a project that started as a voluntary, part-time enterprise and moved rapidly along. A voluntary community association might turn part of its premises into a work-space in order to generate income and offer opportunities to small business as well as providing space for tourist information, a doctor's surgery and running a tea shop or community café. Tentative trading steps at the local market or even through a LETS scheme[5] may lead to the establishment of a new community or social enterprise.

The third system is a disparate collection of organizations which for much of the time often prefer to focus on what makes each subsector different from each other rather than on what they have in common. Recent developments in the UK to establish broad social enterprise coalitions and dialogue initiatives between the enterprise and voluntary organization 'ends' of the continuum are to be very much welcomed. For, in order to become a serious part of a modern mixed economy, the third system must be able to talk when it needs to with one voice and so engage with government and the private sector – and with other institutions. This represents a huge challenge to social economy people – being able to acknowledge common goals and work together to fight for them while respecting the integrity of the many different ways of doing things which constitutes the richness of the social economy.[6]

From community to social economy – a significant shift?

I now wish to explore some of the implications and tensions conse-
quent upon the growing acceptance of the social economy, first by
considering what we might read into the shift in the UK from using
the phrase 'community enterprise' to that of 'social enterprise'.

Most of my active working life has been spent supporting the
development of *community enterprises*, and that term, until relatively
recently, was a broadly accepted description of a range of organizations which sought to tackle social issues by engaging in trade and
which were owned and controlled by the community or the constituency they sought to benefit. Many of the best-known community
enterprises in the UK grew out of community activism – local people
working together to tackle a perceived social injustice or a community
problem. Thus Govan Workspace in Glasgow was created by a group
of residents supported by a community worker who wanted to address
the growing unemployment in their part of Clydeside as the Scottish
shipbuilding industry shrank. In London, Coin Street Community
Builders resulted from the actions of local people determined to
prevent their bit of the South Bank from losing affordable housing
and community space to office blocks and upmarket apartments.
Similarly in London's North Kensington the roots of the hugely
successful development trust was a campaign by residents against
the incursion of the raised section of a new motorway which was to
drive through their neighbourhood.

These and many other community enterprises came to business as
a means of either tackling the problems they had identified (setting
up a managed workspace in the case of Govan) or earning funds so
that they could pursue their community development plans (running
a car park in the case of Coin Street). As community enterprises they
came from the community and sought – and continue to seek – ways
of maintaining their community legitimacy through memberships and
through engaging stakeholders via various accountability processes.
As community enterprises they were not just businesses but institutions able to represent the interests of the local community and to
act as a mechanism through which the community could undertake
actions and set up its own initiatives without depending on the public

or private sectors. In that way community enterprises and the people who supported their establishment saw them as part of a process of community empowerment – giving the disadvantaged and dispossessed the chance to engage with the political agenda and exert some control over their lives and circumstances.

As we have seen a shift from *community* to *social* enterprise I would suggest that there has been a simultaneous or consequential shift from the idea of community development and community empowerment to a focus more on the delivery of specific services. There has been a shift from the idea of community enterprise as an entity for community action to an emphasis on social enterprise as a business model – viewed as not very different in its essentials from private business. The language of the business school has usurped the language of activism and political engagement. Instead of the idea of collective action where the community leaders learn to run business as a necessary tool to achieve their ends, the search is now on for social entrepreneurs – individuals with a business idea willing to develop it for the benefit of a community or for disadvantaged people, but often without any prior roots in that community or constituency. Whereas community enterprises are very much the agent of the people by whom and for whom they have been established, social enterprises can easily become and be seen as the tool of the state as they lobby for more of the procurement cake and are courted by all the major political parties as a means of delivering welfare and other services (often, by implication at least, as a cheaper way of doing that too).

Why do people do social enterprise?

This is the profound and fascinating question. In the heyday of community enterprise the answer was quite unambiguous. It was about empowerment, about community self-help, about a political ambition to redress a perceived imbalance of opportunity and to promote 'another way' of doing things – at Coin Street they proudly displayed a banner across the street proclaiming 'There is another way'. The roots of community enterprise were traced back at least to the Rochdale Pioneers and to the aspirations that ordinary working people should have greater control over their lives and be able to challenge successfully the power both of the state and of the private sector.

I wonder if that political edge is still there in the age of social enterprise as government seeks to co-opt not only social enterprises but the wider social economy as its 'partner' in service delivery? Maybe that does represent an opportunity to become bigger and more respected players in the economy, but surely it is also a threat to the essential independence of a third system which can challenge and which can show that there is a different way of doing things? Therein lies perhaps the greatest challenge facing social economy people in the UK in this first decade of the twenty-first century. The Co-operative movement has always nurtured its independence and indeed formed its own political party to further its social and political goals. Is it too fanciful to imagine the appearance of a Social Economy Party with a genuine alternative programme to offer?

Practical politics

However that fanciful notion plays out, there are some key points to be made regarding the nature of support for the social economy.

As all main political parties in the UK have made commitments to the social economy in recent years, this begs the question: 'What sort of social economy are they seeking, and why?' So far this remains largely unanswered and the social economy sector itself seems wary of making clear exactly what it stands for and why. Therein lies a huge danger of trying to be 'all things to all men', which can only be avoided by asserting independence, articulating the values and principles which make the social economy different, and building the solidarity necessary for political and lobbying clout.

Part of any support programme must address the issue of how to encourage the growth of the social economy through a programme of positive discrimination. There is much talk of level playing fields when in fact what is required are *tilted playing fields* – in favour of the social economy organizations – so that they can more easily win contracts and compete against rivals from the private sector. Part of that positive tilting must ensure that when social economy organizations are delivering services or creating economic activity in difficult areas the full additional costs they incur are factored into delivery contracts. If society wants the positive outcomes, then society has to pay for them.

A support programme must provide for, but not necessarily supply, the technical, legal, financial and other development support required by the social economy. That means acknowledging that the people best placed to understand the requirements of the social economy are those already operating within it, rather than people from the private and public sectors for whom it represents something they are usually unfamiliar with and often unsympathetic to, as it challenges their view of things. Within the wider social economy there are the required skills and experience – the trick which a support programme must pull off is to facilitate the use of that resource; and that, in turn, means paying for it.

At the beginning of this chapter I implied that it should be axiomatic for social economy organizations to report effectively on what they have done and what outcomes and impacts they have achieved. Society has a right to know if they are meeting the objectives they have set and if they are living up to the values they have adopted. That requires both a full '360-degree' picture and engagement with all key stakeholders on an even-handed basis. The UK and Scottish governments' enthusiastic interest in a standard form of Social Return on Investment for the third sector[7] displays a worrying trend towards control rather than support and towards making investing stakeholders (often the public sector) more equal than others – to say nothing of the assumption that all impacts can be financialized and given a financial value. This goes against the old co-operative adage that members should control capital and not vice versa.

Yes, social economy organizations should report on what they do and how they work for the common good, and we, as society, should require such reporting in return for offering a package of fiscal and other incentives to strengthen and grow the third system in our economy. Such might be the basic platform of our Social Economy Party!

Notes

1. In the corporate sector the triple bottom line is taken to be the effect of the corporation on people, the planet and shareholders. Social economy organizations are more interested in achieving a beneficial impact on their local economy rather than financial return on investment and profits to be distributed to the providers of capital.

2. One of the unanswered but intriguing questions about the social economy is its relationship to local government, which tends to view social economy organizations with suspicion and often as a threat. Yet local government represents active democracy at its most local level and no social economy organization can replace that. Developing confident and trusting co-operation between local government and the social economy could strengthen in the face of the powerful interests of both the private sector and central government.

3. These provisions are, of course, central to the recently introduced new UK legal structure, the 'community interest company' especially designed for social enterprises and which requires very stringent annual reports showing how assets are locked and how profits are used, and which also requires a social report each year – see www.cicregulator.gov.uk.

4. Were I redrawing the diagram now I would also extend the term 'social economy' to include all three 'wedges' to the left of the diagram's bottom section and I would probably include a 'family and a grey economy' wedge not only at the end of the social economy continuum but also at the end of the private sector, acknowledging how initiatives which start at domestic level may develop either as private-sector enterprises or as community initiatives.

5. Local Exchange Trading Schemes are associations where members trade with each other using a local, alternative virtual 'currency'.

6. There is a lesson to learn from the private sector, which, for all its talk of competition in the free marketplace, has the ability to pull together when needed and has created the institutions (such as the Confederation of British Industry and the Institute of Directors) to represent its interests strenuously.

7. In the summer of 2008 the governments in both London and Edinburgh announced their intention to commission work to develop a standard form of SROI for the third sector.

References

Handy, C. (1994) *The Empty Raincoat*, Hutchinson, London.

Kay, A., and J. Pearce (2008) *Really Telling Accounts!*, Social Audit Network, Exeter.

Pearce, J. (2003) *Social Enterprise in Anytown*, Calouste Gulbenkian Foundation, London.

PART II

International evidence

3

Building community economies

in Massachusetts: an emerging model

of economic development?

Julie Graham and Janelle Cornwell

The Alliance to Develop Power (ADP) and Nuestras Raíces (NR; 'Our Roots') are two long-standing community organizations growing in the fertile social soil of the Pioneer Valley of Massachusetts. In a semi-rural part of the state, these two organizations have an urban focus: the ADP on institution and wealth-building, affordable housing, fair employment, and financial services for low-income and disenfranchised people throughout the Valley; Nuestras Raíces on urban agriculture, environment, food security, and small business development for the sizeable Puerto Rican community in the small, historically industrial city of Holyoke. This summary snapshot of the ADP and NR belies the broad compass of their daily engagements in community-building and organizing as well as the dynamism of their non-traditional approaches to economic development. Indeed, the liveliness and richness of these organizations make it difficult to treat them simply as case studies of the social economy.

Precisely because the ADP and Nuestras Raíces are difficult to narrate or categorize, they function as a spur to the theoretical imagination. Recognizing them as economic organizations (which they definitely are, though not exclusively) requires us to expand our usual notions of economy, stretching the limits of market-based and capital-tethered conceptions and opening our eyes to a diverse array of economic practices and institutions. Recounting their stories forces us to rework our understandings of economic development and economic dynamics. Understanding them as part of a social economy contributes a sense of innovative dynamism that is missing from familiar treatments of the social economy as a (second-best) provider of social services, transitional employment and bureaucratically mandated social inclusion. Finally, and perhaps most importantly, theorizing them as building 'community economies' (Gibson-Graham, 2006) offers a new lens through which to read the existing economic landscape and, at the same time, suggests a visionary project of economic development for activists on the ground.

In what follows, we first briefly tell the stories of Nuestras Raíces and the ADP from their inception to the present, using ethnographic data from interviews and participant observation.[1] We then examine the community economy that each organization is in the process of constructing – understood as an economic space in which interdependence is acknowledged, negotiated and enlarged. Throughout, traditional notions of economic singularity, dynamism and development are unsettled as alternative formulations and practices come into view. We conclude by recognizing the constitutive role of knowledge production in the shaping, expansion and viability of the social economy.

Nuestras Raíces

> Imagine a little kid that might walk by a vacant lot on her way to school … She sees it full of trash and needles … it looks terrible. Then we start working with people in her neighborhood, maybe her grandparents or her uncles, to make that into a garden. And she sees people cleaning it up, building a toolbox and brightly painting it, putting up a fence, working the soil in the springtime and … things growing in there. Maybe she helps out to plant flowers, or works together with a group of kids to have her own garden in there, and … if you can imagine the transformation of that little kid's outlook on life, from seeing something in the middle of her neighborhood that was so ugly to seeing people that she knows, and even participating in making it be beautiful and productive. It's extremely powerful on the little kid's frame of mind, about what she can do and what her community can do. (Daniel Ross, November 2000)

In the early 1990s a Hampshire College student dedicated his senior project to helping Holyoke residents start a community garden on a vacant lot owned by the city. After he graduated, the gardeners started Nuestras Raíces to sustain the project, with part-time coordinators funded by a local community-based non-profit organization. In 1995, after several difficult years, 23-year-old Daniel Ross came on board as executive director and things started to take off.

By 1996 there were three community gardens and NR had broadened its mission statement to encompass 'community, economic and human development in the downtown wards of Holyoke through projects related to agriculture and food' (Ross, 1996). In 1997, using grants, loans, gifts and earnings, they took a mortgage on a one-storey building which would become the Centro Agricola – housing a greenhouse, a shared-use commercial kitchen, a restaurant, meeting rooms, staff offices, and an outdoor plaza for gatherings and events, with a colourful mural, fountain, plantings and seating for the restaurant. Community members, staff members, college students, carpenters' union apprentices, individuals on prison pre-release and substance-abuse programmes, and casual volunteers worked alongside skilled artisans paid below market rate to renovate the building, using plans donated by a local architect, building materials donated by local businesses, and a general contractor from Orange, more than an hour away, who donated approximately half of his time on the job. The Centro was completed in 2003, with $350,000 in grant money spent on the project.

Currently the Centro Agricola houses El Jardin Bakery, making wood-fired brick-oven organic bread sold all over the Valley; Mi Plaza, a restaurant serving Puerto Rican and American food using locally grown and community garden produce; Marine Reef Habitat, using the greenhouse and supplying fish tanks and reef tanks with corals and invertebrates for educational, scientific and decorative purposes; and four to eight small businesses using the commercial kitchen for catering, food processing and production of sauces. In addition, there's a bilingual library on agricultural, environmental and health topics; meeting space; classroom space for community education; and office space for staff.

In addition to the gardens and the Centro, the other major project of NR is Tierra de Oportunidades (TOP) farm. In 2004–05, after a

summer-long community-led strategic planning process, NR purchased 4 acres of river-front farmland in Holyoke. In 2006, the farm
was greatly expanded when the Sisters of Providence offered to lease
out 26 adjoining acres along the river for $1 per year. The farm oper-
ates as a beginning farmer training project and business incubator.
Each year ten to twelve businesses involved in market gardening and
livestock production (chickens, pigs, horses) are chosen for the season
by a committee of agriculturalists, including the manager of the Food
Bank Farm, from applicants who submit business plans prepared with
the help of NR staff. Customers and community members are drawn
to the farm by additional businesses, facilities and activities on site.
These include a youth-run petting zoo, nature trails, a conservation
area, a farm store, a pig-roasting business using organic pork raised
on the farm (this will develop into a full-scale restaurant over the next
several years), a two-day harvest festival drawing over 2,000 people,
an outdoor stage for events (rented for weddings, retreats, concerts,
family parties, company picnics, etc.). A large greenhouse has been
salvaged from nearby and a nineteenth-century barn has been moved
to the site to house equipment and livestock. In the future, NR plans
to spin off farms, as individuals with three years of successful farming
experience become eligible for beginning farmer loans of $300,000
from the USDA to buy their own farms. Already Francisco Fred, a
successful 2007 incubator farmer, has rented 2 acres of land in Hatfield
for 2008, doubling the size of his farm at TOP.

Today Nuestras Raíces is a national model for community organizations focused on urban agriculture, environmental justice and
economic development. Ten community gardens afford space to
approximately 120 families and produce more than $1,000-worth of
fresh organic food per family. More than twenty small businesses
started through NR's business development assistance are renting
farm plots or space in the Centro Agricola. The organization has
twenty full- and part-time staff members and an annual budget of
$750,000, of which 10 per cent is earned income – largely rent paid by
the businesses in the two incubators. Unlike similar organizations in
other urban areas, they receive no money from the city.

Nuestras Raíces is currently increasing its impact by addressing local and state policy issues, having formed the Pioneer Valley

Environmental Health Coalition and the Holyoke Food & Fitness Policy Council. These policy councils bring together youth, non-traditional community leaders and dozens of agencies to produce powerful community-led movements for healthy environments and infrastructure.

Alliance to Develop Power

When Caroline Murray became executive director of the five-year-old Anti-Displacement Project in 1993, her goal was to transform it from a housing *advocacy* organization to one whose mission is *organizing* tenants to preserve their affordable housing: in her words, changing the question from 'how can tenants be informed about what's happening?' to 'how can tenants control what's happening?' (Caroline Murray, November 2007). Over the next twelve years the ADP won $60.5 million in federal, state and local funds to purchase, rehab and transform 1,450 units of at-risk housing into collectively owned, permanently affordable housing co-operatives, creating the largest holding of tenant-owned housing in the USA.

Today the ADP's scope has expanded well beyond affordable housing. Their mission is broadly conceived as community empowerment, achieved via institution and community building, shared wealth and asset creation, leadership development, co-operative economic development, and mobilizing low-income and disenfranchised people through organizing campaigns to achieve lasting social and political change. In 2007, to capture their wide-ranging goals, they changed their name to Alliance to Develop Power:

> You know, a community organization's main goal is to build power … we added another focus to it which was the people who were marginalized by not having control over any piece of the economy … we use a direct action model of organizing where we go directly to the decision-makers … and that's the heart of who we are. (Caroline Murray, November 2007)

A key focus of the ADP is creating institutions that enlarge the membership, provide a setting for leadership development, support ADP organizing campaigns, and build the ADP community economy.

In 2001, they created United Landscaping and Painting (now United for Hire, UfH) as a worker-owned co-operative to provide landscaping and maintenance services to the housing co-operatives and employment for tenants. The business was capitalized by loans from Spring Meadow housing co-operative, among other local sources. UfH employs from six to twenty ADP members at any one time and grossed $500,000 in 2006.

A more ambitious venture is the Worker Center/Casa Obrera, which opened its doors in June 2007, with sponsorship from the local and national AFL–CIO. The Center organizes unorganized and undocumented workers and offers ESOL, adult basic education, democracy school and leadership training, worker rights training, a food co-operative, a legal clinic, assistance in filing wage and hour claims, and immigrant-based social networks. Currently they have 100 members each paying $52 per year in dues. To provide financial services to the unbanked, they recently introduced a debit card whereby members can load their pay cheques for a small fee rather than paying exorbitant fees to cheque-cashing establishments. Cards shared with distant relatives facilitate migrant remittance transfers and Worker Center dues can be automatically deducted.

The 'ADP has created business and capital holdings worth $45 million' and 'these community-owned assets contribute $20 million a year in cash flow to the local economy' (press release, 26 November 2007). Among ADP assets is 130 Union Street, a 6,600 sq. ft building purchased in 2003 with ADP affiliate institutions (largely the housing co-operatives) putting up the down payment. Currently three housing co-ops each have 5 per cent equity in the building, which houses the ADP staff, United for Hire, offices for one of the housing co-ops, and the Worker Center/Casa Obrera.

Membership in the ADP is for the most part 'institution-based'. Institutional members include the four housing co-operatives, which pay dues to the ADP (ranging from $12,000 to $20,000 annually); United for Hire, which pays dues as well as rent for space at 130 Union Street, and the Worker Center, which pays rent but at this point does not pay dues. For various reasons, United for Hire has transitioned from a worker co-operative to a worker-controlled business wholly owned by the ADP, which appropriates the surplus created by the enterprise. Some 50 per cent of the ADP's operating budget of around $600,000[2] is internally generated, with the other 50 per cent coming from grants. The Worker Center is also a dues-based membership organization, but the members are individual workers.

The ADP and its member institutions have separate governance structures. Each of the housing co-ops is a non-profit enterprise with its own board made up of tenants, which oversees the running of the co-op and decides how to spend the available money collected as rent. United for Hire and the Worker Center are member-controlled, with decisions about jobs and wages (for the former) and decisions about campaigns and services (for the latter) made by the worker members or in consultation with them. Both institutions are represented on the ADP board of directors, as are the housing co-ops, and the board takes a very active role in oversight and planning for the ADP.

The ADP itself currently has six paid staff and a contingent of volunteer leaders. ADP-trained tenant volunteers run many of the services and facilities at the housing co-ops, most notably the food co-operatives that distribute annually 180,000 lb of food, largely donated by the local food bank. Food distributions to 900 tenant families constitute approximately one week's supply of food per month. In addition, every summer the ADP provides two meals a day to 500 children in the housing co-ops, totalling 60,000 meals in the summer of 2006.

One of the major issues the board has dealt with over the years is the tension between the institution-building and the organizing missions of the ADP. The housing co-operatives, for example, pay substantial dues to the ADP and the tenant boards are intensely interested in the question 'what does the ADP do for us?' Caroline notes undefensively that this question arises in part because of the way she directs her talents and energies – 'I'm an organizer!'

> Whenever we had money, we would hire an organizer to do a campaign. And then we didn't necessarily have adequate infrastructure to continue to watch over the fruits of our labors ... in the last year we have focused on hiring different kinds of positions, so we now have a director of operations who's in charge of big picture stuff ... working with all the boards, all the ways we're sharing our money, all of the inflows and outflows. (Caroline Murray, November 2007)

They also hired a community builder to work with the leaders of each housing co-op to 'build *intentional* community'. In her first six months, the community builder surveyed members to see what they wanted and then organized youth mentoring and tutoring (led by co-op members and 'former youths'), brought in social services, facilitated access to government assistance programmes, helped coordinate the food co-ops, and organized social events as well as classes and training.

While the ADP has recommitted to building its community institutions, much of its energy is focused on organizing campaigns. An entire paper could be written on stories of power marshalled by ADP campaigns, which have achieved extraordinary successes, often through showing up en masse in the legislature or at the residence of someone in power – restoring food stamp eligibility to immigrant families, blocking punitive changes in state and federal welfare laws, publicizing abuses in local workforce development programmes, leading the national effort to hold Workforce Investment Act agencies accountable for actually providing job training, helping to pass an Economic Stimulus Bill creating $6 million in resources for community-based job training in Massachusetts, winning changes to Massachusetts labour laws protecting day labourers, playing the major role in national efforts to save the Section 8 affordable housing programme, and gaining over $300,000 in wage restitution for under-paid local workers.

The ADP is currently taking a lead role in the national Campaign for Community Values (CCV), a three-year effort spearheaded by the Center for Community Change and involving hundreds of grassroots groups in reframing the 2008 elections around shared values rather than separate issues. The CCV organized a question-and-answer session between eight presidential candidates and 5,000 members of community groups in Iowa. Because the boards of the institutions paid to send their members, the ADP was able to fly twenty-two leaders to Iowa for this event. As one of three individuals chosen to speak to the candidates on national television, Dedra Lewis of the ADP told the story of her daughter's severe illness and the loss of her job and health insurance because of staying home to care for her. There's footage on YouTube of Lewis speaking to Obama and the candidate embracing the 8-year-old daughter.

Building community economies
as a practice of economic development

Both Nuestras Raíces and the ADP see economic development as an important part of their mission. Yet their pursuit of this mission conforms only minimally to the familiar practice of local economic development that planners and politicians espouse. This cognitive and practical dissonance presents a theoretical opportunity: what if we were to take their self-descriptions at face value, acknowledging their success as development organizations? Perhaps we could begin to trace the lineaments of a new (because not yet recognized or formalized) model of local economic development.

Interestingly, the traditional version of development and NR/ADP-style economic development appear to have the same goal, which is a generalized increase in social well-being. Where they diverge, however, is that NR and the ADP keep this goal constantly in sight whereas traditional development practice has tended to emphasize means and measures rather than ends. Local development planners and policymakers generally do not open up the question of what might be the best way to increase well-being for a particular population or locale. Instead, they trot out the familiar development package – new or expanded firms and industries in export sectors, employment growth, a rise in per capita income. The connection to social well-being is assumed or even forgotten.

When we look at development as practised by Nuestras Raíces and the ADP, nothing from the old model seems to fit. Many of the elements in the picture are non-'modern', even backward-seeming – non-market economic activities, like self-provisioning and gifting, play a major role; unpaid (volunteer) labour is key to every activity; the core sectors involved are non-export (technically, non-basic) industries like housing and locally oriented agriculture. It requires a vaulting imaginative leap to convene these under the rubric of 'economic development', yet development is what these organizations say they are doing. Taking them at their word produces a deconstructive moment, blowing apart our categorical certainties. Suddenly what has been stigmatized as 'outside' development or 'anti-development' is prominently figured in the development frame. Non-capitalist

TABLE 3.I   A diverse economy

MARKET	WAGE	CAPITALISM
Alternative market	*Alternative wage*	*Alternative capitalist*
Sale of public goods	Self-employed	State enterprise
Ethical 'fair-trade' markets	Co-operative	Green capitalist
Local trading systems	Indentured	Socially responsible
Alternative currencies	Reciprocal labour	firm
Underground market	In kind	Non-profit
Co-op exchange	Work for welfare	
Barter		
Informal market		
Non-market	*Unpaid work*	*Non-capitalist*
Household flows	Housework	Communal
Gift giving	Family care	Independent
Indigenous exchange	Neighbourhood work	Feudal
State allocations	Volunteer	Slave
State appropriations	Self-provisioning labour	
Gleaning	Slave labour	
Hunting, fishing, gathering		
Theft, poaching		

Source: Gibson-Graham, 2006: 71.

enterprise, unwaged labour, non-market transactions – elements of what Gibson-Graham call the 'diverse economy' (2006, 2008; see Figure 3.1) – are foregrounded as resources that can be drawn upon to increase social well-being. As we deconstruct development through the experience of these two organizations, it becomes hard to believe (or at least questionable) that such diverse economic resources should be excluded from the development picture, and that the economy should have been so narrowly and capitalocentrically defined. Such is the power of deconstruction – to make the familiar strange.

Via the experience of Nuestras Raíces and the ADP, the domain of economy is enlarged and radically decentred, becoming an unstructured space of diversity, no longer colonized by the master signifier of capitalism. This dramatically opens up the field of economic possibility, bringing into view a wide range of sites and practices as resources for development. For NR, economic development is not a narrow project of capitalist growth but a broad endeavour addressing every dimension of social well-being – health and fitness, food and nutrition, environment, education, arts and culture, useful work, personal growth, community. They are not only creating waged employment for 'working age' individuals but involving people across the generations in productive economic activities that directly benefit them and the community. They are not just building human capital to suit the narrow requirements of the local labour market but reframing the undervalued skills of older men, youth and women as wealth-generating assets.

The ADP's activities are similarly broad and directly focused on enhancing social well-being. They include creating a community-based and community-supporting housing market; winning wage and benefit increases and restitution for existing jobs (as well as generating well-remunerated new jobs); creating shared assets and wealth for the ADP community; organizing the distribution of free food to member families; creating an alternative market in banking services; equipping disadvantaged workers to negotiate the labour market and supporting them through organizing campaigns; integrally linking development with organizing and empowerment. Rather than applying the one-size-fits-all prescription of capitalist growth (assumed to lead, however circuitously, to increased well-being), NR and the ADP approach the goal of increased well-being *directly* – starting where they are (low-income neighbourhoods), building on existing assets (agricultural knowledge and skills, access to affordable housing), and producing what people specifically need (this list gets longer as organizational capacity grows). Their demystifyingly direct approach to development means that each initiative can be scrutinized for its immediate effects on community well-being and adjusted accordingly. There's no generic prescription to roll out, no faith to be placed in mechanical outcomes, no long run to wait around for.

In recognizing these distinctive features of development NR/ADP style, we have moved beyond deconstruction and into the positive practice of renaming/resignification. Here the question becomes, how do we characterize the form of development practised by these two organizations? Is there a concept that could lend its coherence to their multiple, disparate activities and at the same time garner richness and depth from the association? Not surprisingly, given the authorship of this chapter, the concept that leaps to mind is Gibson-Graham's notion of a 'community economy' (2006). In the simplest terms, a community economy is a space in which economic activity constructs a community where interdependence is acknowledged, negotiated and often enlarged. Perhaps the most important 'output' of a community economy is a communal subject, a 'we' that emerges from the activity of building an economy through ethical decision-making and joint participation.

Both Nuestras Raíces and the ADP have the express intention to build a community on an economic base, and to build a viable economy on the strengths of a community. One of the ways they have done this is to ensure that the aspects and activities of the organization are economically linked, in order to strengthen the community economy as a whole. So, for example, a tenant who pays rent in one of the ADP housing co-ops is not only covering the costs of housing provision and maintenance, but contributing to a pool of surplus that the co-op board distributes to support the non-housing activities of the co-op and the ADP. Some of the rent goes to pay United for Hire (whose workers include tenants and other ADP members) to do landscaping and maintenance on the housing complex; some goes to support the food co-ops and the distribution of free food every month to tenant families; some is paid in dues to the ADP and is used to support its organizing mission, mobilizing community power around housing, labour, immigrant and poor people's issues. The rent also pays for the ADP's 'community builder', who organizes activities and support services for tenant members in the housing co-ops; it creates discretionary funds that can be used to pay for member participation in distant conferences and mobilizations; it funds ADP asset-building and equity holdings (one housing co-op contributed a loan to start United for Hire; three co-ops put up the down payment and own a share in 130 Union Street).

As we have seen, the economic links between ADP institutions generate half of the ADP's annual budget. The housing co-ops support the ADP through dues; the Worker Center, United for Hire and one of the housing co-ops support 130 Union Street by renting space; United for Hire produces a surplus that is used to support ADP organizing and staff. Economic activities also link individual members, knitting them into the organization. Weekly 'loading parties' for the debit cards, for example, are held at the food co-ops to bring members together in a space of economic community.

At Nuestras Raíces, a community economy is in part constituted through an internal circulatory system in which outputs from one production process become inputs to another. On the most basic level, the organic and ethnic food produced on the farm and gardens contributes good nutrition and cultural renewal as inputs to local household economies. Produce in excess of what is needed is often gifted to neighbours and other gardeners: 'The tradition of sharing is inside gardening itself' (Jaime Iglesias, garden coordinator, October 2000). The farm and market gardens supply food to Mi Plaza restaurant and pigs for the pig-roasting operation as well as produce for the farm store; small businesses paying rent for commercial kitchen space process foods grown in the community gardens or on the farm; the restaurants and the commercial kitchen produce waste that is composted for use on the farm and gardens; animals raised on the farm are fed farm produce and restaurant scraps and produce manure to be used as fertilizer; farmers join together in a producer co-op to market their produce at farmers' markets and local stores. Courses in business planning are offered by NR staff to community members, who then start businesses on a farm plot or in the Centro Agricola incubator; youth receive environmental education through being involved in diesel exhaust monitoring, opposing the location of a waste transfer facility near the farm, and engaging in environmental restoration, eradicating invasive species and creating nature trails for members and visitors, including customers at the farm store and the pig-roasting operation; young people have gained artistic and design skills through creating a mural that enlivens the Centro Agricola plaza. In these examples the educational work of Nuestras Raíces is either an input to or an outcome of the environmental, agricultural, cultural and community-building work of the organization. Individuals come in as youth with no specified roles or as cultivators of garden plots in one of the community gardens and, over time, become volunteer workers for the organization, leaders or managers of projects, board members, garden coordinators, environmental activists, and integral members of a productive community. The two incubators (TOP farm and Centro Agricola) nurture businesses that contribute rent to support the organization and maintain its assets. As these businesses mature and spin off to other locations, many will continue their affiliation with Nuestras Raíces, enlarging and strengthening the community economy through co-operative marketing endeavours that extend the Nuestras Raíces brand and multiply its markets.

The ethical dynamics of development at Nuestras Raíces and the ADP

So far we have seen how the process of building a community economy involves thinking through the ways that the activities, products and payments of an organization can contribute to strengthening and building an economic community. From the description above, it seems that one way this can happen is through continually 'completing the circle', making sure that one thing flows into another, that energies generated internally are captured by the community rather than allowed to dissipate and leak out. Starting United for Hire was a way of completing the circle for the ADP, eliminating payments to an outside maintenance firm; building the commercial kitchen and the restaurant was a way of completing the circle for Nuestras Raíces, ensuring that value-adding activity takes place within the community. Upon inspection, every aspect of these organizations' activities is geared to contribute to other aspects, strengthening the community as a whole. For the ADP, this is an explicit principle; any proposal for a new project or programme confronts the question, 'does it support the ADP?' But whether tacit or explicit, the vision of completing (and enlarging) the circle is part of an ethical dynamic of development for both organizations. In other words, it is a principle that guides decision-making about what the organizations do.

When we speak of 'ethical dynamics' of development we are stepping onto relatively untrodden ground (Gibson-Graham, 2006; Gibson et al., 2008). Development dynamics are usually understood in terms of structural logics embedded in macro-narratives that unfold

in predictable ways – mechanization, commoditization, proletarianiza-
tion and capital accumulation are the elemental structural dynamics
of capitalist development. Productivity increases, employment growth
and rising incomes are the signs of these structural forces at work. By
contrast to the oft-told tale of logical unfolding that undergirds the
Western development project, the development stories of Nuestras
Raíces and the ADP are unpredictable and idiosyncratic. Their
individual pathways towards increased well-being are governed by
the decisions of a community of stakeholders, not dictated by puta-
tive logics of economic evolution. Rather than attempting to trigger
a familiar transformation in a known economic space, which is the
aim of most development practice, Nuestras Raíces and the ADP
open up the economy as an ethical and political space of unknowing,
a space of freedom and decision in which we choose the forms that
our necessary interdependence will take.

The participants in these organizations have been concerned to
build economies in which the constitutive activities and organizations
support each other – economically, socially, culturally, politically. In
the process they have made many decisions about key issues around
which economic communities often negotiate. Elsewhere we have
identified these issues as four coordinates of ethical decision-making in
a community-based, community-building economy: necessity, surplus,
consumption and commons (Gibson-Graham, 2006). Phrased as questions, these become visible as targets of ethical decision-making that
often involves difficult choices and trade-offs, a process of balancing
between shared but competing goals and commitments:

- What are our unmet needs and how can we meet them?
- How can we generate surplus and how should we utilize it?
- How can our consumption meet our needs, allow for the gen-
  eration of surplus, and augment (or at least not draw down) the
  commons?
- How can we share, maintain and enlarge the commons?

Just a few examples may suggest how decisions around these
coordinates can be seen as constituting an ethical dynamics of
development. In a role play of a housing co-op board meeting at a

recent ADP leadership retreat, the issue on the table was whether or not to allocate more of the rent *surplus* to subsidize the food co-op as a way to address the rapidly rising price of food. Some board members argued that the funds should be used instead to undertake needed property maintenance. Here we can see a very realistic example of a decision whether to meet the *needs* of all tenants for affordable food or to maintain and restore the *commons* – the housing complex itself. In the straw vote taken at the role play, the food proposal won by a small margin. The reasoning was that temporarily deferring maintenance to meet a crisis was justified, but it was also recognized that funds for that maintenance would have to be found, perhaps necessitating a rent increase in the future.

An example that centres on *surplus* and *consumption* is that of United for Hire, which started out as a worker co-operative in which the worker members appropriated any surplus they generated through their work. For various reasons, including the difficulty for workers of running a business as well as doing their jobs, United for Hire is now a wholly owned subsidiary of the ADP. This means that any surplus that remains, once wages and benefits and other expenses have been paid, is appropriated by the ADP and distributed to support ADP operations and organizing campaigns. United for Hire workers, among themselves and through their membership of the ADP board, democratically agreed to this arrangement, which limits their potential *consumption* by excluding them from the possibility of profit-sharing. This limitation is acceptable because they see their *needs* as being met by excellent wages and benefits. So here we have an example of ethical decision-making in which a *surplus* that could have gone into a *consumption* fund for a small group of ADP members is directed towards supporting the operations and organizing of the entire community.

In the words of anthropologist Stephen Gudeman, 'A community makes and shares a commons … without a commons, there is no community; without a community, there is no commons (2001: 27). For both Nuestras Raíces and the ADP the creation and expansion of a commons is a central goal and achievement, integral to sustaining and growing the community. Since 1993 Nuestras Raíces has been 'reclaiming the commons' for a landless agricultural population stranded in a depressed urban setting, engaging in arduous negotiations with the city of Holyoke over access to land and water. This process of wresting garden space from the city has been accompanied by ongoing ethical decision-making within the organization about modes of sharing out the common space. Access to the community's land, infrastructure, equipment, skills and funds, as well as work and meeting space, is governed by democratically agreed-upon rules of entry and behaviour. These are administered in the gardens by elected coordinators, and on the farm and Centro Agricola by the farm director and executive director under the supervision of the board. The rules and programmes of NR ensure that the commons is continually being restored and augmented rather than drawn down or consumed. This allows for the enlargement of the farming community and increased services to members. Space is also allocated at the Centro and the farm for celebration and enjoyment – outdoor seating at the restaurant, annual community festivals, concerts and dancing draw an ever-widening group of people into the NR community as committed customers, gardeners, entrepreneurs, volunteers and appreciators. In the vibrant multi-use spaces of the NR commons, we see the concrete embodiment of an ethically negotiated space of interdependence.

The ADP has likewise created a huge commons in the housing co-ops, Worker Center, United for Hire, 130 Union Street, and the ADP organization itself. They have generated sizeable common wealth: shared and jointly administered assets of $45 million. On an ongoing basis, they create a common identity through a negotiated process of self-recognition (explaining themselves to themselves) and of self-presentation (explaining themselves to the world). This involves developing and disseminating a common language:

> In the past we didn't invest enough in the ongoing training and education of members of the co-ops and our business ... about how everything we do is different, that ... we are creating and we continue to *create this alternative economy* ... We need to do more of that type of thing to institutionalize our beliefs for new people that are moving in and new members of the co-ops and that's the lesson of the moment ... it's not like you win and then you're done ... 'the revolution is continuing'. ...
>
> When we went to Washington DC for fair immigration reform on 19 June [2007] with a busload of people, everybody from all our

member groups came ... this is part of our rebranding efforts about a shared fate – an injury to one is an injury to all and what does that mean? ... We've done some real intentional leadership development and conversations about building bridges, particularly between African Americans and immigrants, who you hear on the radio are pitted against each other ... when it comes to job training or low wage work. But in our organization we've been able to build a multiracial coalition in support of immigration reform because we've engaged in those conversations. (Caroline Murray, November 2007, emphasis added)

Here we see recognition on Caroline's part of the role of a common language in both marking and constituting a community. Through sharing wealth, engaging in joint activities, and speaking a common language the ADP is producing a communal subject, a 'we' whose boundaries are continually enlarged and whose self-recognition is a key to power. The ongoing process of producing that subject is an ethical dynamic of development, one which involves continually choosing to (re-)create ourselves as subjects of a community economy.

Principles and practices of ethical dynamism

Both Nuestras Raíces and the ADP have grown considerably from their beginnings in one community garden and two housing complexes, respectively. Not only have they greatly expanded the scale of their original activities, but they have taken on an ever-widening range of projects and properties. We have treated this process of growth as one of ethical dynamism, in which the ethical coordinates of necessity, surplus, consumption and commons are considered in relation to one another in negotiating the path of development. This may be a conscious or largely unconscious process for either organization or both.

In addition to the principle of balancing among the four coordinates, we see a number of other principles, visions and values as structuring the decisions and pathways of NR and the ADP. Above we identified the principle of 'enlarging and completing the circle'. Here we would like to examine three more, treating each as an ethical dynamic of growth: (1) each organization is 'community-led' and sees straying from this value as dangerous if not fatal; (2) each sees its evolution as 'organic' and 'logical' and places a value on one project growing out of another; (3) each values and fosters individual transformation to strengthen and grow the organization.[3]

1. *Membership-led, community-driven*

Nuestras Raíces and the ADP are both organizations with strong executive directors – this is perhaps an understatement – but at the same time they are resolutely and affirmatively community-led. Each organization has an active decision-making board of directors largely comprising members of the organization or its institutions (and for each ADP institution, there's also a board or leadership team made up of members). Daniel Ross and Caroline Murray see the boards as the voice of the community, and take their directives very seriously. For these community-led organizations, the imperative of growth (if we can call it that) comes from the community.

The unusual composition of the board at NR was a major topic of conversation on 'Institute Day', when other community organizations from around the region received training in the Nuestras Raíces model. Participants in the training were shocked to discover that no prominent business people or professionals or 'other people with money' sat on the board. The issue of community leadership surfaced again that day when one of the visitor groups complained about the difficulty of involving their members in the project of urban farming. Hilda Colon, who was running the training, said 'Maybe you shouldn't be doing that then!'

Asked where ideas come from for new projects at Nuestras Raíces, Daniel Ross responded:

> We're constantly hearing and constantly open to … ideas. It's hammered into staff that they've always got to be asking and always got to be writing down what people say. But we also do formal processes of evaluation and surveys and brainstorming sessions: 'Where do you want to go next? What's your next idea? How can we work together on these things? What help do you need from us?' (November 2007)

The idea of buying farm land came from a community-wide survey funded by the Ford Foundation and conducted by community gardeners and teens from the youth programme.

The reliance on member-led initiatives is not just maintained by ethical commitment but also through the discipline of failure – and the ethic of learning from mistakes. Each organization has experienced the very expensive (in terms of effort and money) failure of outsider-generated projects. El Jardin Bakery started out as an NR-owned business, when a baker from outside the community convinced Daniel they could make a lot of money selling artisan-style organic bread. As soon as they got the bakery up and running, the market changed: 'Everybody jumped into doing artisan bread.' Moreover, it wasn't the sort of bread that Puerto Ricans eat; nor, at $4 per loaf, could they afford it, so they had to market the bread in other parts of the Valley. Principal lesson learned: 'All the businesses that we do now have to come up from within the community' (Daniel Ross, November 2007).

Starting United for Hire as a worker co-operative was similarly an idea from outside, one that was not strongly supported by the ADP community. Members wanted jobs, but they could not afford to underpay themselves until the business got off the ground; nor could they afford to capitalize United for Hire with a personal investment of $1,000, even if it was deducted from their pay in small increments over the first few years. Under the current arrangement in which the ADP owns United for Hire, members run the business democratically but they are free of the co-operative legal structure and responsibilities.

2. *Organic/logical evolution*

The work on Labor Ready [a campaign against an abusive temporary labour service] led to the Worker Center because if we were going to shut them down, we thought that the Center could replace Labor Ready ... but it didn't really work like that so we just started a company for our members [United for Hire] ... And then the idea of going after Pynchon came along because United for Hire made a bid on a contract and ... [Pynchon] undercut the bid and one of our members worked there and knew why they could bid so low and how they were breaking the law ... So we went after Pynchon [eventually winning $130,000 in restitution wages] for fifty-two workers who had experienced wage theft. (Participant observation with Caroline Murray, February 2008)

Every step that's taken has been a logical outgrowth of what previously existed. So it's sort of grown in a logical way to fill a broader and deeper niche in the city. It's added ... not just one garden but more gardens; and it's expanded from mostly old men to youth and women as well. It's built on the original kernel of agricultural heritage and food ... to expand into a bunch of new businesses in an economic development direction and arts and cultural activities that are also building on that ... all of those really come from the same rural heritage – mostly from Puerto Rico. So every step that's come out has kind of built on what was there before. (Eric Toensmeier, farm director at NR, December 2007)

Relying on organic evolution (rather than solely on strategic planning) resonates with the familiar injunctions to community groups to 'start where you are' and 'build the road as you travel'. Often on that unfolding road, serendipity is a catalyst for what will become a major programme. In the early days of NR, a local primary school teacher brought some students down to La Finquita (the first community garden), and immediately

the old men started to teach the youth how to plant some flowers and vegetables, and the youth were very excited ... the next day, those same youth came down on their own on their bikes and brought more friends and they kept bringing more friends so Daniel Ross and the gardeners decided to start a youth program. And it just kind of took off from there. (William Aponte, youth and environmental coordinator at NR, January 2008)

As the youth programme grew, the participants themselves recruited new members, 'so they were all friends ... and to get a new person into the program, it was their decision ... the same way they decided to hire me' (William Aponte, January 2008).

Occasionally the 'logical next step' stretches the organization beyond its limits. At the request of immigrant workers, the ADP Worker Center developed a 'Know Your Rights' curriculum and provides trainings in the neighbourhoods of Springfield. After the training each immigrant is given a card summarizing their rights, with the ADP phone number on it:

So what's happening in our neighborhoods is the local police ... they're racially profiling people and then ... arresting people illegally and calling immigration officials illegally. So one of the results of us doing these 'Know Your Rights' trainings and passing out these cards is that now we're getting calls from people who are in detention – which we don't necessarily have the capacity to deal with. (Caroline Murray, November 2007)

To handle such calls, the ADP staff had to become experts on what to do when someone is detained, and all their time became devoted to rapid response. That's when the leaders of the ADP institutions stepped in:

Whenever staff are pulled in a direction, it's really our leadership that pulls us back to the center ... bringing us back to our mission – that we're not an immigrant response team. We're organizers. (Caroline Murray, November 2007)

Now the ADP has developed an external response team of local social service agencies and immigration attorneys to call when immigrants are detained. As this example suggests, each organization realizes that they cannot rely on organic evolution to operate automatically. Everything requires care and nurturing:

We have to make sure we *establish* what we begin ... We have to make sure that it works before we jump to the other one, and we are very careful in that – keeping in mind everything there is. (Julia Rivera, board chairman of NR, December 2007)

3. *Transforming individuals, developing organizations*[4]

The heart of community organizing ... it's about building power, but it's also about the transformative experience ... when people have their first time speaking truth to power ... it changes who you are. And for our folks – you know, for us – making sure people have that opportunity ... that's what makes it magical. It's not about buying a building. (Caroline Murray, November 2007)

On 30 May ... immigration officials stormed into a house with twenty armed guards and took people away in the dark. ... so Joel went to the house that night and met a woman who had spent an hour hiding in the bathroom, in the shower stall with her son. And he ... talked to her and within forty-eight hours she was speaking to the press ... and then she went to Washington DC and spoke before a rally of 2,000 people a week later. So not only seeing her be able to rise up out of one of the most traumatic experiences ... but also seeing Joel ... It's very few people that can do what he did with her. So for me that's what keeps me going ... the beauty and humanity of what we do. (Interview with Caroline Murray, November 2007)

Joel Rodriguez is a Puerto Rican/Native Canadian who, at the time of writing, had been a staff organizer at the ADP for two years. Before that he was a volunteer ADP leader. And before that, he spent more than five years in prison. Currently Joel is the lead organizer for the ADP's prevailing wage campaign to get contractors who are building affordable housing to obey Massachusetts wage laws.[5] At the Fair Immigration Reform Movement summit in Washington DC, with a busload of ADP members in attendance, Joel talked about building an alliance between the ADP, the unions and different worker groups – Puerto Rican, Mexican, Honduran, African-American – to win wage restitution from an employer. ADP leaders were partnered with union leaders to 'search for the kings' (leaders) among the worker groups, and to visit each one at home. By bringing the group leaders on board, the campaign got all the workers to stand together against the employer:

This was like one of my first goosebump moments that you have as an organizer. One leader stood up and ... said: 'Alright, if we go in tomorrow and we demand our money and they fire us, what are you guys going to do?'

They didn't look at the ADP, they looked at the *other* workers. You know, their co-workers. So one by one, the Puerto Rican leader stood up and he said, 'Well, if they fire you guys, we'll leave.' Until we had everybody in the room – I'm getting goose bumps again – they said, 'Well, we'll shut down the job! WE'LL ALL STOP WORKING!' (Joel Rodriguez, February 2008)[6]

From this successful campaign, the ADP gained several new leaders 'who are still part of ADP today and they go out and they talk to their co-workers and they talk to their communities'. The ADP also cemented its relationship with the building trade unions, which will strengthen the ongoing campaign:

It was a great combination; it was a great relationship ... But the most important thing is you have to maintain it. You have to keep on making it and building it. You have to caress it, feed it and give it water, give it life – just like us, for survival. (Joel Rodriguez, February 2008)

Together, the ADP and the unions got the state Attorney General to enforce prevailing wage laws and agree not to enforce immigration laws (which would exclude many workers from restitution payments). The next step for the ADP is a state-wide campaign to make prevailing wage laws broader in application and easier to enforce. Daniel Ross frequently identifies the central goal of Nuestras Raíces as community building, which involves working 'to help people believe that they can make changes, real changes' and teaching them how to do it within and through an organization:

> So getting people to believe in themselves as leaders and teachers, and getting them to participate in meetings and vote and build a strong organization, it's been difficult. People do like to plant and take home their vegetables, but building people into an organization that's democratic and grassroots and really reflects the changes that people want to make in the community is difficult. I think it's our true mission ... it's a challenge we embrace, but it's hard. (November 2000)

Meeting the challenge of building leadership (or even participation) has strengthened the educational mission of the organization. Not only do they offer courses related to their environmental, economic and agricultural mission – classes on nutrition, organic farming, business development, environmental restoration, and so on – but they have created a distinctive leadership development course culturally oriented to Latinos, a training for community garden coordinators (elected by participants in each garden), and a training for board members, since all members of the board are drawn from the NR community and projects and have little or no experience as directors of organizations.

> One of the things is ... Nuestras Raíces helped me to grow as a person ... First time I joined the board, it was something I didn't even know about – being a board member. And I learned a little bit here and a little bit there, learning and learning and learning and I grow, you know; I have changed ... Every day is a learning day, a time for you. (Julia Rivera, board chairman of NR, December 2007)

At Nuestras Raíces, every programme has involved transforming subjects as a way of also developing the organization, but the youth programme is perhaps most explicitly focused on those goals. Nalany Garcia is an 18-year-old who joined the programme when she was 9. Until the last few years, what kept her attached to the programme were the freedoms it gave her – getting out of the house, hanging out with friends, not having to work at a menial job, having some money to spend. But

> Now it's like, I'm *into* it. I'm really interested to learn the environmental things. ... it's like I'm always in the office; we're doing presentations; we're doing research; we're fighting against the waste transfer facility. ... So I *like* what I'm doing, you know? (Nalany Garcia, January 2008)

In 2007 Nalany was involved in NR's citywide asthma-reduction project, where she learned diesel hot-spot mapping. Over the course of the year the group gave numerous presentations on the project's findings, to community groups and even at Smith and Mount Holyoke colleges.

> One of my [school] principals made a little comment about 'people gotta go flip burgers' ... And I was like, 'No! Not *everybody* does that' ... I felt like telling her, 'No! I work in an office for environmental things and things that will help *you* breathe better in the future.' Sometimes I feel like, 'Damn, Nalany, I can't believe YOU do that! Like out of all people, YOU do that.' So I feel proud. (Nalany Garcia, January 2008)

Considerably less voluble than Nalany but no less involved in NR, Angel Ortiz has been with the youth programme for ten years. He is serious about farming and plans to study animal husbandry in college, and he's also deeply committed to Nuestras Raíces and its growth.

Janelle: When you were little, did you participate in this stuff because it was fun?

Angel: No, I wanted to learn about a lot more things instead of learning just a little bit, and I didn't know half the things that they were talking about at the time.

Janelle: Do you think being involved here has affected your life?

Angel: Yes. If I wasn't here I would be in the streets ... or in jail somewhere ... I used to throw rocks at police and ... we all used to fight all the time and do bad things before I came here. (Angel Ortiz, January 2008)

During the summer of 2007, Angel and an adult NR volunteer were invited to take over an untended plot at the farm. They grew nine or ten types of vegetables and sold the produce at the Holyoke farmers' market.

Angel: The other year we raised pigs and then I got into it more and more and more. I love playing with the pigs ... they tell me I'm the pig whisperer. I've learned a lot of things about animals ... soon enough I'm going to go to college for it.

Janelle: How long do you see yourself staying here?

Angel: I think I'm going to be here ... for a long, long time. Probably thirty years. Probably be the farm manager. Probably own my own farm later on. (Angel Ortiz, January 2008)

Lover of learning, animals, and pigs in particular, Angel sees himself not only as a future farm owner but as a manager, a vision that would have been largely unimaginable for a Puerto Rican boy from Holyoke just fifteen years ago and one that has been wholly shaped by Nuestras Raíces. In return, Angel is a committed member of the organization who puts all his energy into the farm.

Returning to the social economy

The unique successes of Nuestras Raíces and the ADP have allowed (and even persuaded) us to rethink both economy and economic development, placing the diversity of economic activity and the ethical practices of subjects centre stage. In the activities and achievements of these two organizations, we have discerned the emergence of 'community economies' where interdependence is acknowledged and built upon to increase social well-being. We have suggested that NR and the ADP are enacting a new model of economic development, something that we may find already emergent in other sites and settings. (Mondragón in Spain and Mararikulam in Kerala come immediately to mind.) We use the term 'model' advisedly, if somewhat recklessly, recognizing that there may be something transportable and replicable in the experience of these two organizations – if not in the details of what they do, in the more general process of creating community economies to enhance well-being, through an ethically dynamic process of democratic negotiation.

What does this study suggest for the ways in which we understand the social economy? First, it suggests that we can see the social economy as a space of experimentation, where familiar concepts are redefined and novel visions are enacted. For us as academics, orienting ourselves to the experimental quality of NR and the ADP means opening to what we can learn from them, refusing to know too much too soon. It means greeting their claims about economic development with curiosity rather than scepticism. It means treating failures and mistakes as grist to the mill (just as they do), the stuff success is made of, not signs that the experiment can never succeed. It means bringing a collaborative spirit to the academic role of naming and narrativizing their achievements, and those of the social economy as a whole. The goal is to produce a knowledge that strengthens the social economy and helps to build it over time, enlarging its creativity, capacity and credibility worldwide.

Second and relatedly, it suggests that we might treat the social economy as a pool of exemplary resources for communities at every scale. Here we have focused on community-based organizations with an economic development mission, a topic that speaks particularly to the re-localization movement, and to local governments and grassroots organizations working to build community and increase well-being. But the social economy is a treasure trove of innovative governance, social service provision, community-based resource management, conservation and restoration initiatives – indeed an endless list of socially and environmentally beneficial activities in every site and sector. Producing and disseminating an accessible knowledge of this proliferative variety could greatly contribute to the health and expansion of the social economy.

At issue here is the performativity of knowledge, the ways that it participates in bringing into being the realities it describes (Law and Urry, 2004; Gibson-Graham, 2006, 2008). The power of the academy to 'perform' the spread and success of the social economy should not be underestimated. Academic knowledge is transmitted via a global infrastructure of educational institutions whose professional graduates are charged with enacting academic models on the ground. If researchers were truly open to the radical and experimental energies of the social economy, 'another world' could potentially arise from social economy research and the training of social activists and entrepreneurs. Actually, that world is already here – it's just waiting to be strengthened and enlarged.

Notes

We are deeply indebted to Jenny Cameron and Katherine Gibson for their unstinting and supportive feedback during the writing of this chapter, and to Daniel Ross, Caroline Murray and their co-workers for their open and generous responses to our investigation.

1. Interviews with Daniel Ross and Jaime Iglesias of Nuestras Raíces were conducted by Gregory Horvath of the Community Economies Collective in the fall of 2000. In November 2007, the team of Janelle Cornwell, Katherine Gibson, Julie Graham and Ted White (videographer) videotaped interviews with Daniel Ross of NR and Caroline Murray and Mary Lou Symmes of the ADP. All other interviews and participant observation at both organizations were conducted by Janelle Cornwell between November 2007 and August 2008. The Community Economies Collective (www.communityeconomies. org) has had a relationship with both organizations since 2000.

2. This figure does not include revenue generated from United for Hire.

3. Another important ethical dynamic involves networking, alliance-building and collaboration with other organizations, institutions and individuals. Suffice it to say that an entire chapter could be written on this process, for each of these organizations.

4. We have a lot of interview material on the personal experiences of Daniel Ross and Caroline Murray as executive directors, organizers and social entrepreneurs, but decided not to focus on these key individuals because their presence is already so strongly felt in this chapter.

5. Prevailing wage is a standard that is set by a state or local government on projects that are funded with public moneys. Contractors on the project are required to pay the 'prevailing wage', which in most cases is the union rate.

6. Recorded at the Building Alliances workshop, Fair Immigration Reform Movement (FIRM) Summit, Washington DC, 11 February 2008.

References

Gibson, K., A. Cahill and D. McKay (2008) 'Rethinking the dynamics of rural transformation: Representing diversity and complexity in a Philippine municipality', unpublished paper, Department of Human Geography, RSPAS, Australian National University, Canberra.

Gibson-Graham, J.K. (2006) *A Postcapitalist Politics*, University of Minnesota Press, Minneapolis.

Gibson-Graham, J.K. (2008) 'Diverse economies: Performative practices for "other worlds"', *Progress in Human Geography* 32(5): 613–32.

Gudeman, S. (2001) *The Anthropology of Economy: Commodity, Market, and Culture*, Blackwell, Oxford.

Law, J., and J. Urry (2004) 'Enacting the social', *Economy and Society* 33: 390–410.

Ross, D. (1996) quoted in *Holyoke: A Weekly News Magazine*, 11 May.

4

Working for social enterprises:

does it make a difference?

Carlo Borzaga and Sara Depedri

It has long been accepted that economic systems rely on two economic actors: the state, which includes all public bodies; and the market, which comprises exclusively for-profit organizations. Since the 1970s, however, evidence has mounted of the growing inability of the state to respond to new demands for general interest services and to satisfy emerging social needs. At the same time, the market system has come up against difficulties in ensuring adequate income generation, which has exacerbated state failures to collect adequate tax revenue to underwrite public services. These processes have resulted in increasing inequality or poverty and a decreasing level of happiness.

In response to these difficulties, modifications in the role of state and market have been occurring. The state has progressively shrunk from its productive role, with an increase in the activities conducted by private actors in the market. Processes of privatization and liberalization have accelerated in many sectors of the economy. Moreover, although not planned, new spaces for action in the provision of general interest services have been opened up for organizational and entrepreneurial forms that had previously been marginalized or did not exist. In most countries and in many sectors, there has been extensive growth in the number and size of non-profit organizations, which has reinforced their productive role, resulting in many evolving into social enterprises. This development has had a revolutionary impact on the general interest services sector: although liberalization policies were aimed at increasing the influence of private, for-profit enterprises, an unexpected consequence has been the rise of a plurality of suppliers. This has also widened opportunities for citizens, not only in their role as entrepreneurs and investors, but also as consumers and employees of these new organizations.

Surprisingly, economists have not devoted much attention to this emerging pluralism and to the evolution of general interest services. They have insisted that the main effects of privatization have been on the creation of quasi-markets, or they have focused on a few types of not-for-profit organization. A comprehensive explanation of the evolution and institutional setting of welfare systems requires also analysis of why new socially oriented enterprises have emerged and why they have steadily increased in number and strength. Such research is only beginning, still lacking a robust account of social enterprises and the actors involved in them.

This chapter aims to provide a better understanding of individual behaviour in social enterprises by specifically looking at the role of employees. The chapter presents the results of a survey conducted in 2007 of a sample of Italian social co-operatives, a particular form of social enterprise. In order to analyse the evolution of work relations in these organizations over the last decade, the findings are compared to those from a previous survey conducted in 1998, covering a set of public, for-profit and non-profit organizations (including some social co-operatives) in the Italian social services sector. The analysis focuses on employment relationships and worker behaviour in social co-operatives and considers how they have influenced the recent growth of the sector. Some researchers have assumed that surviving the early phases of rapid growth in socially oriented organizations has tended to weaken the long-term ability of these organizations to employ people who are intrinsically motivated and altruistic (see Handy and Katz, 1998; Leete, 2000). If this assumption is true, the analysis of employee behaviour over a period of ten years characterized by strong growth of social co-operatives should reveal a shift towards the prevalence of economic incentives in determining employee behaviour.

The chapter starts with a synthesis of the relevant literature, outlining the basic assumptions and interpretive hypotheses usually applied to work relations in non-profit and socially oriented organizations. The second section provides an overview of the emergence and evolution of social co-operatives in Italy. The third section reports the results of our survey research. The chapter concludes with some observations on the ability of social co-operatives to promote a more plural economic and welfare system.

The state of current research

In recent decades, a body of research has reported the rise and consolidation of the non-profit sector. In quantitative terms, the consolidation of the non-profit sector has been characterized by a growth in the number of organizations, volunteers, paid employees and clients. In qualitative terms, the most significant change has been the spread of a large part of the non-profit sector into productive and entrepreneurial forms – so-called social enterprises. These changes have increasingly attracted the attention of researchers, who have been particularly interested in factors that explain this progressive consolidation. From an economic perspective, a main challenge has been to demonstrate that the presence of non-profit organizations can be explained in terms of efficiency: do these organizations address the failures of both public and private enterprises and do they optimize the usage and distribution of resources? Authors who have tried to demonstrate the higher efficiency of such organizations have focused mainly on the role of the non-profit distribution constraint in overcoming either market failure deriving from asymmetric information from clients and donors (Hansmann, 1980) or the inefficiencies of the median voter in the public provision of welfare services (Weisbrod, 1983).

However, while studying efficiency in non-profit organizations, the specificities of employment practices cannot be ignored. Both empirical and theoretical studies show that while non-profit organizations often pay their employees below-average wages, employee satisfaction and effort are frequently higher than in comparable for-profit and public organizations. Regarding wages, findings vary according to the sector of activity examined. Some general surveys comparing non-profit and public organizations (Mocan and Viola, 1997) and studies of single sectors (Anheier, 1991; Almond and Kendall, 2002; Mirvis and Hackett, 1983) find that wages among different types of organization are not substantially different. However, most empirical studies (Weisbrod, 1983; Leete, 2000; Benz, 2005; Borzaga and Depedri, 2005) show that wages are lower in non-profits than in other organizations – especially public ones.

The literature has sought to explain the combination of lower economic rewards, satisfied workers and strong work motivation by drawing on behavioural economics, psychology and experimental economics, especially their assumption that employee well-being and behaviour are influenced by a variety of factors: intrinsic motivations and other-regarding preferences, and not simply wage and self-regarding preferences. This assumption contrasts strongly with the one in orthodox economics emphasizing self-regarding agents interested only in maximizing off-the-job consumption and minimizing effort. Starting with Akerlof (1982), it has been demonstrated that the decision to accept a job and the behaviour of workers (in terms of effort) are explained by a variety of causes. Sen (1985) has also observed that people make decisions in line with their moral motivations: they undertake an action because it is socially useful, or because the well-being of other people provides them with individual pleasure (hedonistic motivation). As a consequence, different groups and individuals are guided by varying motivations. Furthermore, worker utility depends upon factors other than pay: for employees in non-profit organizations these factors are important, as demonstrated by macro-panel studies by Sousa-Poza and Sousa-Poza (2000), Skalli et al. (2007) and Clark (1997). These non-pay factors relate to individual or group characteristics (e.g. gender or education); characteristics of the job, such as job security (Sousa-Poza and Sousa-Poza, 2000; Blanchflower and Oswald, 1999; Bryson et al., 2005); so-called correlated characteristics of the job, including the size of enterprises (Schwochau, 1987; Miller, 1990), having an interesting job (Clark, 2005) and the level of involvement (Soohne, 2002); social dimensions of the job and altruism, especially when guided by policies of fairness (Benz, 2005; Valentini, 2005; Tortia, 2008); and other intrinsic motivations (as theoretically analysed by Frey, 1997) including social relatedness (Clark, 1997; Borzaga and Depedri, 2005).

Studies of non-profit organizations have adopted elements of these approaches to explain the high level of satisfaction expressed by employees. Attention has mainly focused on three dimensions of job satisfaction. First, other-regarding or social preferences seem to explain why non-profit organizations are able to select altruistic individuals (Preston, 1989) and are inclined to develop group loyalties (Almond and Kendall, 2002).[1] Second, job satisfaction seems to depend upon a mix of incentives such as job flexibility and stability, on-the-job training, and fringe benefits (Steinberg, 1990), and upon wider benefits such as involvement (Michie and Sheenan, 1999), autonomy (Lanfranchi and Narcy, 2008) and creativity (Mirvis and Hackett, 1983). These aspects are frequently identified as intrinsic motivations of workers (Goddeeris, 1988) or intrinsic interest in the job (Weisbrod, 1983) and appear significantly stronger for workers in non-profit than in other organizational types (Mirvis, 1992). Third, worker satisfaction seems to be related to high levels of both distributive fairness (Levine, 1991; Mirvis, 1992; Leete, 2000) and procedural fairness (Benz, 2005; Tortia, 2008).[2]

Summarizing these different approaches, a new model can be said to describe work and work behaviour: non-profit organizations seem to provide a complex and distinctive set of incentives that attract workers who are not predominantly driven by monetary remuneration (Bacchiega and Borzaga, 2001, 2003). In terms of incentives, the characteristics of the work offered by non-profit organizations explain worker satisfaction better than the nature of the organization in itself. Research comparing different types of organizations and the characteristics of the work done show that job satisfaction is only indirectly related to the legal status of an organization. The main determinants are the characteristics of the work that typically distinguishes a non-profit organization: greater involvement, autonomy, social relatedness and fairness (Borzaga and Depedri, 2005; Tortia, 2008; Lanfranchi and Narcy, 2008). Workers choose the organization and decide on the level of effort merited on the basis of motivation, individual and social. Furthermore, self-regarding preferences are complex, since, in addition to factors such as wage and job security, they also include factors such as the quality of social relationships in the workplace and potential psychological benefits. Salary is not the most relevant factor in determining choices, especially in sectors where the outcome is not strictly measurable in quantitative terms (Lazear, 1996). It helps to ensure that workers take a job, but their well-being and behaviour depend upon other factors. Such motivational complexity may well drive workers in different sectors, perhaps even the entire labour market. Rather than assuming they refer to a small group of altruistic people (who prefer to be employed in general interest services and freely donate part of their labour), analyses of employment relationships should consider the presence of an entire population of pluri-motivated agents. However, one of the comparative advantages of social enterprises may be their ability both to attract and to select workers with motivations consistent with the aims of the enterprises or able to change the motivational mix. Due to their proprietary and organizational characteristics, non-profit organizations offer their workers a mix of incentives.

In order to verify the above model of employment relationships, empirical research needs to be developed in two directions: first, by including all aspects of the job that influence a worker's well-being and decision-making; and second, by conducting longitudinal analysis in order to evaluate the development of these employment relationships. We adopted such an approach in a research project conducted in 1998 and a second one conducted in 2007 on a large sample of social co-operatives. Most studies lack such a historically comparative dimension.

The emergence of social co-operatives in Italy

Social co-operatives emerged in Italy during the 1980s and enjoyed a period of rapid diffusion over the next two decades. This was related to state crisis and also to the socio-economic and ideological context in which social co-operatives emerged. Initially, the Italian welfare state was centralized and characterized by a prevalence of cash benefits over services. Public service provision was limited. In the 1970s, the quality of state welfare services in a context of growing demand, and the emergence of new poverties – the so-called 'post-materialistic poverty' – proved to be sources of increasing social dissatisfaction. An ensuing welfare crisis was not only of a fiscal and financial nature, but also reflected the inability of the state to respond efficiently and effectively to the expanding needs of citizens.[3]

In order to respond to the new and growing demand for social services, private citizens began to mobilize by establishing voluntary organizations. The activists who set up these organizations were influenced by the ideas of both the 1968 students' movements, which challenged the traditional forms of social and economic organization, and the Second Vatican Council, which revitalized the social commitment of Catholics. As the organizations began to provide stable and improved services, the only legal form able to reconcile their ideas of solidarity and entrepreneurship was the co-operative enterprise. Recognized as social co-operatives by law in 1991, the organizations started to receive financial support from public authorities (Borzaga and Ianes, 2006; Ianes and Tortia, 2008). As a consequence, social co-operatives came to play a decisive role in driving the growth and supply of social services.[4]

Law no. 381 of 1991 established two types of social co-operative, the common aim of which was to 'pursue the general interest of the community in the human development and social integration of citizens'. Type A social co-operatives were to provide social, welfare and educational services, while type B social co-operatives would undertake agricultural, manufacturing, commercial or service activities to ensure the employment integration of disadvantaged persons. Although non-state welfare organizations existed before the law was enacted, the evidence confirms that the law encouraged the growth and strengthening of social co-operatives. In 1993, the year of the first national survey, there were 1,479 social co-operatives in Italy. The number of co-operatives, clients and employees has continuously grown since the 1990s. According to the most recent census carried out by the National Institute of Statistics in 2005, there were 7,363 social co-operatives; 59.0 per cent were Type A and 32.8 per cent were Type B; with the remaining 8.2 per cent organized mainly as consortia. Type B co-operatives are financially more autonomous, while Type A are strongly dependent upon public funds, with 72.8 per cent deriving their financial resources mainly from local and state authorities. The data demonstrate both the efficiency and the effectiveness of Italian social co-operatives and their ability to supply good-quality services. In 2005 social co-operatives employed about 300,000 workers and served more than 3.5 million clients.

Our 1998 survey of Italian social service organizations identified some characteristics of social co-operatives in the management of employment relationships (Borzaga and Musella, 2005; Borzaga and Depedri, 2005; Borzaga and Tortia, 2006; Mosca et al., 2007). This study investigated 228 organizations delivering social services (54 public bodies, 17 for-profit enterprises and 157 non-profits, 74 of which were social co-operatives), employing 2,066 paid workers (588 in social co-operatives). It compared the characteristics of social co-operatives with other organizational types. Overall, it confirmed many of the claims made in the literature cited in the previous section. For example, the evidence showed that workers in social co-operatives were paid less than in other comparable organizations: full-time employees earned about €770 per month (after tax) compared to about €900 in public organizations, and there were similar differences in hourly wages. Only in a few cases (and less than in public and for-profit enterprises) did workers choose jobs in social co-operatives because of the lack of alternative outlets. The study also showed that workers were attracted to social co-operatives for intrinsic reasons (e.g. the social utility of the activity, or the way in which the organization worked with its clients), but also by the opportunity to balance work with other personal commitments as well as to improve skills and capabilities. However, the strongest positive differential compared with the public sector concerned the opportunity to be involved in decision-making.

These motivations were also linked to levels of job satisfaction with specific aspects of the job. Although the level of job satisfaction as a whole was similar in public, for-profit and non-profit organizations, employees of social co-operatives were more satisfied about job autonomy, recognition of their contribution, job variety and creativity, relationships with colleagues and superiors, and provisions for training and professional growth. The lowest level of satisfaction was with salaries, but not markedly less than among public employees, despite substantial differences in pay. Further modelling comparing public organizations and social co-operatives demonstrated that the determinants of job satisfaction were different (Borzaga and Depedri, 2005; Borzaga and Tortia, 2006). For example, age was positively related with satisfaction only in the public sector, while only in social co-operatives did the level of education positively influence job satisfaction. No correlation emerged between satisfaction and wages in either public organizations or social co-operatives. The strongest influence in both organizational types was exerted by distributive and procedural fairness. Although procedural fairness was perceived as significantly higher than distributive fairness (the former was particularly low in public bodies), the way in which organizations planned incentives and procedures best explained job satisfaction. Furthermore, only in social co-operatives were effort and job satisfaction positively correlated.

Different levels of job satisfaction also corresponded to different degrees of expressed loyalty. Employees of social co-operatives were significantly more willing to stay in the organization as long as possible than were employees of public organizations (47.0 per cent and 36.5 per cent, respectively), even though the latter received higher wages. Furthermore, in both social co-operatives and public organizations age had a positive and education a negative impact on loyalty (Borzaga and Tortia, 2006). This finding suggests that younger and professional people may quit more frequently because of dissatisfaction with contractual conditions, or to pursue other job opportunities. In social co-operatives loyalty, similar to job satisfaction, was also correlated with size of organization (with employees in small co-operatives willing to stay longer) and with procedural and distributive fairness (the former was also significant in public organizations).

Working for social co-operatives in Italy

The aim of our more recent research has been to determine whether these results persist over time or are altered by the evolution of the sector and the growth in size of social co-operatives and the number of workers employed.

Our 2007 study investigated both Type A and Type B co-operatives, and it used a complex process of sampling from all Italian social co-operatives, designed to represent the sector as a whole by typology, region (North-East, North-West, Central, and South Italy) and size (fewer than 15, 15–50, and more than 50 employees). A total of 310 organizations were surveyed: Type A social co-operatives mainly provided welfare and educational services (73 per cent), while Type B co-operatives, devoted to the reintegration of disadvantaged persons into employment, mainly provided environmental (50 per cent) and homecare services (37.8 per cent). Although the latter co-operatives claim to manage their activities autonomously, their revenues usually depend on the supply of services to public administrations (68 per cent on average), with procedures of contracting out often tied to minimum price rules and therefore limiting how far social co-operatives can make independent decisions about economic rewards and wages.

Questionnaires were also administered to 4,134 salaried workers, most of whom were employed in Type A social co-operatives (215 organizations with 3,074 individuals). To allow comparison with the research conducted in 1998, data in the following section refer only to social co-operatives that supply social services (Type A). The results of the comparisons must be treated with a degree of caution, since the two samples do not refer to the same organizations and workers, and the sample interviewed in 1998 was not statistically representative of the sector as a whole.

Characteristics of workers and processes of selection

The workers interviewed in 2007 were mainly female, aged over 40 (36.1 per cent, showing an increase of the average age in comparison to the 1998 study) and highly educated (34.7 per cent with a university degree, in comparison to 17.4 per cent in 1998). Most workers (87.1 per cent) were also members of their organization. The workers also came with work experience: 46.1 per cent came from a previous job (18.5 per cent had temporary contracts and 27.6 per cent had open-ended contracts), while 25.6 per cent had been unemployed but possessed previous job experience. Social co-operatives are therefore able to attract workers from other organizations. Furthermore, people with previous employment consider jobs in social co-operatives a source of intrinsic satisfaction: 32.4 per cent of these workers receive lower wages than in their previous job, but work relations and autonomy have increased for more than 60 per cent, together with work-time flexibility and the match of the activity with professional qualifications.

It should be noted, however, that social co-operatives also have an important role in employing people with fewer job opportunities. The percentage of workers in the sample who were unemployed before taking up employment with a social co-operative is quite high (more than half were non-active), and this finding corroborates the hypothesis that this sector attracts not only intrinsically motivated workers, but also people simply looking for a job.

Motivations

Employees of social co-operatives are motivated by many factors, most strongly by social relatedness and usefulness, followed by job stability and the sharing of ideals with the enterprise and colleagues (see Table 4.1). The employees rank wages and other economic incentives only sixth in importance and other extrinsic aspects even lower.

When choosing where to work (Table 4.2), intrinsic motivations appear of great importance, particularly the social relevance of the job (opportunity to help people ranks first) and other non-monetary aspects (sharing ideals and values with the organization, developing social relationships, and sharing common projects with colleagues). However, extrinsic aspects also are important: the opportunity for professional development ranks second and contractual conditions ranks third in the list of motivations for choosing a social co-operative. Furthermore, a significant proportion of the employees declare that they decided to work in a social co-operative because they needed an income. Therefore, as confirmed by other studies (e.g. Steinberg, 1990; Mirvis and Hackett, 1983), social co-operatives attract employees by offering different types of incentive, both intrinsic and extrinsic. In comparing the motivations of workers who have moved from a previous job with those of previously unemployed workers, it emerges that there are no differences in intrinsic motivations.

TABLE 4.1   Job evaluation factors

Factor	Average score (1–12)	% for whom very important (score >10)
Helping disadvantaged people	9.6	63.9
Relatedness on the job	9.6	63.4
Work stability	9.5	62.3
Relatedness with people outside the job	9.3	57.9
Sharing common ideals and decision-making	9.0	53.3
Wages and economic incentives	8.8	49.5
Professional development and career	8.6	46.7
Autonomy, variety and creativity	8.3	46.5
Physical working environment	7.8	37.8
Flexibility of working hours	7.8	36.8
Job coherent with individual training	7.4	36.0
Social usefulness and visibility of the job	7.2	32.9

However, extrinsic motivations (especially in terms of satisfaction of personal needs) are higher among workers without job alternatives. Finally, the findings of this study, compared with the previous one, suggest that motivations are rather stable over time.

A further step in understanding motivations comes from the evaluation of changes that happen after workers have accepted employment. Employees claim that before entering a social co-operative they were attracted by the opportunity to establish new relationships and by autonomy, but they were also interested in a job that met their economic needs. Working in a social co-operative, however, has increased their view of the experience as one that has enriched them personally, and given them an opportunity to help other people, improve relationships and derive professional satisfaction.

It is therefore legitimate to claim, as asserted in the literature, that intrinsic motivation and interest in aspects of the job other than money are important selection factors. However, the employment of people also interested in extrinsic aspects does not seem to threaten

TABLE 4.2   Motivations for choosing a social co-operative

	Average score (1–7)	% for whom very important (score >6)
No job opportunities	3.0	17.1
Extrinsic motivations		
Opportunity of professional development	5.5	57.9
Satisfying need for income	4.9	44.2
Transparency of contractual conditions	4.3	28.6
Social visibility of the organization	3.9	22.6
Wage and other economic advantages	3.6	18.0
Intrinsic motivations		
Opportunity to help other people	5.5	59.4
Opportunity to share ideals and values	4.6	37.0
Opportunity to share common projects	4.5	37.3
Developing social relationships	4.5	35.1
Answering the needs of the local community	3.9	25.7
Supporting local development	4.9	21.0
Involvement in the decision-making process	4.0	25.0

the survival of the 'co-operative' model, since organizational procedures can modify worker preferences and behaviour over time. By
becoming more intrinsically motivated, workers satisfy non-economic
needs and increase their self-esteem and psychological well-being. As
a consequence, they also achieve a higher level of satisfaction.

Contracts

The duration of employment contracts is a hotly debated issue in
Italy, particularly in the context of increased labour market flexibility
during the last ten years, sparked by legislation allowing new types
of temporary contract. Our survey shows that social co-operatives
do not use temporary contracts more than other sectors and that

the percentage of temporary employees has actually decreased in recent years (falling to 19.1 per cent in comparison to 26.7 per cent in 1998). Instead, social co-operatives employ a large percentage of their workforce on part-time contracts (43.7 per cent in comparison to 29.6 per cent in 1998), mainly at the request of workers themselves (most of whom are female), but also for organizational needs (29.0 per cent of part-time workers declare to have no choice in the matter).

Salaries and perception of fairness

An important extrinsic aspect of a job is salary. The average salary paid by social co-operatives in 2007 was still quite low (see Table 4.3). However, over the decade between the two surveys net salaries increased in monetary terms by more than 30 per cent on average, climbing to about €1,000 a month for full-time employees in 2007. This increase is partially explained by more hours worked, since the hourly wage has increased by a lower margin. The overall increase is still significant in real terms: discounting annual inflation, full-time salaries amounted to €864 per month in 2007, compared to €768 in 1998, while the hourly rate rose to €5.91, compared to €5.14 in 1998.

In the 2007 survey, employees were asked to evaluate their salaries as 'fair' (assigning a score of 4), 'unfair' (scores between 1 and 3) and 'more than fair' (scores from 5 to 7). Table 4.4 shows that employees

TABLE 4.3   Average salaries (€)

	Net wage 2007	% increase 1998–2007
Monthly		
full-time	1010.40	31.5
part-time	688.04	36.8
Hourly		
full-time	6.36	23.7
part-time	7.01	12.9

TABLE 4. 4   Distributive fairness

The wage is fair in comparison with...	Av. score	% score 1–3	% score 4	% score 5–7
Individual aspects				
level of education	3.4	46.8	37.5	15.6
training and experience	3.3	50.4	34.9	14.8
responsibility and role	3.1	56.4	31.7	11.9
effort required	3.1	56.8	31.0	12.2
stress and tension	3.0	61.8	25.6	12.6
loyalty to the co-operative	3.7	38.6	40.9	20.4
Collective aspects				
the wages of colleagues in the co-operative	4.4	22.2	49.1	28.9
the wages of employers in other organizations	4.4	33.7	30.4	35.9
the wages of superiors	4.9	20.6	40.5	38.8
All aspects	3.5	48.7	34.1	17.1

in social co-operatives perceive their salaries as fair (scores near 4) when compared to those of colleagues and superiors as well as market averages. The perception of distributive fairness is slightly less positive: salaries are perceived as less than fair (average scores around 3.3) when compared to educational levels, work experience, job responsibility and effort, stress, and loyalty to the organization.

Although the results are generally positive, it is clear that salaries are relatively low. This explains why workers perceive their salaries to be insufficient for needs and the cost of living (average scores assigned to these evaluations are under 2.5). This perception alone seems to explain any general dissatisfaction with wages expressed in the next subsection.

Procedural fairness is perceived by employees to be higher than distributive fairness, demonstrating the relevance of the working environment and of procedures to satisfy worker expectations. As

TABLE 4.5   Procedural fairness

Your social co-operative...	Average score (1–7)
gives advice and guidelines	5.3
collects complete information on worker activity	5.2
treats its workers in the same manner	5.4
has clear and shared goals	5.0
abides with what has been promised	5.7
Comprehensive fairness	5.9

a whole, procedural fairness (Table 4.5) received high scores (5.9 on a scale from 1 to 7), but this was especially marked for factors such as the quality of advice and guidelines communicated by the organization, the transmission of clear goals, and commitment to the employment relationship ('the social co-operative abides with what has been promised'). Furthermore, compared to the previous study, procedural fairness has improved with the consolidation of social co-operatives.

Job satisfaction

Worker well-being was estimated by asking workers to evaluate their level of satisfaction with their jobs. While average overall satisfaction is high (the same as in the previous study), employees seem more satisfied than in the past about many specific aspects of their jobs (Table 4.6). Average scores increased with regard to some extrinsic aspects, such as the working environment and job stability, but also intrinsic aspects, especially the social usefulness of the job, relationships with superiors, volunteers and the work team, and job variety and creativity. Satisfaction with wages, on the other hand, was unchanged despite the registered increase in nominal and real wages. As a consequence, it can be claimed that social co-operatives continue to supply a mix of incentives to match successfully the expectations and motivations of people employed.

TABLE 4.6   Satisfaction with different aspects of the job

	Average score (1–7)
Extrinsic aspects	4.6
Professional development	4.6
Working environment	5.3
Wage	3.7
Working hours	5.3
Career obtained	3.8
Expected career	3.9
Job security	5.3
Intrinsic aspects	5.4
Social usefulness of the work	5.9
Autonomy in decision-making	5.1
Social recognition	4.9
Variety and creativity of the job	5.3
Relationships with superiors	5.7
Relationships with colleagues	5.7
Relationships with volunteers	6.5
Involvement in decision-making	4.2
The job as a whole	5.5

For a fuller understanding of job satisfaction among employees of social co-operatives, multinomial models were carried out, although problems of collinearity and self-selection mean that care must be taken in drawing final conclusions. The models aimed to verify the principal claims of the literature on non-profit organizations and job satisfaction in general. Furthermore, they approximated the utility function of employees, which provides a basis for understanding the significance of motivations, fairness and intrinsic aspects of the job in explaining employee well-being.

TABLE 4.7 The determinants of average satisfaction in social co-operatives (ordered probit model)

Variables	Coefficient	Standard deviation	Significance
Gender	0.1346	0.0270	**
Age	−0.0183	0.7820	
Age squared	−0.2416	0.8220	
Diploma	−0.0182	0.7550	
Degree	−0.1865	0.0050	***
Over-education	0.0531	0.1270	
Open-ended contract	0.0149	0.8250	
Full-time contract	0.1252	0.1190	
Involuntary part-timer	−0.1415	0.0690	*
Working hours	0.0032	0.5420	
Supplementary hours	0.0080	0.2980	
Monthly wage	0.0001	0.3710	
Distributive fairness with personal aspects	0.0884	0.0010	***
Distributive fairness with collective aspects	0.0115	0.5430	
Satisfaction with wage in comparison with cost of living	0.0500	0.0740	*
Procedural fairness	0.1739	0.0000	***
Relations with superiors	0.3111	0.0000	***
Intrinsic motivations	0.1187	0.0000	***
Extrinsic motivations	−0.0490	0.0470	**
Dimension of organization	0.0545	0.1420	
Age of organization	0.0183	0.9360	

Note: Coefficients statistically significant at: *** = 1%, ** = 5%, * = 10%.

By using an order probit model for employee overall satisfaction (Table 4.7), the linkage between job satisfaction and procedural and distributive fairness emerges as strictly positive and highly significant. Among individual characteristics, the level of education is negatively correlated with job satisfaction, while having specific training does not influence job satisfaction. Good relationships with superiors and intrinsic motivations are highly significant, while extrinsic motivations impact negatively on job satisfaction. Finally, both procedural and distributive fairness are correlated with job satisfaction.

In sum, the data support the interpretation that the variance of job satisfaction in social co-operatives is mainly explained by perceived fairness (as shown in the analyses of Leete, 2000; and Benz, 2005) and by worker motivations, where intrinsic motivations impact positively on job satisfaction. They show that workers mainly attracted by the extrinsic aspects of the job are less satisfied. Furthermore, although wages on their own do not influence employee satisfaction, distributive fairness is considered very important. Finally, the determinants of job satisfaction in social co-operatives do not seem to have significantly changed with the growth of the sector. However, over time, different aspects have emerged as crucial elements in employment relations. For example, social co-operatives seem to have developed better satisfaction procedures, to balance difficulties of increasing wages due to their financial situation.

Loyalty and behaviour

Some empirical studies and theories based on morale models assert that job satisfaction influences worker behaviour, especially in relation to effort exerted and loyalty to the organization. Non-profit organizations and social enterprises, however, have also been considered to be sources of employment for workers without other job opportunities. Our data shed some light on this dual aspect by revealing patterns of declared loyalty of workers (one limitation, however, is that the data do not include the views of workers who have resigned from organizations).[5] Looking at employee intentions to stay or to leave their jobs (Table 4.8), loyalty appears high and seems to have increased over time: 74.1 per cent want to stay in the organization because they are satisfied with their jobs and another 13.5 per cent want to stay at least for some years. Only 6.5 per cent intend to stay because they have no job alternatives. An interesting result also emerges when employees are differentiated by job tenure: less than 10 per cent of workers

TABLE 4.8 Loyalty to the organization

Intend to...	%
stay as long as possible	74.1
stay only some years	13.5
leave as soon as possible	1.9
stay because of no alternatives	6.5

employed for more than ten years intend to search for another job, while 20 per cent of those employed for less than two years look at the experience of working in a social co-operative as a short-term job, in order to improve their skills or psychological well-being.

A multinomial logit model was developed to study the determinants of loyalty. These determinants do not seem to have changed significantly over time, and job satisfaction continues to explain most of the willingness to stay. The model (Table 4.9) shows that, like job satisfaction, loyalty is positively correlated with age and negatively with educational level. Furthermore, the willingness to stay depends upon procedural fairness: the transparency of communication procedures is very important for re-enforcing loyalty and relationships with superiors, who act as intermediaries in the transmission of organizational aims, social norms and behaviours. The correlation is also strong with worker motivation: when workers are interested in economic rewards and extrinsic incentives, they tend to see their job as short-term, while workers who are motivated by intrinsic factors intend to stay. Looking at other extrinsic aspects, while the perception of distributive fairness does not significantly influence loyalty, the level of salary does (although the variable loses its significance when working hours are added into the model). Similarly, people unsatisfied about their salaries are more willing to quit their jobs. Notwithstanding the low percentage of workers willing to quit, the significance of economic aspects confirms that the best human resources policies must be based on a mix of incentives, where both intrinsic and economic rewards satisfy employee expectations and needs. It should be noted, however, in connection with the high percentage of skilled

TABLE 4.9   The determinants of loyalty in social co-operatives today (ordered logit)

Variables	Coefficient	Standard deviation	Significance
Gender	0.0839	0.562	
Age	0.0163	0.026	**
Diploma	0.1672	0.250	
Degree	−0.4367	0.005	**
Open-ended contract	0.1016	0.514	
Full-time contract	0.1750	0.267	
Involuntary part-timer	0.0959	0.584	
Supplementary hours	0.0019	0.917	
Monthly wage	0.0007	0.008	**
Distributive fairness with personal aspects	0.1315	0.066	*
Distributive fairness with collective aspects	−0.0331	0.447	
Satisfaction with wage in comparison with cost of living	0.1399	0.058	*
Procedural fairness	0.1382	0.017	**
Relations with superiors	0.3020	0.000	***
Intrinsic motivations	0.2351	0.000	***
Extrinsic motivations	−0.2298	0.000	***
Satisfaction with the job	0.5207	0.000	***
Satisfaction with wage	0.1105	0.018	**

Note: Loyalty calculated as 0 = willingness to quit and 1 = willingness to stay. Coefficients statistically significant at: *** = 1%, ** = 5%, * = 10%.

and well-educated workers who are attracted into these organizations, social co-operatives do not always seem able to fully recognize younger workers and valorize their professional skills.

Finally, regarding effort, employees assert that their jobs are really demanding (claimed by 65 per cent of those interviewed). They perceive themselves as exerting more effort than other workers given the incentives received (average score 5.5 on a scale of 1 to 7), but they also believe that they exert more effort than demanded by clients and by the organization (average score 5.3).

Conclusions

As a consequence of the crisis of the welfare state and of the opening of welfare provision to private initiatives, the role of social co-operatives has steadily increased. Their ability to respond to unsatisfied social needs depends less upon their efficiency or non-profit nature than upon their success in managing human resources. In fact, employees directly influence organizational performance, in both quantitative and qualitative terms, since general interest services are human capital intensive. The centrality of human resources in the production of serv-ices in general underlines the importance of further research on work relations. This chapter suggests the need for a comprehensive approach capable of monitoring several determinants of worker satisfaction.

The survey data examined here support the hypothesis that employ-ment relationships in social co-operatives are really a different way of working, not because they attract and satisfy a small group of altruistic workers but because they use a larger set of incentives to satisfy agents with multiple motivations. On the one hand, workers make decisions about their choice of job, willingness to stay and behaviour by taking into account a plurality of motivations – both extrinsic and intrinsic – since they need money but are also motivated by social recognition. On the other hand, social co-operatives supply a plurality of incentives, mainly intrinsic but also extrinsic (such as training and flexibility).

Furthermore, social co-operatives seem to follow fair procedures and encourage workers to identify organizational aims on a daily basis. The management of human resources in social co-operatives therefore follows typical patterns. These organizations have the comparative advantage (with respect to other types of organizations) of attracting workers by providing incentives in line with employee social aspirations and intrinsic motivations. Then social enterprises transmit an interest in the social usefulness of the job, which influ-ences both worker motivation and social preference. Consequently, workers are satisfied and tend to provide more than expected. The capacity of social enterprises to attract and efficiently manage their human resources seems to be reinforced over time.

The findings reported in this chapter have three theoretical and policy implications. First, with regard to economic theory, the findings confirm that, at least in the general interest services sector, decisions associated with labour supply do not depend exclusively or even principally on wage levels. Instead, agents are pluri-motivated, with organizations offering workers a mix of incentives so that salary acts more as an incentive to accept a job than as a determinant of job satisfaction. Non-economic motivations can no longer be considered as given or unimportant, but are key elements influencing worker choice and well-being.

Second, public policies should reflect the specificities of social co-operatives. Policies externalizing services to private organizations should not be considered simply as a mechanism to reduce costs or as a solution to an emergency situation. Social enterprises should be seen as an innovative way to provide welfare and general interest services. They are a good institutional form for involving new resources, especially human resources, in the supply of these services. Public policies should take into account the potential of social enterprises and provide the legal framework and incentives necessary to sustain the development of these organizations.

Finally, looking to organizational policies, social enterprises need to develop strategies that respond not only to client but also to worker needs. Intrinsic incentives should continue to prevail, focusing on the quality of work relations, employee involvement in decision-making, task autonomy and creativity, and the social utility of jobs. Simultaneously, extrinsic incentives should be improved to respond to worker needs for security and income, and to increase the loyalty of workers with higher abilities and training. Salaries, therefore, need to be managed carefully by planning for fairness, avoiding excessive turnover, and crowding out intrinsic motivations.

In conclusion, matching worker and organizational needs characteristics seems a good way to organize the provision of general interest services, the demand for which is expected to increase in the future.

Notes

1. These studies reinforce new economic thinking explaining individual behaviour in terms of preferences other than self-regarding or purely economic ones.

2. *Distributive fairness* is the perception of correctness of the level of wages earned in comparison to different aspects of the job (e.g. stress, role) and individual status (e.g. level of education) or a benchmark (e.g. the market wage or colleagues' wages), while *procedural fairness* refers to the correctness of organizational procedures, the transparency in the transmission of information, and the equity in managing careers.

3. Among the causes of the increase in demand for personal services were the spread of drug and alcohol abuse, problems related to the difficult circumstances of Italy's urban hinterlands, and new needs arising from the achievement of certain social advances, including law 180/78 (the 'Basaglia Law') that ordered the closure of mental asylums and orphanages.

4. This was achieved, for example, by creating new services addressed mainly to young people with social problems, the elderly, the disabled, drug addicts and the homeless, but also to people who are unemployed.

5. Although it should be noted that half of the social co-operatives interviewed had no employee departures during the year prior to the interview and in the full sample there was a net growth in employment.

References

Akerlof, G.A. (1982) 'Labor contracts as partial gift exchange', *Quarterly Journal of Economics* 97(4): 543–69.

Almond, S., and J. Kendall (2002) 'Low pay in the UK: The case for a three sector comparative approach', *Annals of Public and Cooperative Economics* 72(1): 45–76.

Anheier, H.K. (1991) 'Employment and earnings in the West German non-profit sector: Structure and trends 1970–1987', in A. Ben-Ner and B. Gui, eds, *The Non-profit Sector in a Mixed Economy*, University of Michigan Press, Ann Arbor, pp. 183–202.

Bacchiega, A., and C. Borzaga (2001) 'Social enterprises as a mix of incentives: An economic analysis', in C. Borzaga and J. Defourny, eds, *The Emergence of Social Enterprises*, Routledge, London.

Benz, M. (2005) 'Not for the profit, but for the satisfaction? Evidence on worker well-being in non-profit firms', *Kyklos* 58(2): 155–76.

Blanchflower, D.G., and A.J. Oswald (1999) 'Well-being, insecurity and the decline of American job satisfaction', www2.warwick.ac.uk/fac/soc/economics/staff/faculty/oswald/ blanchflower.pdf; accessed 20 July 2008.

Borzaga, C., and S. Depedri (2005) 'Interpersonal relations and job satisfaction: Some empirical results in social and community care services', in B. Gui and R. Sugden, eds, *Economics and Social Interaction: Accounting for Interpersonal Relations*, Cambridge University Press, Cambridge, pp. 132–53.

Borzaga, C., and A. Ianes (2006) *L'economia della solidarietà. Storia e prospettive della cooperazione sociale*, Donzelli, Rome.

Borzaga, C., and M. Musella (2004) *Produttività ed efficienza nelle organizzazioni nonprofit: analisi teoriche e verifiche empiriche*, edizioni31, Trento.

Borzaga, C., and E. Tortia (2006) 'Worker motivations, job satisfaction, and loyalty in nonprofit social services', *Non-Profit and Voluntary Sector Quarterly* 35(2): 225–48.

Bryson, A., L. Cappellari and C. Lucifora (2005) 'Why so unhappy? The effects of unionisation on job satisfaction', IZA Working Paper No. 1419, Bonn.

Clark, A. (1997) 'Job satisfaction and gender: Why are women so happy at work?', *Labour Economics* 4(4): 341–72.

Clark, A. (2005) 'What makes a good job? Evidence from OECD countries', in S. Bazen, C. Lucifora and W. Salverda, *Job quality and Employer Behaviour*, Palgrave Macmillan, New York, pp. 1–24.

Frey, B. (1997) *Not Just for the Money: An Economic Theory of Personal Motivation*, Edward Elgar, Cheltenham.

Goddeeris, J.H. (1988) 'Compensating differentials and self-selection: An application to lawyers', *Journal of Political Economy* 96(2): 411–28.

Handy, F., and E. Katz (1998) 'The wage differential between non-profit institutions and corporations: Getting more by paying less?' *Journal of Comparative Economics* 26(2): 246–61.

Hansmann, H. (1980) 'The role of nonprofit enterprise', *Yale Law Journal* 89: 835–901.

Ianes, A., and E. Tortia (2008) 'Creativity and institution building: The case of Italian social cooperatives', ISSAN Working Paper 27, Trento.

Lanfranchi, J., and M. Narcy (2008) 'Difference de satisfaction dans l'emploi entre secteurs à but lucratif et à but non lucratif: Le role joué par les caracteristique d'emploi', *Annals of Public and Cooperative Economics* 79(2): 1346–61.

Lazear, E. (1996) 'Performance pay and productivity', NBER Working Paper No. 5672, Cambridge MA.

Leete, L. (2000) 'Wage equity and employee motivations in non-profit and for-profit organizations', *Journal of Economic Behavior and Organization* 43(4), December: 423–46.

Levine, D.I. (1991) 'Cohesiveness, productivity, and wage dispersion', *Journal of Economic Behavior and Organization* 15(2): 237–55.

Michie, J., and M. Sheehan (1999) 'No innovation without representation? An analysis of participation, representation, R&D and innovation', *Economic Analysis* 2(2): 12–48.

Miller, P.W. (1990) 'Trade unions and job satisfaction', *Australian Economic Papers* 29(55): 226–48.

Mirvis, P.H. (1992) 'The quality of employment in the non-profit sector: An update on employee attitudes in non-profit versus business and government', *Non-profit Management and Leadership* 3(1): 23–41.

Mirvis, P.H., and E.J. Hackett (1983) 'Work and workforce characteristics in the non-profit sector', *Monthly Labour Review* 106(4): 3–12.

Mocan, N.H., and D. Viola (1997) 'The determinants of child care workers' wages compensation: Sectoral difference, human capital, race, insiders and outsiders', *NBER Working Paper* W6328, Cambridge MA.

Mosca, M., M. Musella, and F. Pastore (2007) 'Relational goods, monitoring, and non-pecuniary compensation in the non-profit sector: The case of Italian social services', *Annals of Public and Cooperative Economics* 78(1): 57–86.

Preston, A.E. (1989) 'The non-profit worker in a for-profit world', *Journal of Labour Economics* 7(4): 438–45.

Schwochau, S. (1987) 'Union effects on job attitudes', *Industrial and Labor Relation Review* 40(2): 209–24.

Sen, A. (1985) 'Goals, commitment and identity', *Journal of Law, Economics and Organization* 1(1): 341–55.

Skalli, A., I. Theodossiou, and E. Vasileiou (2007) 'Jobs as Lancaster goods: Facets of job satisfaction and overall job satisfaction', Centre for European Market Research, Discussion Paper 2007–02, Aberdeen University.

Soohne, K. (2002) 'Participative management and job satisfaction: Lessons for management leadership', *Public Administration Review* 62(2): 231–41.

Sousa-Poza, A., and A.A. Sousa-Poza (2000) 'Well-being at work: A crossnational analysis of the levels and determinants of job satisfaction, *Journal of Socio-Economics* 29(6): 351–72.

Steinberg, R. (1990) 'Labour economics and the non-profit sector: A literature review', *Non-profit and Voluntary Sector Quarterly* 19(2): 51–169.

Tortia, E.C. (2008) 'Worker well-being and perceived fairness: Survey-based findings from Italy', *Journal of Socio-Economics* 37(5): 2080–94.

Valentini, E. (2005) 'Psychological factors in job satisfaction', Università delle Marche, Dipartimento di Economia Working Paper No. 225.

Weisbrod B.A. (1983) 'Non-profit and proprietary sector behavior: Wage differentials among lawyers', *Journal of Labor Economics* 1(3): 246–63.

5

Experimenting with economic possibilities: ethical economic decision-making in two Australian community enterprises

Jenny Cameron

Community (or social) enterprises are a form of endeavour within the social economy that can be framed in two ways, with implications for how we view the economy more generally. In one framing community enterprises are a way that communities respond to the negative impacts of economic change. Community enterprises do this by providing employment opportunities and much-needed social services, especially in areas that have been economically and socially marginalized. In this view, the economy (particularly through capitalist economic activity and related process of economic globalization) acts on people and communities, and community enterprises are one small means of responding. In a second framing, community enterprises are an avenue for communities to act on concerns about economic equity, social justice and environmental sustainability. Community enterprises are a way of experimenting with forms of economy that explicitly take into account social and environmental questions. In this view, the economy is something that can be actively shaped by people and communities as a means of building not only a better present but a better future.

In this chapter I take the example of two Australian community enterprises and explore how these enterprises are experimenting with economic practices in order to act on social and environmental concerns. Certainly these two enterprises could be framed as local responses to global economic change. Both could be framed as part of the intermediate labour market providing employment and training opportunities for economically and socially marginalized groups, particularly recently arrived refugees, long-term unemployed and public housing tenants. However, I would argue that this framing only touches on what these community enterprises have to offer. From them we can learn how communities are actively building initiatives that meld economic, social and environmental concerns, and we gain insights into the types of economies that are possible.

I start by briefly outlining the Australian context in which community (and social) enterprises develop. I then discuss the two community enterprises in terms of three strategies they are using to take the economy into their own hands and practise economic experimentation: using a learning-by-doing approach to experiment with what is possible; making ethical economic decisions to address economic, social and environmental concerns; and innovating with a diversity of economic practices to sustain their operations.

Community enterprises in the Australian context

In the Australian context, community enterprises are generally characterized by four features:

- They focus on producing direct community benefit (e.g. 'employment' in either paid or purposeful work, social connections, environmental outcomes).
- They use economic activities as a means to help achieve their aim (and this can be through a conventional economic approach whereby paid employees produce goods and services for the market, or through a diverse economy approach where goods and services are produced and transacted through a range of economic practices that include alternative and non-market transactions, and alternative and unpaid forms of labour).
- They produce surplus for the enterprise, but not profit for individual gain.

- They are accountable to their identified constituents (usually through shared decision-making).

In Australia community enterprises have generally arisen out of two contexts. The first is through grassroots community activism, a process in which small groups band together to experiment with economic possibilities. Examples of enterprises that have developed through community activism include:

- CERES Community Environment Park, a 25-year-old enterprise that started as an inner city community garden in Melbourne but has grown to include a bushfood and permaculture plant nursery, an onsite organic café, a certified organic farm that supplies the café, a solar power plant and a host of other activities. In 2007 it had a budget of almost $4 million, 150 staff (70 full-time equivalent positions) and 110 volunteers on regular placement (CERES, 2007; see also www.ceres.org.au).
- SpeakOut, a not-for-profit organization that works with disadvantaged young people to foster their creativity and confidence. It started in 1995 with T-shirt design and production, then moved into graphics, training young people in digital literacy and visual design, and in enterprise development. Its programmes are now largely funded by three profit-for-purpose enterprises that offer digital and visual design services (see www.speakout.com.au).
- Reverse Garbage, Bicycle Revolution, Eco-Geek and Papernet, all initiatives of Friends of the Earth, developed since 1997 to offer more environmentally sustainable forms of economic activity (see www.brisbane.foe.org.au/projects.htm).
- Food Connect, a community-supported agriculture (CSA) initiative in South East Queensland that links city consumers with rural producers. Consumers purchase an upfront subscription (from 4 to 52 weeks) guaranteeing farmers a stable market but also meaning that consumers share in any shortfalls due to drought, pests and so on. Currently 1,500 households are active members; there are over 80 volunteer households that act as distribution centres, 30 paid employees and 70 core farmers, all within a five-hour radius of Brisbane (personal communication, Robert Pekin, managing

coordinator, 29 August 2008; see also www.foodconnect.com.au). The initiative also runs other activities, including a programme to enable low-income households to become subscribers, a programme to support young farmers, a catering enterprise and an education programme.

The second context that has given rise to community enterprises is through government and large non-governmental organization (NGO) programmes. Since 2000, for example, the Victorian State Government has allocated $9.2 million to its community enterprise strategy (Department for Victorian Communities, 2006) and, in partnership with the Brotherhood of St Laurence, is supporting forty-two localities across the state to develop community enterprises (Brotherhood of St Laurence, 2006; see also Barraket, 2008; Simons, 2000; Talbot at al., 2002). This is a relatively recent development, and compared to programmes in other countries Australia's endeavours are 'patchy and piecemeal' (Lyons and Passey, 2006: 90). For example, in the UK social enterprise (as it is generally known there) 'is a "brand" which has become an important plank of government policy', with the Blair Labour government establishing a Social Enterprise Strategy, a Social Enterprise Unit and a Social Enterprise Action Plan to develop social enterprises in England and Wales (Spear et al., 2007: 2). Given that there is so much 'policy borrowing' between Australia and the UK (Lyons and Passey, 2006: 98), there is no doubt that what is being done in Australia has been heavily influenced by this 'branding' of social enterprise in the UK.

One concern is that in the process of policy importing what has been lost from sight are the lessons we might learn from the community enterprises that already exist in Australia. Indeed, much attention has been paid to the start-up of community enterprises, but less to what happens as community enterprises develop, as they consolidate their operations and confront new challenges. What might we learn from existing community enterprises in the post-start-up period? What challenges do they face? How do they sustain and consolidate their activities? What development pathways do they follow? How are these development pathways shaped by their economic, social and environmental commitments?

In this chapter I turn to the experiences of two community enterprises that were initiated through grassroots activism and outside of any government or NGO start-up programme. Both enterprises are past the start-up phase and are currently going through a period of change and consolidation, and assessing their development pathway. They therefore provide insights into the sorts of challenges that community enterprises can face in the post-start-up period. These community enterprises also help us understand some of the features of this area of the social economy, and ways of conceptualizing the role of community enterprises in the contemporary setting.

The material presented in this chapter draws from two sources. The first source is my observations of the two community enterprises over a number of years. I first came in contact with Sustainable Gardening Services (SGS) through New Mutualism, an informal support and network group for community enterprises, and when SGS was going through a period of change I was part of a small group that provided input, advice and support. In the case of Flying Eagle Facilitators (FEF), I have employed the group to train final-year university students in workshop facilitation and recording skills, worked with members on a community enterprise participatory action research project, been present at annual general meetings and kept in informal contact with group members. The second source of material is from interviews conducted with key people in the two enterprises in December 2007 and September 2008, and follow-up email discussions around drafts of this chapter. My aim in this work and in this chapter is to support these (and other) community enterprises, and to provide insights to help affirm and strengthen current and future endeavours.

Learning by doing

Sustainable Gardening Services (SGS) started in 2003 as the idea of a community activist. Having worked in community development, Paul was looking for a change in direction and was particularly interested in pursuing his environmental concerns. A conversation with a friend who worked in refugee services led to the idea of an environmentally sustainable gardening service that would employ refugees. So the overarching ambition for the enterprise was twofold: to develop a more environmentally sustainable approach to gardening and to provide opportunities for recently arrived refugees.

To start, Paul got into the federal government's New Enterprise Initiative Scheme (NEIS), a programme to help unemployed people start their own micro- or small businesses. Even though the NEIS programme is oriented towards mainstream micro- and small businesses, people like Paul have used it to start community enterprises (examples include a social change agency to train and support environmental, union and community activists; and an organic food co-operative for consumers). This meant the enterprise's initial legal structure was a sole-trader business, with Paul as the only worker. Then, as Paul describes, as the work became too much for him, he employed some people he knew who needed a bit of work, but once the work grew and stabilized, he looked to employing more marginalized people.

Within six months long-term unemployed people were being employed, and within twelve months a part-time position was available for a refugee worker. Since its inception in 2003, SGS has provided employment and training for some forty-five people from refugee, migrant and long-term unemployed backgrounds.

SGS developed through an experimental learning-by-doing approach, as Paul started with an initial enterprise idea that was then refined and modified based on what he learned through 'trial and error' (as Paul characterizes it). Here, for example, Paul describes one of the early changes:

> There was always a vision but it probably did keep changing. At first I just had this idea that it would be me and a whole bunch of refugees working. Then it started to come into this idea of, well, a whole range of issues around capacity, supervision, around what refugees really want … So we started to build more of a capacity-building approach. We really didn't want to produce a generation of migrant gardeners like they have in the south of the USA. We wanted to be developmental, that this was a stepping stone into the Australian work culture.

As Paul learnt through the practice of running the enterprise, the vision shifted from providing permanent jobs for refugees to linking refugees into other forms of employment. But as the enterprise developed, this vision was modified even further. Paul found that SGS did not have the capacity to provide all the support that recently arrived refugees needed. Also the political context changed and refugee networks were offering more support services, including links to established businesses that had permanent full-time positions. Gradually Paul started employing other marginalized groups such as people who have been long-term unemployed. So over its formative years, the enterprise has developed through an experimental learning-by-doing approach. It started as a small one-person operation to see what was possible, expanded once Paul established the operation and learned more about running the enterprise, and then incorporated participants from a wider range of backgrounds as again Paul learned more about what was feasible.

In September 2007, the enterprise went through another major change. After five years of running as a sole-trader business (with input from a loose advisory group that included people in the community development field), SGS changed to a not-for-profit company overseen by a board of directors. This occurred for a number of reasons. Paul was, in his words, 'close to burnout' and looking to step back from his role as manager. Also it was time to align the enterprise's legal structure with its practice as a community enterprise. This means that Paul now has more of a back-seat role on the board of directors, while one of the staff with horticulture and community sector experience, Asger, has stepped into the manager's position. The change to a not-for-profit company was made with considerable input and advice from a range of sources (including community members, staff and a social enterprise support service); nevertheless it is a step into the unknown where learning-by-doing (and 'trial and error') continues to be important. Indeed, the new manager Asger characterizes the new arrangement as 'another whole area of learning'. For example, Asger reflects what this means for him: 'moving into this new role was basically learning everything again … there's all these skills and techniques and knowledge that I didn't have beforehand to make it [the enterprise] happen. I've had to learn that.' The board of directors (including Paul) is likewise learning about its role in reviewing and supporting the enterprise's activities. Even the workers are learning about what the new structure means for them, as Asger describes:

Now that it's a non-profit company, I've made it quite clear to all the workers that 'Well, your continued employment here is pretty much reliant on SGS still being able to return a surplus and operate efficiently, so you have a direct stake in making this work.' And everyone's gone 'Yeah that's right.' And that changes your outlook, and your work and what you do there. And people still sort of need to get what they need out of the business, but it just increases the responsibility you have to it.

At the same time as learning-by-doing (or 'trial and error', as Paul describes it, or 'learning the hard way', as Asger describes it) is important in the enterprise, Asger also makes the point that planning is equally important:

I think it's a mistake if you don't try and plan for where you want to go. Otherwise you're just in a situation of constantly reacting to what happens to you and it's just really stressful. Also you don't necessarily grow or go anywhere. SGS would just end up staying where it is, sort of hit this level and size that unless we start pushing something else we're just going to sit here and we may well end up just frittering away and we won't actually do what we want to do – which is ecological landscaping.

So the enterprise has reached a stage where both learning-by-doing and forward planning are contributing to the enterprise's current and future activities.

Like SGS, Flying Eagle Facilitators (FEF) also started through an experimental approach. In 1999 Wendy Sarkissian, a private planning consultant, was working for the state health department in Eagleby, a largely public housing suburb on the main highway between Brisbane and the Gold Coast. As part of her commitment to participatory planning, Wendy trained a group of local residents in facilitation and recording skills so they could staff stalls at a community workshop using a SpeakOut format (Sarkissian, 2005; Sarkissian et al., 2003). From this initial experiment with local people facilitating workshops, the group went on to facilitate more workshops and events, and in 2001 the informal group incorporated as a not-for-profit association. At the outset there was no plan that the group would formalize into the community enterprise that it is, and now almost ten years old. Instead the group of residents trained for one event, but found not only aptitude for the work but political commitment to making sure that fellow residents' views were accurately recorded and reported to decision-makers. Like SGS, the early years of the FEF were characterized by an experimental learning-by-doing approach, starting with a small trial and then building one step at a time as members acquired skills and knowledge about their 'business' activity, and developed confidence in what they might be able to achieve.

The start of SGS and FEF is characterized by an experimental approach of 'giving something a go', seeing what results, and then using what is learnt to develop further actions. At the outset, neither had strong plans to direct their actions; rather, actions led to reflection and planning. There is evidence from other sources of the value of this experimental approach. For example, out of a participatory action research project working with groups that had been economically marginalized through the downsizing and privatization of the state-owned power industry (Cameron and Gibson, 2005a, 2005b), the community enterprise that continues to this day (Santa's Workshop) started as a modest two-month experiment to see whether local residents turned up to make large outdoor Christmas decorations. Almost ten years later, the enterprise is open for most of the year, with people making Christmas decorations to sell; the money from sales is used later in the year to provide local residents with free workshop access, advice and materials for making their own decorations. In contrast, the enterprises that were guided by more ambitious and detailed plans folded within three years.[1] Similarly, at a recent workshop on community enterprises in the food sector, practitioners talked of how their enterprises started through learning-by-doing, organic and experimental approaches (Cameron and Gerrard, 2008). This is not to say that business or community enterprise planning is not important; however, it raises the issue of the type of planning that is appropriate, particularly at different stages of community enterprise development. For those community enterprises that arise out of grassroots community endeavour, it seems that actions and experimentation at the outset are an important means for people to initially test ideas, and then to develop and refine them on the basis of what they find.

Ethical economic decision-making

The second way these two community enterprises are taking the economy into their own hands and experimenting with economic possibilities is through ethical economic decision-making. The economic decisions that Sustainable Gardening Services and Flying Eagle Facilitators make are guided by social and environmental ethics and concerns.

From the outset, SGS has been strongly committed to providing opportunities for marginalized groups – initially refugees and more recently other marginalized groups like the long-term unemployed. This social commitment has shaped how the enterprise operates. For example, SGS pairs workers. This practice is rare in garden maintenance and landscaping as the field is primarily made up of sole operators. Initially, the practice was partly a response to the political context in which the conservative federal government was provoking public resentment and fear about so-called 'illegal' and 'queue-jumping' refugees. The practice offered another way of coexisting with difference by having recently arrived refugees and long-time Australian citizens working alongside each other, interacting, sharing and learning together. The practice continues, even though workers now tend to be the long-term unemployed, as it builds social connections between workers. However, the practice of pairing workers has economic implications. More 'dead time' or economically non-productive time is spent travelling between an increased number of shorter jobs, and this reduces the amount of surplus (or 'profit') the enterprise generates. But for a community enterprise like SGS, where profit maximization is not an overarching goal, there is still sufficient surplus for the enterprise to operate, and economic 'profitability' can be subsumed to this social ethic and social practice. Moderating how much surplus is produced in order to achieve social benefit illustrates the community economy at work. As discussed by Gibson-Graham (2006: 82), the community economy is a space of ethical decision-making where the question of how we are to live together is negotiated. And one of the coordinates for ethical decision-making is the issue of how much surplus is produced. In SGS, ethical economic decision-making has determined that a little less surplus can be produced in order to gain social benefit.

SGS has made other ethical economic decisions to generate social benefit. These range from small forms of support (such as allowing workers to borrow work vehicles to move things at weekends) to more ambitious plans (such as having dental insurance for workers and developing a housing co-operative for workers). The commitment to strong social goals is valued by workers. For example, the current manager, Asger, reports on how one former worker, a refugee who had to leave because of health reasons, misses the companionship that came with the practice of pairing workers: 'One of the workers, H, he still phones back and has a chat to me and says "Yeah, I liked that part of it at SGS. That doesn't exist anywhere else."' Asger similarly values the opportunity to work in, and for, an enterprise that is socially committed to supporting workers:

> I can identify with what the business is trying to do, and I can see it as a vehicle to achieve all these other goals that I want to see – social goals. And I don't see a better vehicle around at all. And that will keep me with SGS, and if it turns out that it's just not going to happen, then that's a reason to stop. But I think it is quite inspiring to have this. It's a business model, it's an organizational vehicle and it's sort of in our control. You're not just a worker and that's not going to happen anywhere else. That's quite unique, and that's going to keep us around.

SGS's social commitments are reflected in economic practices that limit the enterprise's ability to generate surplus in the first place (by pairing workers so that 'dead time' increases and subsidizing private use of the enterprise's vehicles), and then direct how surplus is to be distributed (potentially to dental insurance and housing). These ethical economic decisions contribute to building a community economy in which surplus production and distribution become a means of enacting social commitments.

Along with its social goals, SGS also has strong environmental values, and is committed to more environmentally sustainable forms of gardening, as Asger describes:

> We have actually had a few meetings about this and tried to make things more formalized and put it on paper. But, explicitly, we won't

do certain types of job. If I'm called out to do a landscaping job and they ask me to do a formal ornamental garden with all these different sorts of plants, I'm going 'Nah, these are the sorts of gardens we do.' We put the emphasis on indigenous plants, which have habitat and bush food value. They're all organic methods when we set up the garden and we're not interested in making high maintenance hedges or McMansion sort of gardens. We're not doing that.

This environmental position potentially has two very different economic impacts. On the one hand, if SGS is missing out on landscaping work, then this has a negative economic impact for it is landscaping work (rather than mowing and garden maintenance) that generates surplus, a resource that could potentially be used to support social goals like dental insurance or a housing co-operative. On the other hand, having a strong environmental (and social) ethic might attract clients. Asger explains that one of SGS's tasks at the moment is

> finding new work and … *competing in the marketplace, within the ethical framework that we've given ourselves*, which is what makes us different, and makes us special as well, gives us an edge. The people interested in the work we do, I think, are also supportive of the fact that we're doing all this other stuff and it's not just a profit business. That distinguishes us. (emphasis added)

Here we can see how economic practices (in this instance, competition in the marketplace) are moderated by SGS's ethical framework. This standpoint distinguishes SGS from other operators and potentially attracts clients who support another way of 'doing business'. A further potential benefit of SGS's environmental and social stance is that it also attracts workers who are committed to the enterprise. Again, Asger explains:

> With SGS, the people who work here I think they ideologically agree with what the business is trying to do, and that's the thing that they want to do with their life, and so SGS offers a vehicle that they can do that with their life and still get a wage.

Asger's experience is that these workers who are committed to the enterprise's environmental and social values are more likely to stay longer term, a situation that has positive economic benefits. Indeed, Asger's ambition is to deepen the enterprise's social and environmental practices with not only dental insurance and a housing co-operative, but a multi-purpose timber farm that would absorb carbon while providing a rural retreat for workers. For Asger 'These are all possibilities. And it's up to us to try and make that happen if we want it to happen.' If such possibilities are to be realized, surplus has to be produced; and for a community enterprise like SGS surplus has to be produced in a way that is consistent with its ethical framework. Thus SGS is constantly engaged in ethical economic decision-making that takes into account both economic imperatives and social and environmental concerns. Such decision-making constitutes a community economy where surplus production and distribution are governed by the social question of how we are to live together *and* the environmental question of how we are to live together on the planet.

Like SGS, Flying Eagle Facilitators has made ethical economic decisions about how it operates. Indeed only recently the enterprise made an extremely difficult decision. FEF has been highly successful in training and employing Eagleby residents as facilitators, and being a vehicle for people to move into full-time paid employment. Over twenty people have moved into paid employment as a result of their work with FEF, and these jobs have included management-level positions in the community and government sectors. Paradoxically, however, success in getting people into paid work has eroded the enterprise's very ability to operate. With members moving into paid employment there are fewer and fewer people to do the jobs that come in, to recruit and train new members, to tender for jobs, and even to be active on the committee of management. As a result, the enterprise has been picking up work that comes to it rather than actively seeking new work. Along with this change within the enterprise there has been an important change in the context in which FEF operates. At the time the enterprise started, the state government was running a highly participatory Community Renewal programme in disadvantaged areas like Eagleby. Residents had a high degree of input, and there was a strong sense that government was working in a very different way in disadvantaged communities and that an enterprise like FEF could act on its motto to 'Deliver the voice of the people.' However, the second iteration of Community Renewal has less opportunity for input from residents. This changed context has impacted heavily on FEF, as one member highlights:

> It's also about … 'What is our purpose?' 'Has our time come?' Flying Eagles did a whole lot of work outside of Eagleby, sort of Community Renewal stuff … and so when you were out there doing consultation and engagement and stuff in communities that were similar (or we thought they were similar) there was that real drive and commitment and it's really about whether that's still there or whether that's gone. But the initial stuff was a catalyst for something that's no longer … but now we're eight years down the track, so unless you have some other real driving force, or purpose, you know, 'Is this something you want to continue with?'

So FEF confronts the major ethical economic decision about whether to continue, a decision all too easily read as community enterprise failure. But as one member sums up:

> *Rob*: It is all about how people want to look at things. I think the fact that they've continued going for the time they have, they've achieved an enormous amount in that time. They took out a business achievement award a few years ago, and had really some quite significant amounts of money go through, and lots of people have gained employment that they wouldn't have otherwise gained. It may be spasmodic but at the same time…
>
> *Jenny*: It's been a stepping stone.
>
> *Rob*: Yes, when you've not got much income and you suddenly find yourself able to earn some money, that's really something. So I don't see that if the decision is to fold completely, I don't see that that's a negative, I don't see that that means failure, just that your time's up, you know. And you have to think about it. Do you want to become just another NGO that provides government services, government-funded services? That wasn't what this was about in the first place. More and more you look around you and organizations are having to do that to survive. …
>
> *Jenny*: And you're going just for the sake of doing it. You have to ask yourself, what did we set out to do originally?
>
> *Rob/Lynn/Peter*: Yeah!

Rob: When we set out in the beginning it was all about delivering the voice of the people. And ensuring that, no matter who or what their role in that community was, their voice was heard. That was the purpose!

In this discussion in December 2007 members raise the possibility of closing. As one member points out, if FEF was to take a purely economic perspective then the enterprise might well be able to continue by changing direction and providing government-funded services. But this would mean rethinking ethical commitments and *delivering government services* to so-called needy populations rather than delivering the voice of the people to government. In mid-2008 FEF decided to close, a decision that meant staying with the original ethical commitment rather than modifying the commitment and becoming a service-oriented enterprise, albeit one that could be more certain of government funding.

This recent decision to close provides an opportunity to reflect on 'the Eagles' achievements, which, along with the employment outcomes, include:

- managing two government-funded projects which provided accredited and non-accredited training for over five hundred residents over a three-year period;
- facilitating and recording at over fifty different community engagement and community consultation processes for local and state governments, private consultants and developers;
- participating in myriad community forums and activities lobbying for grassroots involvement in government decision-making;
- training university students and other community organizations in skills related to workshop facilitation and recording.

As one member reflects:

This has been quite an achievement and a real success story, that people who were largely unskilled could achieve this much and leave the legacy they have in the communities they come from. The real legacy is that of more informed residents who are better connected into their community and who know how to have their say about those things that matter to them.

In summary, FEF has clearly done more than deliver the voice of the people; it has enabled people to have a voice in the first place.

Both SGS and FEF are making economic decisions about the operation and future of their enterprises, but these are *ethical* economic decisions shaped by each enterprise's ethical commitments. In so doing, SGS and FEF are experimenting with what is possible when economic practices are driven by ethical commitments and concerns. They show us how (to paraphrase Gibson-Graham, 2006: 98) people are starting where they are and with what they have at hand to build ethical and community economies. In the process of building these economies, community enterprises are tested. In the two examples discussed here, the characteristics of SGS and FEF change, as does the context in which they operate – with implications for both enterprises' commercial activities. As they negotiate their way through the changes, ethical commitments come to the fore. For example, SGS contemplates the type of work it is willing to do, and decides to refuse work that compromises its environmental commitments – even if this jeopardizes the enterprise's ability to produce surplus that might be used to develop social programmes for workers. Similarly, FEF contemplates – and decides upon – closing, an outcome we perhaps too readily associate with failure; yet, as members make clear, it is an outcome better matched with the enterprise's ethical commitments than the pathway of expansion and diversification that we might more usually admire.

Diverse economic practices

The third way in which SGS and FEF practise economic experimentation is by innovating with a diversity of economic practices to sustain their operations and enact their ethical commitments.

Table 5.1 locates SGS in terms of its diverse economic practices. As a community enterprise operating as a sole-trader business and then as a not-for-profit company, SGS has the structure of an alternative capitalist enterprise. It is like a capitalist enterprise in that employees produce surplus labour that is appropriated and distributed by someone else (the sole trader in the first structure, and the manager and board of directors in the second structure). However, unlike a capitalist enterprise, profit-maximization is not the driving imperative; rather, as discussed in the previous section, social and environmental commitments drive the enterprise.

In terms of transactions, SGS uses the market, but also alternative markets and non-markets. For example, to get the enterprise started Paul's father loaned money and took out a credit card in his own name for Paul to use for the business, and Paul's father-in-law lent a vehicle – both non-market transactions that reflect an ethic of caring for family.[2] Other expressions of care were prevalent in the early days: a friend also loaned money, a neighbour loaned gardening equipment, and a Catholic community worker donated gardening equipment when a community house closed. The new manager, Asger, describes these types of alternative and non-market transactions as 'embedded gifting', and he points out that 'SGS has been built on that [embedded gifting] in lots of ways, and that's in there in the process and the materials we have and in the relationships that have existed in the past, and are very much part of the informal way that SGS works.' Indeed, the tradition of gifting was part of the transition from the old to the new legal structure. The new not-for-profit company purchased SGS from Paul through a no-interest loan arrangement with him. Paul also lent money to the new entity to cover operating expenses, and this second loan is being repaid through a low-interest arrangement (which allows Paul to make interest repayments on this money, which he borrowed from another source).

In terms of labour arrangements, SGS employees are paid a wage based on the number of hours worked. When it was a sole trader business, the owner was paid a share of the surplus that was generated. This was a variable amount, depending on how much surplus was generated each week or fortnight. The owner also contributed his unpaid volunteer labour to the enterprise. In the new legal structure, the new manager is paid a wage based on the number of hours worked, usually around forty hours per fortnight (which suits Asger as he also has shared care of two children). Like Paul, Asger also contributes unpaid volunteer labour, usually between five and eight hours each fortnight. The new board of directors recognizes that this is not ideal, and in Asger's words the board's view is that 'SGS should not be built on free labour, as that would create a false

TABLE 5.1 The diverse economy of Sustainable Gardening
Services

Transactions	Labour	Enterprise
Market	*Wage*	*Capitalist*
Sells gardening services to clients (e.g. property management firms, local council, individual households) Purchases business inputs from suppliers (e.g. fuel, equipment)	Employees paid a wage based on an hourly rate	
Alternative market	*Alternative paid*	*Alternative capitalist*
Father took out credit card in his name for the business Former owner borrows money from a source and lends to the new legal entity at low interest	Owner paid a share of the surplus (a variable amount) Self-employed landscapers paid a share of jobs	
Non-market	*Unpaid*	*Non-capitalist*
Father and friend loaned money to help start enterprise Father-in-law lent vehicle to help start enterprise Neighbour loaned gardening equipment to help start enterprise Catholic community worker donated gardening equipment to help start enterprise Philanthropic support from Social Enterprise Hub (e.g. computer)	Former owner contributes volunteer labour Current manager contributes volunteer labour Board of directors contribute volunteer labour Volunteer advice and support provided by supporters (e.g. Social Enterprise Hub, large corporations, other community enterprises, community members, owner of mowing franchise)	

economy.' Nevertheless Asger also recognizes that SGS works in an
extremely competitive market where other operators, particularly sole
operators who do not have the same costs of managing staff, will
charge less in order to secure jobs. To change the situation SGS is
working on decreasing mowing and garden maintenance work, and

increasing landscaping work, as this area is more specialized and clients are willing to pay more. The ambition is for SGS to move completely into landscaping as this would not only pay for all Asger's labour, but would increase the amount workers are paid each hour and enable the enterprise to accumulate surplus that can be used for social and environmental benefits such as workers' dental insurance, a housing co-operative and a timber farm.

SGS also has labour inputs from other sources. When there are larger landscaping jobs to complete, SGS calls on its network of self-employed landscapers to assist, and the self-employed landscapers receive a share of the payment for jobs. SGS also has volunteer contributions of advice and support from a number of sources. SGS is part of a mentoring programme run through the Social Enterprise Hub (a joint initiative of Brisbane City Council, Social Ventures Australia and PricewaterhouseCoopers) (see www.socialenterprisehubs. org/node/11) and through this SGS receives input from Hub staff and mentors in large corporations. SGS also benefits from the volunteer input of its board of directors and from other supporters, including community members and even the owner of a franchise mowing operation who could be seen as a competitor in the marketplace but who willingly advised SGS.

Another way of representing the range of diverse economic practices that sustain SGS and through which SGS practises its ethical commitments is illustrated by Figure 5.1. This figure demonstrates the range of networks that SGS has developed through its diverse economic practices. The diagram shows how, far from being isolated and marginal, SGS is embedded in a network of relationships with other enterprises (including capitalist, alternative capitalist/community and non-capitalist/self-employed enterprises), government bodies, and community and family members. And, rather than being dependent on these relationships, they involve reciprocity and *inter*dependence. For example, there is a reciprocal relationship between SGS and the local council (SGS provides mowing and landscaping services that the council needs to acquire); between SGS and community and family members (SGS receives support in various forms but also provides an avenue for community and family members to express and act on their social and familial commitments); and between

FIGURE 5.1   The diverse economy: networks of
Sustainable Gardening Services

SGS and large corporations (SGS receives free mentoring but also
provides an opportunity for large corporations to practise corporate
responsibility).

The example of SGS shows how community enterprises can be
embedded in networks of reciprocal and interdependent relationships
that are based on diverse economic practices. For SGS the outcome
of these relationships is that the enterprise is able to operate as an
employer of economically marginalized groups like recently arrived
refugees and the long-term unemployed. Like SGS, FEF also relies
on diverse economic practices – particularly *within* the enterprise. For
example, in terms of labour arrangements, when members facilitate
and record workshops for clients they receive a payment based on
an hourly rate. However, the possibility of this paid work is under-
pinned by the unpaid volunteer work of members or by work that

is alternatively paid. One of the members who was injured in an industrial accident describes such an arrangement:

> I was put on the pension in 2000 due to an industrial accident and I was told 'Can't work on a building site'. So where does that leave you? You've got no other skills, so where does it leave it? So I was fortunate enough the first twelve months; I had bit of a think about what I was going do to and then in 2002 I thought 'Okay, let's do this'. I did my Certificate 2 in IT. And I started doing some courses and thought 'Hang on, I can actually work in an office. I can work with computers and all that sort of thing.' So I just decided 'Well, how about I start putting my time towards the Flying Eagles.' Who in return paid for my training to be completed, which was good because we both got something... And that's the opportunity I got, all those years ago. There were a couple of people working in the office on a roster and I just came in, worked with them, learnt from them but also got trained up in how to use the computers, and then gradually over the last four years have gone to various courses and have gone from just sitting at a desk to coordinating projects, making sure the office is managed properly and things like that, anything that needs to be in on time.

So Peter initially started by volunteering his time to help out FEF, and then was remunerated by having his computer training paid by FEF – a reciprocal arrangement in which, as Peter describes, 'we both got something'. Since then, Peter has continued to volunteer his time running the office. In return, Peter is provided with a sense of purpose and social connection by working alongside others. Indeed, when asked what he would do without FEF, Peter replied: 'Sit at home and stare at four walls'. So, along with the paid work that comes through workshop facilitation and recording, FEF provides unpaid but *purposeful* work. Indeed, one member estimates that the amount of unpaid work would match the amount of paid work generated by the enterprise. The distinction between paid and purposeful work raises the issue of the role of community enterprises. Are community enterprises a stepping stone into 'real' (i.e. paid) employment? Or are community enterprises something more? Is their role also to generate diverse and meaningful forms of work based on valuing the contribution that people are able to make and providing social connections through both the paid *and* purposeful work context?

Conclusion

This chapter has argued that community enterprises can be framed as a form of economic activism through which community members are experimenting with economic possibilities based on social and environmental commitments rather than a narrow economic emphasis. This means that community enterprises are reshaping economic practices in light of their ethical commitments, and in the process they are building community economies which are concerned with the social question of how we live together and the environmental question of how we live together on this planet. This is by no means easy; the examples of Sustainable Gardening Services and Flying Eagle Facilitators show how community enterprises are always reviewing and reflecting on their practices as circumstances change and as they learn through trial and error. There is no single development pathway for community enterprises to follow; rather, as SGS and FEF demonstrate, it is through a process of ethical economic decision-making that development pathways and possibilities are opened up.

This raises the question of the role of academic research in contributing to building ethical economies, particularly in terms of how we represent community enterprises like SGS and FEF. One approach is to frame these as marginal endeavours that not only have little impact on the main game of capitalist economic development and globalization, but are economically weak and even unsustainable. Another approach, the one I have taken in this chapter, is to frame community enterprises as a form of economic experimentation through which we might learn about the economic possibilities that are available to us when social and environmental concerns drive economic practices. From SGS we learn how an enterprise can moderate the amount of surplus it produces in order to generate social benefits or enact its environmental commitments, and we learn about the novel ways that surplus can be distributed for social and environmental benefit – for example, for workers' dental insurance, for a workers' housing co-operative, or for a multi-purpose timber farm. From SGS we also learn about the forms of economic diversity and economic interdependence that can be used to sustain enterprises. From FEF we learn about the value of unpaid but purposeful work, and to query the usual development pathway of growth and appreciate that success might also mean acting with integrity and making the difficult but ethical decision to close.

Notes

1. There are other reasons why the other enterprises folded; nevertheless there is no doubt that the modest experimental approach meant that Santa's Workshop could quickly start operating and that there were tangible outcomes that could then be built upon.
2. This use of family financing is not unique to community enterprise; researchers point out that many, if not most, small and entrepreneurial businesses use financial bootstrapping of this type not only to get started but to keep operating (e.g. Lahm and Little, 2005).

References

Barraket, J. (2008) 'Social enterprise and governance: Implications for the Australian third sector', in Jo Barraket, ed., *Strategic Issues for the Not-for-profit Sector*, UNSW Press, Sydney.

Brotherhood of St Laurence (2006) 'Community enterprise development Initiative', Brotherhood of St Laurence, Melbourne, www.bsl.org.au/main. asp?PageId=3561&iMainMenuPageId=3561; accessed 12 April 2008.

Cameron, J., and J. Gerrard (2008) 'Report on the workshop on community enterprises in the food sector', Centre for Urban and Regional Research, University of Newcastle, NSW, Australia.

Cameron, J., and K. Gibson (2005a) 'Alternative pathways to community and economic development: The Latrobe Valley Community Partnering Project', *Geographical Research* 43(3): 274–85.

Cameron, J., and K. Gibson (2005b) 'Participatory action research in a poststructuralist vein', *Geoforum* 36(3): 315–31.

CERES Community Environment Park (2007) *2007 Annual Report*, CERES Community Environment Park, Brunswick East, Melbourne.

Department for Victorian Communities (2006) 'Enterprising communities: The Victorian government's community enterprise strategy', Victorian Government, Melbourne, www.dvc.vic.gov.au/Web14/dvc/dvcmain.nsf/allDocs/ RWP0C47790245D57B16CA257045007FFBE3?OpenDocument; accessed 12 April 2008.

Gibson-Graham, J.K. (2006) *A Postcapitalist Politics*, University of Minnesota Press, Minneapolis.

Lahm, R., and H. Little (2005) 'Bootstrapping business start-ups: Entrepreneurship literature, textbooks, and teaching practices versus current business practices?', *Journal of Entrepreneurship Education* 8: 61–73.

Lyons, M., and A. Passey (2006) 'Need public policy ignore the third sector?

Government policy in Australia and the United Kingdom', *Australian Journal of Public Administration* 65(3): 90–102.

Sarkissian, W. (2005) 'Stories in a park: Giving voice to the voiceless in Eagleby, Australia', *Planning Theory and Practice* 6(1): 103–17.

Sarkissian, W., A. Hirst and B. Stenberg, with S. Walton (2003) *Community Participation in Practice: New Directions*, Institute for Sustainability and Technology Policy, Murdoch University, Western Australia.

Simons, R. (2000) 'Social enterprise: An opportunity to harness capacities', Research and Advocacy Briefing Paper No. 7, The Smith Family, Sydney, www.smithfamily.com.au/documents/Briefing_Paper_7_6CB8C.pdf; accessed 12 April 2008.

Spear, R., C. Cornforth and M. Aiken (2007) 'Governance and social enterprise', paper presented at the Ciriec Research Conference on the Social Economy, Victoria BC, October, http://conference.se-es.ca/wp-content/uploads/2008/02/roger-spear-chris-cornforth-mike-aiken-re.pdf.

Talbot, C., P. Tregilgas and K. Harrison (2002) *Social Enterprise in Australia: An Introductory Handbook*, Adelaide Central Mission, Adelaide, www.ucwesley-adelaide.org.au/publications/resources/Social_Enterpse_Part1_2.pdf.

6

Building community-based social enterprises in the Philippines: diverse development pathways

The Community Economies Collective[1]
and Katherine Gibson

Community-based social enterprises offer a new strategy for people-centred local economic development in the majority 'developing' world. In this chapter we recount the stories of four social enterprise experiments that have arisen over the last five years from partnerships between communities, NGOs and municipal governments in the Philippines and university-based researchers from Australia. The concept of social enterprise coming out of the 'Western' social economy context is relatively unfamiliar in Asia. In practice, however, social enterprises, in the form of co-operatives, have long played a central role in rural development in countries like the Philippines. Moreover many customary, indigenous, traditional and local practices of mutual assistance form a social economy 'on the ground' that provides well-being and an informal social safety net for millions of people. We argue here that community-based social enterprise development that builds on local forms of social economy has much to offer, especially as mainstream economic development options are failing to narrow the gap between rich and poor.

At the national level dominant political factions in the Philippines continue to support greater openness to global economic forces as the main development option – condoning the exit of up to a million citizens each year on limited-term migrant work contracts around the world and welcoming foreign investment in export-processing zones, minerals extraction and export plantation agriculture. But increasingly even the mainstream economic analysts who advocate greater global integration have to admit problems with this development scenario. Balisacan and Hill (2007: 29) document the extreme and increasing regional inequalities in the Philippines, noting that the country's 'unenviable record on poverty reduction in recent years is the outcome not only of its comparatively low per capita GDP growth rate but also its weakness in transforming a given rate of income growth into poverty reduction'. Other, more radical, political factions that agitate for regime change still advocate nationalization of key sectors of the economy and are dismissive of local attempts to reshape economies. Meanwhile, international development agencies working in the Philippines remain committed to individual micro-enterprise development and micro-credit programmes, backed up by infrastructure projects (led by selected national and international construction companies) and governance support (e.g. property titling and GIS-based strategies for increasing urban tax collection).

Municipal governments charged with the responsibility for local economic development since the decentralization of governance in 1991 are increasingly turning to the NGO sector to form partnerships for local economic change. In this chapter we examine some experiments with social enterprise development that local communities might replicate. These initiatives take up a number of different challenges. First, they are offering a new and somewhat alternative opportunity for local people to 'get ahead'. In the mindset of local communities, development means striving to make ends meet by getting a family member to migrate as an overseas contract worker or starting a small family micro-enterprise, such as a tiny grocery (*sari sari*) store or tricycle business offering public transport. For those households able to gather the finances to afford migration or a micro-enterprise, these strategies help them to get by and make ends meet, but few are able to generate enough surplus to really get ahead. Social enterprises draw on the collective effort of many people and partnerships and have a greater capacity to produce not only income for those involved, but a surplus that can be distributed to social ends (Pearce, 1993).

Second, social enterprise development relies on the active participation of community members who take charge of planning and problem-solving. There is no 'one-size-fits-all' governance format that is imposed from outside, so organizational structures are worked out as the enterprise is formed and grows. This challenges the norm. Many rural people in the Philippines are members of credit, consumer, marketing and service co-operatives. In 2007 there were 59,765 registered co-operatives with a membership of almost 3 million (Griffiths, 2007). Over the past decades producer marketing co-operatives with state-mandated bureaucratic structures have been advocated by the national government as a way of managing small farm production, securing agricultural product for the export market, and improving livelihoods in rural areas. But many rural people criticize the lack of participation in governance by grassroots membership and the absence of accountability. In recent years, however, the co-operative sector has worked to provide a more independent and alternative voice (Teodosio, 2003). As part of this revitalization of economic alternatives a small number of NGOs have become interested in social enterprise development as a strategy of economic intervention that emphasizes community participation.

In the first part of this chapter we discuss two experiments conducted by Unlad Kabayan Migrant Services Foundation Inc., an NGO that has pioneered social enterprise development in the Philippines. In the second part we turn to two other experimental interventions piloted in an action research project that emerged from a partnership between Unlad Kabayan, a group of researchers based at the Australian National University, the Municipality of Jagna in the island province of Bohol and community members in a number of *barangays* (neighbourhoods) in the municipality. The four enterprise stories presented here were written collectively by NGO workers from the Philippines and ANU researchers at a writing and reflection workshop held in Australia in December 2007 designed to create a more accessible knowledge about this innovative development pathway.[2]

NGO-facilitated social enterprise development

Unlad Kabayan began in 1994 as a project of the Asian Migrant Centre in Hong Kong to harness migrant savings for alternative investments. The idea was to direct the investments of migrant savings groups organized all over the world into productive enterprises in the Philippines. The hope was that these enterprises would help migrants reintegrate into their home economy and not be forced into cyclical migration. Remittance funds are usually spent on individual household consumption and education expenses of family members back home. More often than not they are used to equip the next generation of workers to leave and seek overseas contracts. Unlad set up as an NGO in the Philippines in 1996 to facilitate migrant savings and investment mobilization and take on the role of business incubator. By 2000 it was supporting migrant investor groups with investments in businesses all over the country from Ilioilo in the north to Davao in the south (Gibson et al., 2001). The range of businesses included merchandizing (school supplies, agricultural-veterinarian supplies), agriculture-related (organic chicken raising, rice milling, integrated farming) and some manufacturing (noodle making, ube-aromatic yam confectionery). The choice of locality for business development was largely driven by the allegiances of certain migrant savings groups to their home communities and Unlad had little control over the geography of their activities. There was no substantive connection between the different enterprises, and at that time relations with local government units were distant or non-existent. The businesses were run along relatively traditional lines with the emphasis on returns on the investments made by migrant savers.

Over the past eight years or so this has changed as Unlad has learnt from its successes and failures. The key expectations that fuelled the initial vision have had to be reassessed. One is the expectation that migrants will be able to return to work in their investment enterprises in great numbers. Generating employment in small businesses is difficult, and while returnees might aspire to a management role, they often do not have the specific skills necessary to take over management of the enterprise. As the story of the Matin-ao Rice Centre shows, some migrants have been able to return to run businesses successfully, but as yet the number is small. Another expectation is that the migrant savers are the best judge of what kind of business to set up or invest in. Increasingly Unlad has taken on the strategic role of identifying business opportunities, marshalling migrant investor interest and acting as a business incubator. It has gradually concentrated its activities in the southern regions of the country (Bohol and Mindanao). Over time has come the realization that migrant investment needs to be combined with local communities willing to spearhead enterprise development and take on the responsibility of making this work.

Throughout this learning process Unlad started to conceptualize social enterprises whose objectives are to achieve direct community benefit as well as a return on investment. Its interest in this kind of 'alternative' investment was crystallized with the establishment of the Linamon SEEDS (Social Entrepreneurship and Enterprise Development) Centre, a social enterprise set up in partnership with Linamon Municipal Council in an abandoned agricultural training centre donated by the Council. Through such partnerships with local governments and other community-based NGOs, Unlad is pioneering social enterprise development in the Philippines. Recently May-an Villalba, the executive director of Unlad Kabayan, was named as Philippines Social Entrepreneur of the Year 2007 by the Schwab Foundation in recognition of her groundbreaking role. As the following two stories show, Unlad is finding its way as a social enterprise incubator, treading the fine line between responsible investment of migrant savers' funds and providing direct community benefits via social enterprise activity.

The Matin-ao Rice Centre:
from migrant small business to social enterprise

'The community needs social enterprises; it does not simply need employment.' Over the past years Elsa, the driving force behind the Matin-ao Rice Centre, has struggled with this statement. Elsa's story exemplifies the tension felt by entrepreneurs who want to develop an enterprise that will generate a good return for a community of international investors, but who are also pulled by the local community's needs and aspirations for a better life. For Elsa and her group of migrant savers working in Taiwan the Matin-ao Rice Centre is an avenue of investment, a way to move from being an employee to being an investor and, for Elsa, a manager. For the Matin-ao community the Rice Centre has extended beyond a source of employment and trade in rice to become a focus of community life, meeting basic food and farming needs, with Elsa herself providing community leadership and counselling. While Elsa has brought the migrant investors and the Matin-ao community together, this is not what she had in mind at the outset.

Elsa has always had strong business aspirations. She took up a contract as a migrant care worker in Taiwan as a way of 'getting ahead' after finding it hard to secure paid employment in the Philippines. While working overseas she began saving and joined a migrant savings group. Her employer in Taiwan owned a rice mill, and this gave Elsa the idea to direct her savings group to invest in a foreclosed co-operative rice mill in her home town of Matin-ao in Surigao del Norte Province, Mindanao. By the time bidding opened for the rice mill the savings group had gathered half of the money being asked. They sought additional credit from Unlad Kabayan and Quedancor (Republic of the Philippines Department of Agriculture Rural Credit Corporation). After two attempts the bid put in by Elsa's savings group was successful. The seller and another bidder, a *barangay* captain, 'completely underestimated Elsa as a serious buyer', recalls May-an Villalba, executive director of Unlad Kabayan.

In early 2003 the business was reopened to supply rice milling services to local farmers. Elsa came home to make the mill profitable and generate income for her investors, and she was willing to sacrifice her own income to meet this goal. Unlad Kabayan sent a staff investment adviser and an engineer to appraise the property and discovered that it was worth more than the migrant investors paid for it. This gave the group of investors, including Elsa, assurance that their money was well invested.

After the first rice harvest in 2003 the mill suffered losses. Elsa had underestimated the competitive environment into which she had ventured and the costs of overhauling an old mill to get it reliably operational. A business plan was developed with Unlad Kabayan. The planning process revealed that 'milling rice seasonally is not enough' to sustain regular returns. After visiting other rice mills to see how they operated Elsa began buying *palay* (unhusked rice) from farmers, stockpiling it and milling it throughout the year to be sold as processed rice wholesale and retail. However, there wasn't always more rice to buy as rice farmers already had relationships with traders and Elsa did not have enough cash to out-price them. So in the second year of operation Elsa took out a loan, mortgaging and risking the entire enterprise. She also asked farmers, 'Why aren't you coming to my rice mill?' Farmers told her about their indebted relationships with other commercial traders. Elsa responded by providing credit to farmers, especially for farm inputs. After talking to farmers' wives, Elsa decided to provide credit in kind, so that cash wouldn't be diverted to gambling and drinking.

From the business plan and listening to farmers, Elsa knew that she needed to generate other enterprises. After accessing further investment, she opened an agrivet (agricultural and veterinarian) supplies store and, later, in the fourth year, a grocery store. Elsa was confident in initiating these enterprises because she knew farmers wanted them. These new enterprises rented space from the rice mill, providing an income stream to the mill and generating a profit for investors. All of the businesses lacked capital, so in 2005 Elsa returned to Taiwan to promote enterprise investment by migrant workers.

Economies of scale are critical to the viability of the rice milling business and this requires substantial capital. As a social enterprise, the Matin-ao Rice Centre has been able to draw on the relatively patient equity investment from Elsa's fellow migrant workers and soft loans from government and the NGOs. But Unlad needed to educate migrant investors to be patient as part of their savings and investment mobilization work. Many migrants think that investment is something you put in and take out any time, like savings in a bank. Others expect a quick return on investment and demand 'instant and substantial' dividends. While they lack an understanding of mainstream business principles, they know even less about how an alternative economy might work and how they could be contributors to and beneficiaries of alternative wealth-creating and distributing businesses.

With additional funds, in 2006 the Rice Centre opened a farm machinery service in response to farmers' requests so that they could plough early before the rains stopped. In 2007 it bought a hauling truck. Today the Rice Centre includes six affiliate businesses: the rice mill, a farm machinery hiring service, farm credit, an agricultural and veterinarian supply store, a mini grocery store and a *palay* trading business. In 2007 the business had a net worth of P3.5 million (Au$91,000 or €51,000), annual sales worth P4.4 million, and made a net profit of P207,000 (Au$5440 or €3,000). In the rural Philippines context these are sizeable amounts. The Centre employs 11 people full time, 1 part-time and 8 seasonal workers; services the needs of 129 local farmers; and is a focus of investment by 66 overseas migrant workers.

Elsa has the spirit of an entrepreneur. She has been 'driven' to build up the Rice Centre as a business that attracts ongoing investment and has demonstrated that sacrifice, hard work and creativity are key to new enterprise development. Entrepreneurs, however, do not work in a vacuum. Nor is their market shaped solely by competition and supply-and-demand factors. What makes a *social* entrepreneur is the willingness to recognize the multiple and diverse factors that influence enterprise success and to direct business activity so that it contributes to and develops a community around the enterprise. The community thus shapes the enterprise, creating further opportunities for development by instigating ventures that branch out in avenues that might not otherwise have been pursued. The community's aspirations have been intertwined with those of the rice mill and its migrant investors to generate the Matin-ao Rice Centre. But one cannot assume that there are pre-existing communities that will contribute to the development of a social enterprise. Both investment communities and local communities often need to be created and maintained. In this case Unlad Kabayan took a leading role in calling forth the communities that support and finance the Rice Centre and making sure that people are at the centre of the enterprise's mission.

Incubating social enterprise: the Davao Oriental Coco Husk Social Enterprise Incorporated (DOCHSEi)

DOCHSEi is a coconut-husk processing plant that was established by Unlad Kabayan as a business incubation project in July 2004 in the municipality of San Isidro, Davao Oriental Province in Mindanao. It was begun to improve the livelihoods of economically marginalized tenant farmers and landless people and contribute to economic growth in the municipality. Furthermore, it was designed to provide opportunities for Filipino migrant workers to invest their remittances, not only for profit, but in a way that would provide social benefits to the broader community. The plant was established with an initial investment of P5 million (Au$130,000; €73,700) in partnership with a local NGO, Kalumonan Development Centre, which focused on livelihood development projects for local coconut farmers, fishers and the Muslim community. While Unlad Kabayan provided expertise in social enterprise development and funding to support the establishment of the plant, office and equipment, Kalumonan gifted land for the production site and counterpart funding. Most of the financial support has been sourced from foreign donors, including Christian Aid, the Inter-church Organization for Development Cooperation, and the CARE's Canada Fund for Local Initiatives, but some funding was donated locally by the family of former mayor Tina Yu, executive director of Kalumonan. San Isidro was an ideal location for a coconut-husk processing plant, not only because of the poor economic conditions in the municipality, but also because it was the number one coconut-producing province in the Philippines and so had an abundant supply of coconut husk.

In addition to the aim of generating economic benefits for the community, DOCHSEi was also established as an environmentally friendly enterprise. Before it was established, coconut husk was a waste product of the local copra industry, clogging local creeks and rivers and washing into the ocean, killing fish, coral and other marine life. DOCHSEi provided a way for farmers to make money from this waste, turning it into coco fibre, which is used for twine, erosion control matting, flower pots, hats, bags, wall decorations, door mats and mattress filling. Today the plant is producing fibre that is exported to China and used in car seat upholstery and mattress-making; geo-netting for the growing national market of local governments that use it for erosion control along roads and river channels; and handicrafts for the local market.

As with most social enterprises, the development of DOCHSEi has been punctuated by crisis moments where ethical commitments to social objectives rather than hard-headed business judgements have guided actions. At the outset competitors derided DOCHSEi when they came from across the province to see the new coco coir plant. 'You won't last six months with that old equipment!' they claimed. They were nearly right. After only six months of financial losses, the management board recommended that the NGOs supporting the fledgling social enterprise close down the coco coir operation. But the NGO staff of Unlad Kabayan, the business incubator, refused. They did not want to be just another NGO deserting the community after the funding had run out. NGOs had a reputation in the region as failures in sustaining business and livelihood activities and they wanted to prove the critics wrong. Furthermore, they felt responsible for the welfare of the thirty local workers who were employed by the plant at that time.

Uncertain of what to do next, the Unlad staff discussed the situation with the workers and asked their opinion. 'Do not worry,' the workers said, 'we will just work without a salary now and then we will be the ones to sell the products. After we are able to sell the products that will be the time we will receive our salary.' So the workers took charge. No longer were they beneficiaries, passively receiving handouts from an NGO or salaries from an employer, but partners working alongside the managers to keep the enterprise alive.

Others, too, have come to the aid of the enterprise to sustain its activities over the last three years. First, there was support from other NGOs, which offered technical assistance to improve production efficiency and management protocols in order to increase overall output. The Canadian Executive Services Office, for example, assisted DOCHSEi by sending a volunteer mechanical engineer to advise on efficient production and management processes. He helped cut down on time wastage, which has contributed to increased productivity, and helped DOCHSEi become more competitive and profitable. The corporate volunteer programme of the Philippine Business for Social Progress also sent a volunteer, who assisted by compiling a production and operations manual that serves as a guide to implementing the rules and policies of the enterprise efficiently. Then there was support from the Department of Agriculture, which granted funds to improve the solar dryer. Support, however, has not been limited to NGOs and formal agencies. When another privately owned coco coir plant opened in the municipality, local suppliers, workers and others in the community stayed loyal to DOCHSEi. They did not want to lose the many benefits that the social enterprise offered them as a community, such as health insurance; free training on gender, health, technical skills and other topics; flexible working conditions; and monthly incentives for workers who meet production targets. The relationships formed between management and workers, community members, government departments and NGOs have been the key to nurturing and protecting the growth and sustainability of the DOCHSEi vision.

It has been critical that both workers and others within the local community understand that DOCHSEi is a social enterprise and that they have a stake in its long-term viability and success. Activities that have helped to foster this sense of ownership and commitment include team-building exercises, social entrepreneurship training, skills training and weekly meetings between workers and team leaders. The responsibility for decision-making is not held by the management team and board alone. Staff in different production units contribute ideas, make recommendations and even implement their own decisions at different levels to help improve the productivity of individual workers and the enterprise as a whole. The weekly and monthly meetings keep the management team updated so they can discuss crucial problems that may lead to poor performance. Trusting the capability and initiative of workers motivates them to work more efficiently and productively.

In addition to the 125 production, technical and office staff now employed at the DOCHSEi plant, up to 90 homeworkers are employed on piece rates to spin the fibre into string that is then woven into geo-matting. Fibre is delivered to women at home in the surrounding area. Groups of two to four women share the use of a simple spinning wheel to make string. They transport the wheel from home to home and spin in their spare time, as one reported, 'instead of watching television or gossiping'. This brings added income into the household and spreads the effects of the DOCHSEi plant deep into the community. Further income for the households of tenant farmers comes as payment for what is otherwise coconut waste product. They receive 100 pesos per truckload of husks. At the plant there are plans to introduce a profit-sharing system so that workers have an ongoing stake in the social enterprise. This venture shows that even during times of financial difficulty, when normal business enterprises would have decided to cease operation, it is possible for a social enterprise to remain committed to building sustainable livelihood options for the poor and marginalized sections of the community.

These two stories illustrate a development pathway in which an active NGO takes a leading organizational role. The Matin-ao Rice Centre and DOCHSEi have been able to operate on a relatively large scale by drawing on the capital resources of a dispersed international community of migrant savers and investors. Importantly, Unlad Kabayan has taken on the pioneering tasks of convincing migrant workers that they can become social investors, working with migrant entrepreneurs to become responsive to local community needs, and working with community members to enrol them in an unfamiliar form of business.

Grassroots social enterprise development

The question that our action research explored was whether rural people in economically marginalized areas could develop community-based social enterprises that built on local resources and provided well-being directly.[3] The insights gained from the experience of Unlad Kabayan pointed to the need for communities to be mobilized so that migrant investment, if it could be marshalled, would flow into an environment fertile with enterprise ideas that were being tested and were ready for financial support. Initial research in communities such as that of Jagna showed that some people, often inspired by a charismatic returnee, were matching migrant remittances donated to the community with volunteer labour to produce benefit for all – for example, paving farm-to-market roads or improving local facilities. The action research aimed to see if this kind of spontaneous initiative could be directed towards social enterprise development.

The concept of a community-based *social* enterprise – that is, a *business* explicitly focused on improving well-being of community members and not just on business goals – was foreign to most rural Filipinos. More familiar were small private businesses and co-operatives, but both were associated with problems. Many had seen small businesses fail due to lack of capital and intense competition in oversaturated markets. And while many were members of co-operatives, they had experienced dysfunctional and dishonest management and did not feel involved or confident enough to challenge this to make changes. The idea of working together, within and across *barangays*, in a business venture was novel. Yet all rural people had experience of ritual practices of mutual assistance in which they regularly came together to share labour and resources, support the weak and celebrate important life and community events. People were curious that such practices might be harnessed for social enterprise development.

The Jagna Community Partnering Project (JCPP), as our action research intervention came to be known, worked on shifting the focus of community members from the needs and problems of the municipality to its natural and social assets that could be harnessed for enterprise development. The diverse practices of a still viable social economy were represented as an asset that the action research could tap into and build from (Gibson-Graham, 2006). The second shift in focus we worked on was from the traditional preoccupation with individual micro-enterprise to experimentation with collective, community-based enterprise.

The following stories recount how two small community-based enterprises developed from the grassroots in Jagna with the supportive assistance of a local NGO and the municipal government. It must be noted that in Jagna, as in many rural areas, community benefit was primarily defined in terms of an increase in cash income. In poor rural communities, where households or extended kin networks are connected to the land, most people are assured access to rice, the basic staple, and vegetables. What they lack is any access to cash to buy other foodstuffs or to pay for transportation and cover medical and school expenses. Cash is usually obtained via complex loans from local moneylenders or relationships of patronage. Involvement in a community enterprise enables people to generate cash income outside of these intricate debt relations. But community enterprises are not limited to this outcome. They make many other contributions to strengthening the resilience of community economies and increasing the quality of civic involvement of those usually marginalized from public life.

'Starting with what we have': the Laca Ginger Tea Community Enterprise

In the rural community of Jagna, many negative stories circulate of small enterprises that fail or are not sustainable. This has made people apprehensive about new enterprise initiatives in their community. The 'wait and see' mentality lives on because people see substantial financial capital as necessary to begin an enterprise and they have very limited (if any) surplus cash. But one group of women in the *barangay* of Laca decided to stop waiting and take steps to generate income. They were open to discovering assets other than money and building on them to develop a new enterprise.

The women of Laca were active members of the local municipality's Jagna Council for Women and had previously organized fundraising events to support their community. When the JCPP began its action research in the municipality, this group of women was identified as a community 'asset' with potential for mobilization. One of the group volunteered to be a Community Enterprise Researcher (CER) with the project and it was she who broached the idea with the others of starting to process the ginger that is grown in the cooler upland areas of the municipality. Two women had, in the past, received training in making sweet ginger tea powder, what's known locally as *salabat*, and occasionally produced it for their families and friends. All of the women were interested in starting a community enterprise, although they had little knowledge of what this meant.

As part of the JCPP the enterprise group was supported to go on a fact-finding mission. They visited another group of ginger-tea producers in Bohol and observed production. They went to a supermarket in the provincial capital and researched the cost of the equipment they would need to get production going. They saved their travel allowance and walked to town to speak to traders in the local market to see if they would agree to sell their *salabat* and at what price. After conducting their own research, they used their travel money to buy inputs and began trial production of ginger tea powder in their local community hall.

Guiding the women's approach to the development of their enterprise was the realization that they already possessed knowledge and experience that they considered valuable even if mainstream employers did not. While they might not have university degrees, they had a wealth of life experience. Through group discussions and informal conversations, the women effected a philosophical shift, turning the 'wait and see' mentality on its head. In terms of mainstream employment, the women had passed their use-by date. Advertisements for government and private-sector positions specify age limits that exclude older people. Ranging in age from 47 to 81 these women decided that, despite their age, they would take stock of the assets they already had in order to begin a productive enterprise. Their goal was to achieve a regular income. This was not specified as a particular amount. What they were focused on was having a reliable source of income that would allow them to plan, access credit, repay debt and, most importantly, maintain or improve their health and that of their families. Overcoming the seemingly intractable barrier of age, they chose the more active philosophy of 'even though we are old, we can start with what we have'. They started the Laca Ginger Women's Group with a 'nothing ventured, nothing gained' attitude rather than the more defeatist 'why bother?'

From the outset, the women have exemplified the 'start with what you have' approach. In order to raise the capital to pay for the initial production run, they pooled their bus fares provided by the JCPP and walked the 4.5 kilometres into town to conduct their market feasibility study instead of catching the bus. They did not have to struggle to win the approval of the council members in their community to use the local hall as a venue for meetings and, subsequently, ginger processing.

Their production practices draw on local work traditions that are understood and respected. If one worker cannot attend the production day because of ill health or other commitments another household or kin member will attend in her place, following the rules of *hungus* or reciprocal labour exchange practised in local agriculture. Again, following local custom, all workers are fed lunch and snacks on the production days. Participants bring a cup of rice each to share and enterprise funds are set aside to buy toppings and snacks. The group are putting aside 10 per cent of their earnings from the sale of *salabat* to pay for supplies and marketing costs and have set up a small credit facility that incorporates principles of *repa repa*, the local revolving credit practice.

To market their product the group began by drawing on the longstanding *suki* system, whereby the seller and buyer develop a relationship that ensures the customer purchases exclusively from the one seller. They also targeted the local market rather than aiming directly for the larger national and international markets.

To date, the women earn roughly P90 (Au$2.30) per production, with two or three production events per week. They have used this new cash income to purchase glasses and pay for health check-ups. Three women have paid for their husbands to stay in hospital and receive treatment for hypertensive heart disease. By acting and doing, rather than waiting and seeing, the women have attracted the attention of government and private investors. This, in turn, has inspired other women in their community to join in the production process.

From these beginnings the philosophy of the group is changing and growing along with their enterprise. Diversification is now key to their approach. They have identified a gap in the market: no ginger tea powder was previously available without sugar. With a high incidence of diabetes in the community there were many potential customers not buying ginger tea powder due to the sugar content. The women now struggle to keep up with the demand for sugarless ginger tea powder.

This successful foray into product diversification has seeded ideas for other ginger-based products including ginger cookies, ginger candy, and even ginger exfoliating scrub made from the by-product of the ginger-tea-making process. To expand, the women must scale up production, which means moving out of the *barangay* hall. They are soon to move into a designated processing centre built with development funds from the local government, which will also serve as a site for meetings, experimentation, storage and product display. Starting with what they had – a vital local social economy – the Laca ginger-tea makers have developed a small but successful social enterprise.

Jagna Nata de Coco Community Enterprise: 'awakened through nata'

The Jagna Nata de Coco Community Enterprise Organization was founded with the assistance of the JCPP. It produces and processes *nata de coco*, a white gelatinous food product made from the bacterial fermentation of coconut water. *Nata de coco* is a favourite Filipino treat, best served as a dessert; it is an excellent ingredient for fruit salads, pickles, fruit cocktails, drinks, ice cream, sherbets and other recipes. It is a nutritious and healthy food that contains high fibre and zero fat and cholesterol.

The founding vision of Jagna Nata was to establish a community-owned and -operated producer enterprise that would provide an opportunity for group members to earn income and improve the quality of their lives. The original twenty-three members were all members of the Small Coconut Farmers' Organization (SCFO), mostly economically marginalized men and women farmers, local government workers and housewives drawn from six different *barangays* across the municipality. Before starting their social enterprise the Nata group underwent capacity-building activities. They went on a fact-finding trip to small communities with related enterprise activities, made visits to the Department of Science and Technology (DOST) and Philippine Coconut Authority, and obtained technical training on *nata de coco* production and processing. They conducted a feasibility study into marketing, the technical aspects of production and processing, financial and organization management and the potential socio-economic benefits.

Following this they conducted experimentation to produce prototypes and product samples. Market testing was done in the locality of Jagna and the group found that their product was very saleable and profitable. The only other supplies of *nata de coco* came infrequently from Mindanao and were quite expensive. The group found that it was easy to produce *nata* in the unique cooler climate conditions in the upland areas of Jagna municipality. Inputs for production could be easily accessed – appropriate mixtures of coconut water, refined sugar, water and glacial acetic acid. With the assistance of JCPP the organization accessed funding support from the Jagna LGU (P21,107; Au$500) to be used as start-up capital and an experimentation fund for processing the *nata*. The DOST provided initial and ongoing technical assistance and the Technical Education Skills Development Authority provided training. The Agricultural Training Institute provided the *nata* starter, the agent for bacterial fermentation.

All members have experienced transformations that have occurred as a result of their involvement with the Jagna Nata de Coco Community Enterprise Organization. Francisca is a member of a *barangay* livestock association, an income-generating micro-enterprise scheme whereby the local government allocates each member one pig to raise in return for three piglets to be paid back to the programme after weaning. Members then keep the rest of the litter and the three pigs will be distributed to other members in the *barangay*. While this programme generates food and income for the household, Francisca noted that it doesn't bring her out into the community to build connections between people, as she only interacted with the central organizer. Through involvement with the Jagna Nata enterprise she has become more comfortable in society and is proud of her civic involvement.

Others have similarly been '*Sa nata... nagmata*', 'awakened through *nata*'. For example, Visitacion Galgo, or Venie as she is fondly called, worked as a CER with the JCPP in 2005. For Venie, it was a big accomplishment to gather together people from different *barangays* and take the lead in managing a small community enterprise. She gained more and more confidence as she dealt with different kinds of people, first members of the SCFO and *barangay* officials, and then even business people. Through her work, Venie developed skills in facilitating meetings, negotiating, communicating and producing and processing the *nata de coco*. As a CER, she displayed great leadership potential. Now the rest of the members follow her example, to the extent that they call her 'Ma'am', locally a title indicating tremendous respect. Says Venie, 'I am very happy that I'm called Ma'am because it shows that people respect me.' For Venie, her new outlook started with *nata* and the realization that she had the potential to do something for community development.

At the start, 36-year-old Sesinio Madera Jr was very shy, silent and lacking in leadership skills. Single and living with his parents doing farm work, he seemed to be a 'typical' Filipino farm worker with no exposure to the world and little interaction with people around him. He was the type of person who never cared to get involved in village activities until the JCPP started and the *nata* enterprise group was organized. But Sesinio's regular attendance at meetings, training, the exposure trip, production and other organizational activities helped him develop his personal and professional skills. He recognized his potential as a leader. As the vice president of the *nata* group he has developed his public-speaking abilities to the point where he can actively talk and share his ideas. Sesinio now is head of the production committee and in charge of fermenting the *nata de coco* before it is brought to the town for processing and marketing.

The members of Jagna Nata have all enjoyed their greater civic involvement and are proud of their cross-municipality organization – a rare thing in a rural society still structured around kin-based villages. But this very strength has also been the group's downfall. The cost and difficulty of travel around the municipality, especially in wet weather, have proved a problem. The different production phases are in separate places, with fermentation and processing in the upland *barangay* of Cambungaan, and packaging and marketing closer to the Municipio (centre of Jagna). The lack of available equipment in the right place sometimes hinders the production process. Coordinating, communicating and organizing meetings and production have proved difficult and this has impacted on output as the timing of stages of the *nata* production process is crucial to its success. Without the support and guidance offered by the JCPP, production stumbled to a halt in 2008. The remaining group of nine have become registered as an association and are still keen to access funds for a new processing site where all members can meet and work together. At present the group are considering how to meet the challenge of the lack of clear facilitation by an NGO or arm of local government. Given the awakening that has occurred for selected members and the sense of belongingness as part of the group they have generated, they may well resolve this issue as there is strong motivation to continue to contribute their time, resources, energy and ideas.

Conclusion

These four stories present very different development trajectories. One of the enterprises incubated by Unlad Kabayan, the Matinao Rice Centre, began as a simple rice mill that was one migrant returnee's dream business. Over time and in response to social and economic challenges the business has become a cluster of interlinked social enterprises servicing the multiple needs of poor farmers. The Centre is now a focus for community activity, farmer advice and enterprise development. The other enterprise, DOCHSEi, began as an initiative of two NGOs concerned with the plight of the landless and poor tenant coconut farmers. It has been developed as a relatively large social enterprise from the start. As they have developed, both enterprises have forged greater integration with local communities and a clearer articulation of the social returns on investments made by an internationally dispersed community of migrant savers. Each enterprise is trying to balance the multiple demands of accountability to donors and investors, capital raising, high equipment costs and, in the case of DOCHSEi, a large labour force.

The enterprises begun as part of the JCPP are much smaller in scale and are defining themselves against the prevailing norms of micro-enterprise and rural co-operatives. The Laca Ginger Tea Community Enterprise has evolved from a previous organization of local women, many of whom are close neighbours or kin. Shifting focus towards a community-based social enterprise has been relatively easy as the group members are already linked in networks of support and mutual assistance. They have formalized their enterprise as a co-operative and registered with the provincial government. Already they are showing the benefits of active participation, as when they dared to challenge a provincial official who assumed that she would become a member of the co-operative. In contrast, Jagna Nata is struggling with a multi-sited membership, the lack of money to get together regularly and the absence of a forceful coordinator. There is community support for the enterprise, but there is a need to shore up partnerships to replace the facilitation offered by the action research team.

What is distinctive about all these cases is the conscious intervention that is being made to strengthen community economies in place. All enterprises are building on relations of interdependence between, for example, the natural and social environments, farmers and processors, shared community resources and community enterprise. They are building on diverse practices of mutual assistance and developing novel collective initiatives that are increasing well-being directly for local people. They are contributing affordable products and services to local consumers, as well as to more distant markets. Importantly they are generating income for cash-poor people. In each enterprise the learning curve has been steep for community members and NGO incubator staff alike. Most rewarding has been the flowering of confidence among people who never saw themselves as entrepreneurs or philanthropists or leaders.

Building the social economy could well form a focus for migrant remittance funds that would begin to address the extreme poverty and regional inequality in the Philippines. As we have seen with the stories presented here, social enterprise development in the majority world can be targeted at producing food and fibre products for the local market that will lower costs and increase access to desired consumption goods. Once the local market has been supplied, it is up to the enterprise to see if it wants to expand into regional, national and international markets. It is expansion of community well-being that is at the centre of the enterprise vision, not expansion for its own sake.

By documenting these experiments in community enterprise development we hope to assist in the formulation and consolidation of new development pathways that build more resilient local economies. Producing discourses of the social economy and social enterprise in the Philippines is an important way of influencing debates and policies around development. The writing workshop that produced the enterprise stories presented in this chapter teamed up NGO activists and scholar activists to overcome the communication barriers that often stand in the way of reporting the successes of community initiatives. Since that workshop, an interactive CD-ROM that outlines the action research steps of the Community Partnering Project has been developed for use by communities, NGOs and others wishing to replicate this pathway for local development.[4] A DVD that features three of the social enterprises discussed here, as well as three others, has been produced for dissemination to local governments, policymakers, development agencies and universities in the region and internationally.[5] In the conclusion of this film May-an Villalba outlines a range of policy initiatives that could significantly assist social enterprise development and build community resilience. The 30 per cent corporate tax rate that is applied to social enterprises and prevents them from scaling up is one area for policy change. Another is the coordination of marketing so that small community-based enterprises do not undercut each other. Academic and activist networks such as those constructed in this volume can contribute powerful representations that help to make social enterprises more viable and the social economy that sustains life more visible.[6]

Notes

1. The Community Economies Collective Kioloa Writing Group included May-an Villalba and Benilda Flores-Rom, executive directors of Unlad Kabayan Migrant Services Foundation Inc.; Maureen Balaba and Joy Miralles-Apag, founding members of Bohol Initiatives for Migration and Community Development; and Australian National University academics and graduate scholars Katherine Gibson, Deirdre McKay, Amanda Cahill, Jayne Curnow Michelle Carnegie, Ann Hill and Gerda Roelvink. The collective wrote the accounts of each social enterprise. Katherine Gibson has reworked these stories and framed them in this chapter within a discussion for which she, rather than the collective, is responsible.

2. The workshop was funded by a grant from the Australian Research Council's Asia Pacific Futures Research Network (PA030703).

3. The project, 'Negotiating alternative economic strategies for regional development in Indonesia and the Philippines', was conducted between 2002 and 2006 and was funded by the Australian Research Council and AusAID, Australia's international aid agency (ARC Grant No. LP0347118). In the context of recently decentralized governance, the four-year research programme tested the utility of the Community Partnering model, an approach that was piloted as part of an action research project in the Latrobe Valley of Australia (Cameron and Gibson, 2005a, 2005b; McKay et al., 2007).

4. *Community Partnering for Local Development*, an interactive CD-ROM, available from Katherine Gibson, Department of Human Geography, RSPAS, ANU, ACT 0200 Australia.

5. *Building Social Enterprises in the Philippines: Strategies for Local Development*, a fifty-minute DVD available from Katherine Gibson, Department of Human Geography, RSPAS, ANU, ACT 0200 Australia.

6. As a result of this network May-an Villalba has visited the US social enterprises discussed by Julie Graham and Janelle Cornwell in Chapter 3

and has taken insights from these visits back into her practice as a social entrepreneur in the Philippines.

References

Balisacan, A.M., and H. Hill (eds) (2007) *The Dynamics of Regional Development: The Philippines in East Asia*, Edward Elgar, Cheltenham.

Cameron, J., and, K. Gibson (2005a) 'Alternative pathways to community and economic development: The Latrobe Valley Community Partnering Project', *Geographical Research* 43(3): 274–85.

Cameron, J., and K. Gibson (2005b) 'Building community economies: A pathway to alternative "economic" development in marginalised areas', in P. Smyth, T. Reddel and A. Jones, eds, *Community and Local Governance in Australia*, UNSW Press, Kensington.

Gibson-Graham, J.K. (2006) *A Postcapitalist Politics*, University of Minnesota Press, Minneapolis.

Gibson, K., L. Law and D. McKay (2001) 'Beyond heroes and victims: Filipina contract migrants, economic activism and class transformation', *International Feminist Journal of Politics* 3(3): 365–86.

Griffiths, D. (2007) 'Co-operatives in the Philippines: Information sheet', Information and Documentation Centre, International Co-operative Alliance-Asia and Pacific, www.australia.coop/artman2/publish/ICA_ROAP_30/Co-operatives_in_the_Philippines.php.

McKay, D., A. Cahill and K. Gibson (2007) 'Strengthening community economies: Strategies for decreasing dependence and stimulating local development', *Development Bulletin* 72: 60–65.

Pearce, J. (1993) *At the Heart of the Community Economy: Community Enterprise in a Changing World*, Calouste Gulbenkian Foundation, London.

Teodosio, V.A. (2003) 'Keeping the spirit of 1896 alive: The cooperative movement rising', *Philippine Journal of Labor and Industrial Relations* 23(1/2): 178–97.

7

A path to the social economy in Argentina: worker takeovers of bankrupt companies

José Luis Coraggio and María Sol Arroyo

This chapter examines a specific process of social enterprise emergence in Argentina, about which there is little knowledge. It discusses initiatives by blue-collar workers to rescue their disintegrating companies, eventually turning them into co-operatives. Our interest lies in a new subjectivity born of this process, and its potential for developing a social economy some way distant from market-centred capitalism.

Between 2000 and December 2001, the crisis of the Argentinian neoliberal model caused thousands of companies to suffer real losses or embark upon capital flight through 'asset stripping'. Rising debts and the failure to invest eventually led to the cessation of payments to creditors. Production facilities were not maintained and stocks became depleted. The workforce was destabilized by cuts in benefits, long delays in wage payments and, ultimately, dismissals. In some cases, workers did not wait until they were dismissed but reacted by taking over and trying to save the businesses. As the businesses went bankrupt, workers – faced with few alternative options in Argentina's generalized economic crisis – forced their way into businesses and occupied them, slowly putting them back to work. Initially, the response of the owners was mixed: some let go of the failed business, while others did not wish to forgo their property rights. In turn, the government and the courts did not formally recognize the takeovers, and although later some enterprises, especially those that received help from unions, universities and specialist organizations, came to acquire partial or full legal recognition, today the majority of the occupied ventures remain in a precarious state in terms of the ownership rights of the worker collectives. They still run the risk of the original owners attempting to repossess the now successful worker-run businesses.

Though limited in number and scale (around 200 companies currently employing 10,000 workers), these 'recovered' companies turned into self-managed co-operatives – despite their precarious legal standing – are showing the possibility of a different arrangement of social and private property rights; when collective actors can, with legitimate effort, redistribute assets and decision-making power. These shifts also show the possibility of symbolic change: new values, attitudes and capabilities to undergird a different kind of economy. The irresponsibility of private owners fighting for their freedom to make as much profit as possible but unwilling to face the social costs of their actions has been pointedly revealed through the experience of the companies' ability to operate under worker management. By openly confronting private capitalism and its property rights' regime in the midst of an economic crisis, the new co-operatives are showing that the social economy can help to build a new kind of economy.

This chapter draws on studies that were carried out between 2003 and 2007 on five recovered companies located in the Metropolitan Area of Buenos Aires, all of which were still in existence at the time of writing in late 2008. These are small to medium-sized companies that were slowly downsized in the years prior to being taken over, with most involved in the textile, metalworking or plastics industries. The chapter draws on powerful testimonial evidence collected throughout the process of factory occupation and reactivation in the five enterprises. The evidence is testimony to social subjectivity, motivation and meaning in a new 'moral' economy that does not shy away from market interaction. It shows that workers were not motivated by an ideology of self-management as an alternative to subordinated waged labour, but by a desire to confront social injustice, when threatened with dismissal without payment of due/severance wages in a context of widespread unemployment. A new subjectivity of work and reward has gradually emerged, as the process of recovery has passed through different stages.

Four stages clearly stand out in each case. First, the factory was occupied and wages that were owed were claimed. The workers resisted eviction by the police and courts as well as the enforcement of bankruptcy resolutions to sell off machinery and equipment as part of debt payment to creditors.[1] Second, the workers deliberated over the appropriate course of action, in view of the absence of external solutions (neither the owners nor the state provided help). Proposals were made to process existing raw materials and to supply products already ordered. Work hierarchies were set aside and production processes reorganized. Slowly, wage payments and commercial relations were reinstated. Third, there ensued a legal battle to recognize worker rights to use and acquire the means of production, thereby giving shape to the ventures as co-operatives and incorporating the formal rules of democratic management. Fourth, new production projects were developed.

The provincial government (the autonomous City of Buenos Aires or Buenos Aires Province in the case of the five enterprises considered here) responded differently according to who was in power between 2000 and 2007. However, a common stance adopted was cautiousness towards former owners' property rights, mindful of future threats to such rights.

Motivations and meanings

Worker motivations and feelings were initially characterized by reactive response to the fear of unemployment, outrage at the injustice committed, and the idea that workers had been cheated by employers:

> Staying was not planned, but then we were so furious ... For instance, they asked that we work really hard and demanded a lot of output ... Where did it all go and why wasn't there any money if we had so much work to do? People can say a lot of things out of spite, but when you're in need, it is tough being told 'what do you want? That I bring you the money from abroad?' As if making fun of you. I felt wounded, as if by a mortal blow. (Inés, quoted in Fernández Álvarez, 2006)

The thing is that we didn't really have a choice. [Occupation] was our last resort. It was obvious we were going to get thrown out onto the streets. (I, quoted in Petrelli, 2004 and 2005)

In the process of reorganizing the takeover, a marked re-signification of work has occurred. Current practices are compared by the workers to two previous stages of experience as wage earners: when work relations could be called 'normal'; and when the company's crisis and work instability built up. The meaning of work is tightly linked to the right to basic necessities and to life and dignity, as opposed to idleness, unemployment or mendicancy:

> Work is everything, because without it you can't get by. Having a job you get a paycheck, and with that you can pay your bills, support yourself, feed your kids ... the main thing for me is to have a job ... I'm underpaid but at least I can support myself ... nobody has to be sorry for me. To have work is to have dignity. (Rosana, quoted in Fernández Álvarez, 2006)

> All we wanted was to work. Because working is part of a human being's dignity. Losing our jobs, we automatically lose our dignity. For me work means everything. (Mirta, enterprise 2)

> Many fellow workers got depressed being at home, some of them have even died. (Luis, enterprise 2).

Workers compare their present situation with that of those who receive social aid. They discuss the employment benefits they enjoyed before the crisis, and their eventual withdrawal:

> It's a thousand times better to be employed than receive social aid, for work is the only thing that dignifies the man and the person. (legislator of the City of Buenos Aires)

> For me, work means life. ... because to have a job is not the same as being in search of one ... or being in a Plan.[2] I don't criticize people who are in a Plan, but I couldn't live with 150 pesos and a handbag [containing food]. I think that they don't have a life, because you have to work, there's no way out. (E, quoted in Petrelli, 2004 and 2005)

> In the good old days we received a paycheck every fifteen days, there was a lot of work, we even had some bonuses – for being punctual, so we would arrive early, for being productive ... We even had food vouchers, very good benefits, we were well paid and, all of a sudden,

we started to lose our rights, little by little. Even the vacation time was paid for, but soon they wouldn't pay for vacations or a Christmas bonus. All the benefits ended ... because there wasn't any money. (Clara, quoted in Fernández Álvarez, 2006)

Slowly, the attitude to pay and benefits as an entitlement has changed. Now the view that the employer provides rights and duties is in most cases perceived as humiliating, replaced by a more open attitude to work emphasizing earned entitlement. Working is also seen as more dignified and a free act, and workers talk about overcoming challenges through their own and joint effort:

We couldn't foot a lot of the bills and that's where we learnt to be creative, negotiating with suppliers as well as with those who owed us money ... little by little we paid off all of our debts ... today we've doubled last year's output. (E, quoted in Petrelli, 2004 and 2005)

Hearing the noise of the machines working ... was moving, a tremendous joy. (Reci, quoted in Bialakowsky et al., 2005)

You see the effort you make reflected in your pay check. It wasn't like that before. Although I had always worked the same way, being very responsible in my job, even my best effort did not mirror what I earned at the end of the month. Now it does, so one wants to put in even more effort. (E, quoted in Petrelli, 2005)

Behind such shifts in attitude towards work lie different views on the co-operatives and future expectations, linked to age, gender and personal history. Viewpoints are not consistent: some view the co-operative[3] as a temporary shelter, some as their own established project, and others as an asset to be handed down to future generations:

For fear of what would happen, we couldn't decide on resuming work. At the time, there were people living far away and just to subsist needed money. Some of the people wouldn't agree to do it ... but if you start asking the women around here you'll find out that most of them are divorced, widowed, or single mothers ... it is like they are the only source of income in the house. (Manuela, quoted in Fernández Álvarez, 2006)

This is a recovered company for those who come after us, because these kinds of companies employ elderly people. Here many of us are almost ready for retirement, we even have retirees and they are people who had already walked the path. This will go on for the future of others, for the next generation. (Luis, quoted in Garcia Allegrone, 2005)

Not only a work source has been saved, but we've also saved the manufacture of torches in Argentina. Otherwise, people would've had to import them at a higher price and pay in dollars … Indirectly we've helped a lot of people and also given jobs to a lot of people. (E, quoted in Petrelli, 2004 and 2005)

A moral economy?

Even this brief summary of changes in motivations and values suggests the rise of a 'moral economy'. The takeovers were not intended as a means to private ownership, but as a way of maintaining a source of labour. The expression 'recovered enterprise', referring to factory occupation and a return to production, signals something different from worker expropriation of the means of production. It has to do with recuperating or mending moral rules: machinery and investments are there to foster production, to employ workers who get paid to make their living. There is a strong sense that employers failed to fulfil their obligations, leaving it to workers to restore a work ethic.

At first, the steps taken were hesitant, with workers fearful of breaking the law. Public actions (the occupation itself, picketing, blocking traffic, taking goods to the streets, camping outside the factories guarded by the police, arguing with legislators, etc.) gradually helped to redefine legal boundaries. What appeared fair and legitimate in terms of protecting livelihoods became the guide to confront and stretch legal criteria. Such 'awakening' is clearly evident in the following comment:

Because it's not like a lot of people say: 'they've taken over the factory'. We never took over the factory, we stayed inside. It's not like with the other factories that had been shut down and were broken into. That's not our case, we had been protecting it. We had always been looking after it. In family businesses like this one, you know them [the owners], but they are kind of inaccessible. Well, it was difficult when we had to throw them out. Throw out the 'owners' is just a figure of speech, right? Legally, they weren't the owners any longer, but the people didn't know that ... the bankruptcy proceedings were going on ... and finally one day we just had to tell them: 'you have to go, you have no business being here.' The machinery had been saved by us, it was about to be taken, the police were here. Yet, it was us, the people, who prevented it from being taken. It's not that we took the factory away from him, he lost it and we recovered whatever was left, whatever was being auctioned off. (E, quoted in Petrelli, 2004 and 2005)

The worker accounts are consistently disapproving of employer behaviour, at times from a paternalistic understanding of the work relationship:

The owner and I got along pretty well ... I was really disappointed with him, I thought he was a better person. But, in short, he tried to degrade us and belittle our intelligence and capacity. (H, quoted in Petrelli, 2004 and 2005)

The difference between now and then is that in the past we didn't care about how it [the product] came out, because it was done for someone else and nowadays we do it willingly, with more attention and care so that the material won't be rejected. (Reci, quoted in Bialakowsky et al., 2005)

The early struggles gradually turned the workers into self-identifying groups. Such collective orientation varies from one enterprise to another, depending on the effort made to construct meaning from contradiction. It is also influenced by attitudes towards the trade unions, partly in reflection of union involvement in previous struggles, which contrasts with reliance on workers identifying with each other and local communities. The support of the unions for the recovered companies has not been strong (studies show that only 15–20 per cent of companies mention having received support from unions, while more mention having received help from other recovered companies). The cluster of comments below reveals the varying views on community, colleagues and the unions:

Managers, hierarchical staff, administrative and sales people stayed out in the street. Only the blue-collar workers joined in the act [of occupation] to protect their jobs. The owners were nowhere to be seen. We organized ourselves into groups and took turns. (Pedro, quoted in Fernández Álvarez, 2006)

Many had the mindset of still being workers and would not understand that they were now partners or owners of a co-operative. Then, when they stayed after hours because there was a lot of work they demanded to be paid extra. Someone had to explain to them: 'Who are you going to charge for overtime if you're working for yourself?' (E, in Petrelli, 2004 and 2005)

Nobody has a position higher than the next person. If you sweep the floors, you'll make as much money as me ironing at the press. That's the difference from having a boss. (Carolina, quoted in Fernández Álvarez, 2006)

They [the new workers] have to pay their due until they've learned. Then, after three months, if they are well-behaved and learn, they are allowed to join the co-operative ... although there will remain a wage difference, since they have not been there for the same time as us. (Reci, quoted in Bialakowsky et al., 2005)

This factory has a tradition of struggles ... like when the Metallurgical Labour Unionists would come with their 'logic': 'You're talking about fighting for a raise, but the statute says that you should earn $1 per hour and you're making $1.20.' (Juan, quoted in Garcia Allegrone, 2005)

Subjectivity, time–space and the assembly line

Everyday notions of space and time have gone through significant changes. In a short time, a culture separating home and work and waiting for the fortnightly wage has given way to one of 'the factory feels like home'. The time-and-space distances of factory, neighbourhood, home and work have merged, to replace the heteronomy of the capitalist production line and its distance from the life-world. At the centre of this process is a change in working patterns, from one based on qualifications or repetitive tasks executed under the eye of a watchful management and with scant communication among workers, to one based on task rotation (multiskilling), and production organized in a way permitting new tasks to be learnt (multitasking) and enabling horizontal consulting and openness to knowledge exchange. Additionally, the new organization allows staff to fill temporary vacancies and to assign critical tasks to specific workers at certain times; old and new efficiency criteria intertwine with these changes. Yet social subjectivity has changed, no longer harnessed to capitalist work (pay in exchange for labour) but to a principle of worker solidarity.

Consider this situation: Carolina is 'cleaning jackets', a job familiar to her, but no longer her sole responsibility, as in the past. Meanwhile, her 1-year-old son, who was born during the rescue phase, is taking his morning nap. In spite of the endless noise of the machinery, Lucas is fast asleep and his mother looks just as calm. Now she does not have to run to her sister-in-law's house in the morning to leave her baby, but can nurse him at work. Next to her, standing by a table in the jacket production area – which has become more varied in task composition – Manuela is busy marking a front piece and refining a necktie. This is her main task, but she alternates it with administrative jobs she has had to pick up, including sales, which she definitely does not enjoy, and banking, which is a favourite of hers since it allows her to get out of the plant. Rosa, sitting across from her, passes on the front piece when she has finished. Meanwhile, she puts a tape in the cassette player to listen to a singer she could previously listen to only on her Walkman. Now she can listen at the highest volume, singing along every once in a while. On the other side, Julia places waistbands in a machine she has been using for a few months, under Adriana's watchful gaze. Since the takeover, Adriana has had to oversee the machines as best she can, alternating between them, sometimes handing over to someone else. This is not all that has changed in her life. She has had to negotiate with her partner about staying on at the factory for some night shifts. She has also had to learn how to participate in meetings, something unfamiliar and alien in the past.

In the middle of the shop floor, a group hurries to speed up work on batches just received from the cutting area. Workers who have been at their machines leave them momentarily to give priority to the more urgent task at hand. In a corner, José discusses with Maria about how best to deliver a new order. He does relish the task since it is one he is experienced at, but he knows that the new order will allow them to break even and pay the bills. Behind them, on the blackboard located in the middle of the third floor where now production of jackets and trousers has been unified, a notice announces: 'Meeting Friday 2 p.m.' Dolores knows that on that day she will arrive home later than usual. She must plan who will pick up Gisella, the younger of her two daughters, from school.

At 11:45 a.m. the lights go off to signal the lunch break. Rosana invites one of us to sit with her in the small adjoining room, where she has eaten with her co-workers ever since taking 'production into their own hands'. While we are eating she says that in the afternoon they will be going to the Legislature, like every other Wednesday, and invites us to come along. They will discuss the recovered companies' bill, which has still not been passed by the 'Development Commission'. Minutes before 3 p.m., while most of the staff peel off their working clothes and change into those they wore from home, Margarita, Celeste and Rosana sweep the floors. Although they do not like this chore, it is their turn for a few weeks. Hours later, when many paid workers are already at home, the group enters the Legislature to discuss once again the chances of the law being approved. The meeting goes beyond 7 p.m. and it is too late for Edith and Rosana to get home. They will spend the night at the factory.

We end this section with statements on how a new sense of responsibility and possibility has emerged during the transition from paid work to workers' control. First, a view on work and home:

> To me personally, this factory is like my home. I have to be here to maintain my house; this is the daily work, the dignity of every day. This is my second home, the one which supports my family, so I have to be here all the time. (Roberto, enterprise 2)

> At the moment, this is my whole life ... I mean, when I'm home I think of my work – that is, you unify everything at your home. In my case, my wife is with me during the occupation, at the court, at the Legislature ... she takes people to visit other businesses when I can't ... the home environment, in my own case, revolves around the factory occupation, around this new struggle. (NN, quoted in Bialakowsky, 2003)

Next, some views on professional responsibility and its demands:

It is one thing to put together a co-operative, and another to go to work, but something quite different to defend it. For us it was important … and it turned out OK … without much planning. (NN, quoted in Bialakowsky, 2003)

If the factory fails, so will the cultural centre and the relationship with the neighbourhood. (ZZ, quoted in Bialakowsky, 2003)

We feel more responsible and capable and we get to learn many things. Before, the issue of money was in the hands of the owners, secretaries were in charge of the administration, the sales people cared for commercial issues, they would sort it out. But now we find that we have to do it all … it's a huge responsibility. (Pedro, quoted in Fernández Álvarez, 2006)

For instance, my area is trousers and ironing, which is pretty heavy work. Now we have two new shifts, therefore no one is stuck standing up for nine hours. (Inés, quoted in Fernández Álvarez, 2006)

In the beginning, we were more concerned about the orders and we'd work to meet demand. Production was subordinated to orders and it was inefficient because we worked on short batches. People had to bear with us for three months while we explained that we had to adapt production to our rhythm. Then, we started working on longer batches. Sometimes we get an order and we can turn it around right away. (anon.)

Finally, some views on how a new relationship with the market has emerged, based on continuous learning and adaptation, further changing subjectivities:

It was a learning experience … We are not organized as we were before, when there was a person dedicated only to quality control. So, each one of us has to be conscious and pay attention. We are all part of the process. A piece undergoes many operations before arriving here to be assembled, but you have to make sure all of the pieces get here at the same time. (E, quoted in Petrelli, 2004 and 2005)

In the past, if we found that there was no raw material to work with, we would badger the administrative staff constantly. Now we do not wait until they decide to buy! We all know what we are supposed to do … and we do the best we can. Nobody is following us around, rushing us, that's the difference. (Reci, quoted in Bialakowsky et al., 2003)

The thing is to take care of your work, get the best out of it; for instance, we're not here cracking the whip or anything like that. We'll have our coffee, I'll read the paper, make sure the product is OK. You see, the product has many pieces, but once the line is well organized it runs smoothly; it's really amazing – I have my coffee, read the paper, but then I'm very productive. (J, quoted in Petrelli, 2004 and 2005)

Strikingly, the workers describe the atmosphere as relaxed, democratic:

We used to work faster because we were rushed to do more. Nowadays, we work at our own pace ... we do what we have to, nothing else. (A, quoted in Petrelli, 2004 and 2005)

It makes you aware of your rights and of the fact that you can speak up because you have the right to do so. You're a worker defending your job. (NN, quoted in Bialakowsky, 2005)

Synthesis

In this study, salaried workers had fallen into a spiral of instability, facing the threat of losing their jobs, struggling to maintain their positions while they went through a sorting process, during which the most skilled and management workers left. Supported by their families, the workers went through the experience of taking their case to the local community, to government institutions with decision-making power, or to the legal system. In many cases they had to confront the police. They came up against company owners as well as creditors, whilst trying to maintain their jobs (at the time of the takeovers it was clear that unemployment would be long-lasting or even permanent for those aged over 40). Their future would depend not only on the market but also on legalizing their position as self-managed workers under a formal co-operative structure and with community support.

In addition to obsolete and segmented facilities, the workers inherited knowledge of how to work in a given technological system (assembly lines with fixed positions, based on surveillance and vertical hierarchies). Employer practices during the economic crisis had reinforced such rigidities.[4] Workers surviving a bankruptcy had to fill in for workers who had left certain positions, and they had to build knowledge of the production process as a whole, thus developing new notions of space and time, allowing them to make collective decisions. Identities and communication structures also went through changes. A new mode of horizontal communication grew, concrete work proposals were incorporated, and workers learned to spontaneously take turns to cover for vacancies. A new work ethos emerged privileging shared responsibility and motivated by job sustainability and collective economic outcomes. Although absenteeism is not tolerated and late arrivals have their wages deducted, dismissal is seen as the last resort and is no longer posed as a constant threat.

The workers of the recovered companies have come to value learning opportunities provided by participation in management, job rotation and involvement with external actors (market actors, public bodies, the media and social organizations). The workers often mention 'speaking and arguing in public' as an acquired ability. Values of justice have been added to those of self-management (e.g. that one person alone will not be responsible for undesirable tasks; that workers will be paid fairly even though they perform different duties). Pay levels vary according to the task set or the level of technical expertise. There is also some evidence that in predominantly female workforces wages tend to be more equal, possibly due to a stronger sense of social justice or tacit understanding that wages need to cover common household needs. What in a capitalist enterprise might be seen as 'snitching' (informing managers about someone who is not working) now becomes a matter of peer pressure, with underperforming colleagues openly shown the consequences of their actions. The allocation of coordination tasks is agreed upon in assemblies, on the basis of a person's competences and common sense. Such changes have made routine work less tedious, as a sense of belonging to a collective venture helps to raise workers' satisfaction and inculcate an ethos of harmony.

The crisis of private enterprise brought to light a 'moral economy' (Thompson, 1993); upon reflection on the recovery process, workers condemned their ex-bosses, not for having exploited them, but for not having fulfilled their duties as capable entrepreneurs and persons in charge of the company's sustainability. Workers saw themselves as entitled to manage their factory, convinced that a company should be active in producing, selling, creating employment and paying decent wages to workers.

It is important to bear in mind that most of the workers of the recovered companies were blue-collar workers, which differentiates them from other actors in the social economy dependent on government or NGO initiatives to create jobs (which the workers do not consider as genuine). It is no coincidence that most interviewees were over 45 years old, with some conscious that 'old' workers have led the recovery of companies, fighting against neoliberalism. They know that younger workers did not take part in this struggle, which they justify as a fight for national industry, a legacy for future generations.

Conclusion

The testimonies gathered in this chapter do not necessarily share the view common among social economy advocates that the logic of the sector is anti-capitalist (but see below with respect to property rights). The workers see their role as that of putting the plant back to work and generating justly distributed rewards. It would be interesting to know whether such distributive justice can be retained while keeping the same basic forms of production, and whether new management practices will change the form of production itself. What is clear, however, is that the content and form of collective action have changed. The mechanical modes of union representation or negotiation with bosses have been replaced by intersubjective relations based on participatory self-management, public protest, solidarity with other recovered companies or social actors in similar emergency situations, and engagement with the media or with public bodies. Other studies (e.g. Flores 2002; Fajn, 2003) confirm that recovered companies act in solidarity with other popular protests, looking for the minimum from politicians, and striving instead to enforce their own rights or to change the law to prevent the progress of neoliberalism. As the testimonies show, this way of building the social economy inevitably ends in an open conflict over property rights (e.g. protection of private property rights) and the social right to work. Building the social economy requires both the lawyer and the engineer.

Imaginative suggestions for new public policies have arisen, including reforms to the Bankruptcy Act to ensure workers are paid due wages, to facilitate expropriation in cases of deceptive liquidation of companies, and to provide sustained support to recovered companies in order to help promote their survival. Since thousands of businesses go bankrupt every month, social justification for a handover to workers should be linked to the full restoration of workers' rights in cases of dismissal. The proposals also include management issues – for example, governance of a recovered company by a trust involving workers, public banks, local government, technological institutes and/or co-operative organizations. Reinserting productive resources into a vibrant social economy requires attention to the ways in which workers can become self-managed. There is need for a more comprehensive policy vision, one that goes beyond specific cases and considers the social economy as a still incomplete system that can gain in strength by integrating entire supply chains into its orbit.

In a plural social economy, different actors can play varying roles. Trade unions can incorporate bankrupt company workers into specific action plans, by mobilizing resources and developing solidarity activities, such as providing worker access to social security (the Central de Trabajadores Argentinos, the Argentinian Labour Union, is already working along these lines). Local governments tend to respond to the social economy according to the political orientation of the party in power. We would suggest that recovered companies need to work with political parties and to influence public opinion so as to build greater legitimacy for worker co-operatives in the Argentinian economy.

An important finding of this study relates to space. It has been shown that, especially for women, the workplace has become a multifunction site: rhythms of the domestic economy – childcare, eating, social meetings, cultural activities – are becoming integrated into factory life. Similarly, the street has become a site of protest and, occasionally, workers calling for citizen solidarity. Notions of time and space and the division of domestic labour are also being redefined by new work relations. All of these changes need to be recognized in future policy effort, by seeing the social economy as a mode of existence.

Public and social actors interested in the social economy can help workers in recovered companies see themselves as part of a wider transformation of economy and society. The recovered companies, paradoxically, are showing that the social economy can solve many social and economic problems neglected or intensified by prevailing capitalism. The potential for radical change is there to be seized, though many contingencies will determine the final outcome.

Notes

1. According to the Argentinian Bankruptcy Act, workers come last after the banks, the government and suppliers in priority to receive payment for debts in companies under liquidation.
2. This refers to the Plan for Unemployed Heads of Households, which offers 150 Argentinian pesos per month in exchange for communal work or involvement in associative enterprises.
3. Under the influence of left-wing organizations, one of the companies pressed the state to acquire the factory and put it under workers' control while retaining the obligation to buy the output. Politicians opposed the idea, so the outcome was a co-operative, operating in the market but with the option of public-sector contracts in the future.
4. In the years prior to the crisis, productivity was not linked to financial incentives to workers, but to the threat of dismissal.

References

Bialakowsky, A. (2003) 'Identidades, cultura y formas de conciencia en el mundo del trabajo', presentation to 6th National Congress of Labour Studies, ASET, FCE-UBA, Buenos Aires, 13–16 August.

Bialakowsky, A., Grima, J. and Zelaschi, C. (2005) 'Identidad y conflictos entre trabajadores en empresas autogestionadas. La recuperación del método', presentation to 7th National Congress of Labour Studies, University of Buenos Aires, 10–12 August.

Fajn, G. (ed.) (2003) *Fábricas y empresas recuperadas. Protesta social, autogestión y rupturas en la subjetividad*, Cultural Centre for Co-operation, Buenos Aires.

Fernández Álvarez, M.I. (2004) 'Proceso de trabajo y fábricas recuperadas: análisis a partir de un caso de la Ciudad de Buenos Aires', presentation to 2nd Meeting of Investigations in Social Anthropology, Faculty of Philosophy and Letters, University of Buenos Aires, 5–6 August.

Fernández Álvarez, M.I. (2006) *De la supervivencia a la dignidad. Una etnografía de los procesos de 'recuperación' de fábricas de la Ciudad de Buenos Aires*, Ph.D. thesis, Faculty of Philosophy and Letters, University of Buenos Aires and École de Hautes Études en Sciences Sociales, Buenos Aires.

Flores, T. (2002) *De la culpa a la autogestión*, MTD Editora, Buenos Aires.

García Allegrone, V. (2005) 'La 'necesidad de trabajar': entre la supervivencia y la inserción social. La experiencia de los trabajadores en una empresa recuperada', presentation to 3rd Meeting of Investigations in Social Anthropology, Faculty of Philosophy and Letters, University of Buenos Aires, 3–5 August.

Petrelli, L. (2004) *Recuperando los sentidos del trabajo: las percepciones de los trabajadores de una cooperativa metalúrgica*, Graduation Thesis, Faculty of Philosophy and Letters, University of Buenos Aires.

Petrelli, L. (2005) 'Los sentidos del trabajo y la recuperación: las percepciones de los trabajadores en una cooperativa metalúrgica', presentation to 3rd Meeting of Investigations in Social Anthropology, Faculty of Philosophy and Letters, University of Buenos Aires, 3–5 August.

Thompson, E.P. (1993) *Customs in Common*, New Press, New York.

PART III

Policy challenges

8

Organizing for the solidarity economy in south Brazil

Noëlle Lechat

In Brazil, the term 'social economy' is not well known. The most common terms are 'third sector' and 'solidarity economy', both considered to be quite distinct, even if it is acknowleged that a part of the latter belongs to the former. The third sector is seen to have public objectives, but juridically speaking its entities are seen to be private, consisting of foundations, non-profitable associations and co-operatives. According to Boaventura de Sousa Santos:

> 'Third sector' is a residual and vague designation intended to cover a vast set of social organizations which neither belong to the state nor are commercial; that is, social organizations that, on the one hand, are private, but do not seek profits, and, on the other hand, are motivated by social objectives, public or collective, but do not belong to the state. (Boaventura de Sousa Santos, 2001: 250–51; my translation)

In Brazil, third-sector activism took the form of co-operativism, mainly in the South, during the twentieth century (even though the very first co-operative, inspired by Charles Fourier, appeared in 1847 in the State of Paraná). In its early days, co-operativism was essentially a rural phenomenon, the work of peasants who were descendants of non-Iberian European immigrants. Urban co-operativism, on the other hand, appeared after the proclamation of the constitution of 1988; co-operatives that focused on health, work, housing and other areas of welfare flourished everywhere. It is also from this date that the autonomy of co-operatives, which until then had seen strong intervention from the state, was acknowledged. Today, many co-operatives are managed as companies. For this reason, they are not recognized as part of the solidarity economy, because their members have little say in their administration and since their employees receive salaries; while in the solidarity economy, self-management and ownership or co-ownership of the company by workers are fundamental principles.

The solidarity economy, according to the Brazilian Forum of Solidarity Economy (Fórum Brasileiro de Economia Solidária, 2008), is composed of enterprises, organizations providing advocacy and support for the enterprises, and the network of public managers who establish, execute or coordinate public policies for the solidarity economy. This understanding is close to thinking in new economic sociology (Lévesque et al., 2001; França Filho and Laville, 2004; Abramovay, 2004) and economic anthropology (Caillé, 2000; Godbout and Caillé, 1992) critical of neoclassical economics for considering only the market and individual interests as valid regulators of production, distribution and consumption in the modern economy.

In Brazil, the solidarity economy as a social movement and as an object of study has grown since the First World Social Forum in 2001, although it is possible to find thousands of workers organized in a collective way, managing their own work and fighting for emancipation prior to 2001. Solidarity enterprises have taken various forms, including the initiatives of non-governmental organizations (NGOs) interested in collective projects, co-operatives, networks and financial institutions helping popular enterprises, bankrupt companies recovered by self-organized workers, family-based farming co-operatives, services co-operatives, and so on. The rise of a social movement led to the establishment of a Secretariat of the Solidarity Economy in the Ministry of Labour, in June 2003. The Secretariat consisted mainly of university teachers involved in the movement, with little support from government itself. In Brazil, there is a strong relationship between the crisis of the state and the appearance of new actors in civil society and new modes of managing public affairs. (Nascimento, 2000).

This chapter presents a brief account of the solidarity economy in Brazil, followed by an ethnographic study carried out in the south of the country, to reveal the heterogeneity of this social movement, its weaknesses, its challenges, and its hopes for inclusive and sustainable social development (Sachs, 2004). The chapter begins with a summary of the size and nature of the Brazilian solidarity economy, and an account of significant policy developments. It then examines the ethnography of two enterprises, one involving family farmers, the other involving recyclable waste collectors. The chapter ends with some considerations on the strengths and weaknesses of this kind of economy.

The solidarity economy in Brazil

At its inception, the Secretariat of the Solidarity Economy had the job of carrying out a large-scale survey to create a national database on the solidarity economy. The first national census (2005–07) tried to count the number of enterprises as well as supporting organizations, and it identified 21,578 enterprises, involving 1,687,035 workers, of which 630,083 were women. Enterprises with up to 20 workers were the majority: 9,244 in total. These enterprises employed 53,061 women and 39,934 men.[1] The majority of the enterprises are organized as associations (52 per cent), followed by informal groups (36 per cent) and co-operatives (10 per cent), with the small remainder organized as commercial companies. Bankrupt private companies recovered by workers represent only 0.71 per cent, yet happen to be the most studied type of organization. Enterprises in rural areas account for 48 per cent; while those in urban areas account for 17 per cent, while 34 per cent perform their activities in both areas. Thus, currently, the solidarity economy is mainly a rural phenomenon in Brazil, and as Kraycheyte notes:

> It seems that there is a bigger tradition and ease of organizing [such] enterprises in rural areas. These enterprises have distinctive characteristics in comparison to typically urban ones. If, for example, a family farm looking to collectively commercialize or manufacture its products does not succeed, it has the option of returning to the traditional way through which it entered the market, even if this means

selling to local profiteers. In the case of urban enterprises, ensuring economic success is of greater urgency, especially when there are no other sources of income. (Kraycheyte, 2006: 7; my translation)

The fact that there are more men than women in the solidarity economy, and that men are mainly employed in enterprises with more than twenty members (the minimum number to form a co-operative), can be partially explained by the preponderance of rural enterprises. It is the breadwinner, usually the husband, who has the association with the co-operative. This might explain the relative absence of women in the statistics, even though they remain active informal participants.

The surveys show that many enterprises formed after 1990 (40 per cent between 1991 and 2000 and 28 per cent between 2001 and 2007) were motivated primarily by looking for an alternative to unemployment (cited by 30 per cent of the enterprises), followed by the hope of attaining higher profits in an associative enterprise (15 per cent) or the search for a complementary source of income (14 per cent). Developing an activity in which everyone is an owner was cited by 7 per cent of the enterprises, while 13 per cent mentioned access to finance or other advantages as a reason.

In Brazil, as Guerra (2002), Lechat (2004) and França Filho and Laville (2004) observe, the solidarity economy is more 'alternative' and politicized than in other countries. Thus, the Solidarity Economy Movement, for instance, insists that this kind of economy is much more than an answer to unemployment. It is seen to represent a new philosophy of life, a new economy, or even a new way of organizing production (Tiriba, 1997; Singer, 2000; see also Chapter 7 of this volume). The Movement's first conference (2006) declared the solidarity economy 'a strategy for a new model of sustainable and inclusive development'. Gaiger comments:

> Some sections of the left, echoing the historical ideals of the workers' struggle or of popular movements, started to integrate the solidarity economy into their debates, their social change programmes and their strategic visions of socialist construction. (Gaiger, 2003: 183; my translation)

The most common activities are agriculture and cattle breeding, followed by textiles and craftwork. Classified in order of importance, corn, beans, rice, manioc flour, clothing, milk, bedroom, bathroom and kitchen goods, and fresh produce are the main products of the Brazilian solidarity economy – the basics of popular consumption. Some 30 per cent of the enterprises do not sell their goods and services on a commercial basis. The monthly income of 40 per cent of the enterprises is lower than €1,666. In 13.5 per cent of the cases, the monthly income is between €1,666 and €3,333, while 13 per cent have an income between €3,333 and €16,666. Only 8.25 per cent have monthly incomes higher than €16,666. More than half of the enterprises sell directly to consumers. A third reuse part of the waste they produce. These figures indicate a local, craft or peasant form of economy, producing basic goods for personal consumption or for the community.

In addition to mapping the solidarity economy in Brazil, the Social Economy Secretariat has sought to strengthen organizational arrangements and supply chains, promote fair trade and ethical consumption, encourage the formulation of public policies, facilitate research, and enhance the public visibility of the solidarity economy. In fact, the mapping exercise gave powerful impetus to establishing a movement. The Secretariat has also facilitated cross-sectoral policies, in conjunction with the National Bureau of Social Assistance, the Ministry of Agrarian Development via the Secretariat of Territorial Development and the Secretariat of Family Farming, the Secretariat for Racial Equality, and other departments.

Incubators of the solidarity economy

Informal groups, associations and co-operatives that characterize the solidarity economy require support, both at their 'birth', in order to organize themselves, and during the phase of consolidation. Various entities in Brazil (NGOs, universities and state departments, among others) have developed tools of advice and support, called incubators.

An agency of the Science and Technology Ministry called FINEP (Financer of Studies and Projects) has created a programme to support the start-up of social enterprises by university incubators, by funding techno-scientific teams in many parts of the country. By 2007, 1,200 enterprises had declared to have received support from a university. The incubators support all the stages of forming the enterprises, in line with the core principles of the solidarity economy, slowly moving into operational, professional and administrative aspects in order to facilitate self-management. The support at incubation focuses on mobilization, advice, training and technical support, but explicitly for a different ideal. As Frantz (2005: 33) notes, 'education to cooperation starts in understanding the co-operative phenomenon and in producing knowledge'. For example, the incubator from Universidade Regional do Noroeste do Estado do Rio Grande do Sul (UNIJUÍ) is part of a university extension programme. It promotes citizenship, work and social inclusion, supported by the principles and values of the solidarity economy (co-operation, self-management, solidarity, valorization of the worker and sustainable development). These are woven into support of an economic orientation, such as facilitating start-up or the establishment of commercial networks (Lechat et al., 2003).

The incubator consists of a multidisciplinary team of teachers, technicians and students aware of the necessity to integrate knowledge in order to intervene on the ground. An important pedagogical tool is a register of every single intervention and theorization of different aspects of the incubation process. Knowledge and action spring from a shared ideal called the solidarity economy. The teams provide education on the solidarity economy and the collective economy in general. This reinforces a feeling of belonging to a bigger project. The teams are goal-oriented, with all actors involved in plenary discussions. All participants are encouraged to bring their knowledge and experience to the table, evaluating situations and activities and proposing new analyses and actions. The meetings and activities are recorded and evaluated. The incubation process is as much about setting up a social enterprise as it is an exercise in 'world-making'. According to Lechat and Barcelos, at the heart of the exercise is

> An intelligence or democratic commitment to dialogue, and respect for experience, tacit knowledge, and the culture of the excluded, in service of a sole concern to preserve life, despite adverse surrounding circumstances. (Lechat and Barcelos, 2008: 100; my translation)

The process involving experts from the incubators visiting enterprises and helping the enterprises to meet each other and the public has proven to be very productive, for expression, participation and personal growth: making individuals stronger as social enterprise actors. Similarly, the collection of data, books on the solidarity economy, reports, press releases and summaries has become a tool for reflection and grounding; a way for the solidarity economy to place itself within debates on local and regional society. Publicity for an alternative way of generating work and income has served to question assumed social values, by proposing the possibility of a harmonious work–life balance and collective action. Although in material terms incubator support for social enterprises has been limited, it is unquestionable that new attitudes have emerged regarding the value of associations and/or co-operatives, sustainable consumption habits, and care for the environment (Lechat and Barcelos, 2008).

The incubators build on a methodology inspired by Paulo Freire's principles of empowerment through popular education and participation. It is recognized that learning and knowledge formation are essential for self-management and democratization. In Brazil the expectation is growing that social enterprises can become sites of socio-economic inclusion for people who are discriminated against because of their gender, age, ethnic group and/or education. It is assumed that development occurs when environmental sustainability, social justice, citizenship and cultural diversity are integrated into economic activities. These principles were reaffirmed by the National Conference of Solidarity Economy in June 2006, when a final text was agreed, after months of discussion all over Brazil. The Conference also confirmed the need for specific public policies for the solidarity economy as well as specific juridical regulation.

Solidarity economy in the far south of Brazil

In the far south of Brazil, small farmers, indigenous families, outskirt dwellers and recyclable waste collectors have begun to organize themselves to sell natural or semi-industrialized farming products, commercialize craftwork, produce and sell clothing, cleaning products, personal hygiene materials and food products, collect solid waste, or offer collective services. With support from public and private organizations, 378 enterprises have emerged, seeking new or supplementary sources of income, or escape from unemployment.

This section examines the trajectory of two social enterprises located in the city of Ijuí in Rio Grande do Sul, based upon the author's participation in university incubation projects (Thiollent, 1997).

Ijuí's Recyclable Waste Collectors' Association (ACATA)

In 2003, a young street sweeper dreamed of organizing the recyclable waste collectors of Ijuí. He held a number of meetings with the collectors and gathered the support of many people and agencies in the local community. Then, thanks to the UNIJUÍ incubator, on 1 June 2005 twenty-two waste collectors living in the north of the city founded an association called Ijuí's Recyclable Waste Collectors' Association – ACATA. The members possessed absolutely nothing. They needed carts; a contract was signed with Ferradura, a plastics recycling company, which lent them eight carts on agreement that in return all material collected would be sold to Ferradura, for a price negotiated every other month. It was also decided that every associate would give 7 per cent of profits to the Association. A management board was elected and the president gave each associate a smock with the name ACATA printed on it, an ID tag and a pair of gloves, purchased with money borrowed from the incubator.

The search for contracts was a constant concern. In October 2005, Ferradura was forced to close until it complied with new environmental regulations. Other recycling companies began to take advantage of the situation by forcing down ACATA prices even more. Ferradura carts, however, remained available to ACATA, in the expectation of a future renewal of the contract. However, many carts were damaged and the Association did not have enough money to repair them. Continual reduction in the price of recyclable materials, due to the devaluation of the dollar, and the growing availability of recyclable products brought further losses for the collectors. They needed land, a storage place and money to repair the carts, buy uniforms and personal protective equipment, and a drop press. It was deemed essential to find buyers for the materials and to make the community aware of the need to separate recyclable waste at home and deliver it to the collectors.

In November 2005 the Association was registered legally, allowing it to receive help from commercial and industrial entities, co-operatives and other philanthropic organizations. Many attempts were made to persuade the municipal authorities to support the Association. The authorities were invited to various celebration events, but a relationship was only established at the end of 2007, after pressure from the Public Prosecutor's Office and from the public regarding agreement on a selective garbage collection service in the city.

An important development was help from a neighbourhood state school, which offered space to the Association. It was in this school that most meetings took place, as well as workshops, end-of-the-year celebrations and a fair to sell second-hand clothes. These activities helped to bring together members and their families, and families from surrounding neighbourhoods, as well as garner the support of many institutions. In January 2006, the president of the local syndicate of storekeepers offered to loan the Association a piece of land located two blocks from the school. However, the members decided to rent space elsewhere because it was already fenced and came with water, electricity and a small house that could serve as a residence. In order to raise funds, the Association organized dinners to help repay some debts, raise rent for the land, and repair some carts. Soon after, however, many collectors gave up their membership of the Association; some moved to other cities, while others looked for different sources of income. Workshops on associativism were offered with the purpose of providing, in a simple and accessible way, guidance on the importance of collective organization in the search for alternatives to unemployment and shortages of work and for income opportunities. The importance of education was also stressed, and as a result many collectors started to study at night.

In June 2006, thanks to a proposal sent to an NGO, the Association raised €1,233 to build a storage place. In August of the same year some members of ACATA attended a course with workers from other solidarity enterprises, aiming to share experience and knowledge, as well as identify partnerships and sources of support. However, it was only in 2007 that the few remaining members of ACATA reunited to restart the process of receiving and sorting waste materials, with no remuneration, even using their own money to pay for initial costs. One of the collectors moved into the small house with his family to become the night guard.

In January and February 2007, ACATA took active part in the preparation and organization of a Solidarity Fair. The fair brought donations of clothes, blankets and mattresses, sold for token prices to people in the neighbourhood. Some twenty organizations participated, collecting and receiving clothes and other materials, organizing the event and working all day long, and over a thousand people bought the products on show. Most of the money raised (€900) was used to buy a weighing scale and to build a bathroom. The Association managed to convince many people and institutions to reserve their recyclable waste for them. It was also given furniture, kitchenware, clothes and other goods.

Today, as an enterprise, ACATA takes part in regional and state forums, conferences and fairs on the solidarity economy. Its members are called to speak in public and academic events. In two years, more than two dozen articles on ACATA have been published in local newspapers, and the Association often receives visits from students and environmental entities.

The experience of ACATA can be considered positive, although its future remains uncertain, since a permanent nucleus of members has yet to be constituted. Members leave because of disagreements, to find more attractive alternatives, or to move to other cities. Some forty-six collectors have taken part in the Association (totalling 138 people when family members are taken into account). In evaluating ACATA, it is important to note that members who have left the Association did so with the help of the social capital and experience they acquired during their involvement.

The members of ACATA are going through a long learning process, which needs to be renewed from time to time because of shifting membership. It was only with the acquisition of the storage compound that a group identity began to take shape. The compound also created new problems. Many families have lived in the small house, responsible for the night watch, but for people who have lived on the streets it is hard not to want possession of something that belongs to the group. The practice of democracy, for those who have never had voice and opportunity, is another difficulty. For example, family, home and property arrangements are extremely fluid, with distinctions of duties and obligations towards bringing up children and recycling goods getting blurred.

The trajectory of the NATUAGRO co-operative

The members of the Co-operative of Family Farmers of Agro-ecological and Natural Products in the Northeast of Rio Grande do Sul, NATUAGRO, are small family farmers building on a trajectory of co-operation among farmers begun a decade ago. NATUAGRO was formed in August 2005, with twenty members. The initiative was welcomed by the farmers. According to Frantz (2005: 50), 'farming families, somehow, have always put their faith in associativism and in co-operative organization as a way of improving their social standing through multiple practices.' Similarly, as Singer notes, 'there is no doubt that, if family farming still predominates today in most countries, among small and medium size farms, it is because of the effects of co-operativism, which strengthens competitive potential' (2002: 87). This seems even more the case of 'a kind of co-operative that has been growing steadily, becoming a "new trend", that is, organic food co-operatives' (2002: 95).

Co-operation in NATUAGRO started in May 2006 with the inauguration of a space where the farmers could sell their home-grown products, although preparatory meetings had been taking place since 2005. The space belongs to a school, lent by the Association of Parents and Friends of Mentally and Physically Disabled People, APAE. The building and the infrastructure were installed with the support of a state programme.

The only activity that all members have in common is commercialization. Each family brings what it produces to the co-operative store many times a week, where three employees sell the goods. The three employees are also responsible for the maintenance of the store. Members also help each other with other joint activities, such as transportation and manufacturing. For example, nine families have formed a subgroup aiming to improve the production of sugar cane and its by-products. Once the group was formed, the incubator at

UNIJUÍ offered its assistance.[2] The group chose a coordination team and signed an agreement with the incubator, which led to a process of diagnosis and support. A survey was carried out to learn about the size of the cultivated area, the experience of the farmers in producing sugar-cane by-products, what they produced, and how and where they sold the products. Expectations to increase the cultivated area and the required expertise were also addressed.

In May 2006, a course on the solidarity economy and self-management was offered by the incubator team, along with another course on agro-ecology and sugar-cane handling, offered by technicians from the Association of Syndicates of Rural Workers. These educational activities were complemented by a study trip to the city of Porto Xavier, where the farmers visited three agro-industries: two family-owned and the third an association. In addition to learning about production and organizational processes, the farmers also visited sugar-cane plantations, to look at the diverse ways of handling the crop and its varieties.

The methodology for planning was participatory. The diagnosis started by mapping options and difficulties, classified between the ones that depended on the intentional acts of the group and those that did not depend on the group. This resulted in a view that the cultivated area was not large enough to supply the needs of NATUAGRO, that the co-operative lacked seedlings to plant, that an experimental study was needed to identify the most adequate varieties of sugar cane for the local soil, climate and seasonal conditions, and that a facility to produce sugar cane by-products was needed. It was noted that the period between starting a sugar-cane plantation and final processing was long – three years or more. Accordingly decisions were made, for example, to change product varieties and production methods to facilitate the processing and sale of by-products on a collective basis.

The farmers have not found it easy to see themselves as researchers of different varieties and experimenters with different production methods who are not dependent upon external expertise. In June 2006, some members participated in a course on how to produce molasses, dark brown sugar and *rapadura* (a sweetmeat in the form of a brick produced from the pure dried juice of sugar cane) offered by technicians from the National Service of Rural Learning, SENAR. The course was delivered at a farm and tested different mixes of expert and lay knowledge. Sugar-cane syrup, molasses, dark brown sugar, *rapadura*, sugar-cane brandy and liqueur became the by-products that farmers learned to supply to the co-operative store. Since this required an increase in raw material, the group purchased about a tonne of sugar-cane seedlings from farmers in another region, to enlarge the plantation area. During the second semester of 2006, the members of NATUAGRO participated in four fairs and exhibitions that took place in Ijuí. This facilitated the commercialization of by-products, the exchange of experience among producers, and feedback from consumers.

The importance of the participation of the group in the solidarity economy movement was discussed. In September, NATUAGRO and other enterprises were invited to participate in the incubator's stand in the Regional Fair of Innovative Technology. Slowly the external visibility of NATUAGRO has grown, through its participation in fairs, in the municipal forum of solidarity economy in Ijuí, and in the Regional Forum, from which two of the members have been elected as the movement's regional representatives to the National Assembly.

The group advances through continual reflection, an essential factor for both associative renewal and economic performance. This has allowed the group to become more co-operative and partici-pate in the solidarity economy movement. The donating of 10 per cent of profits to the School for Mentally and Physically Disabled Children of Ijuí demonstrates the social aspect of the co-operative. The producers, who are descendants of European immigrants, have settled in the region for almost a century in homogeneous family, ethnic and religious communities. Social capital is strong and plays a very important role, since mutual trust is indispensable for making an association work. Cáritas, a progressive wing of the Catholic Church, also plays an important role in strengthening adhesion to the principles of solidarity economy.

At present, the group of sugar-cane producers has no possibility of producing on an agro-industrial scale. They need three or four years to do so. Although the members of the group have collaborated for almost a decade, they have progressed slowly in terms of collectively defining cultivation priorities and a division of labour. Some members are convinced of the need to advance in this direction, while others prefer to follow old patterns of family production and come together simply to sell. The latter members are reluctant to change farming practices, for example being asked to process sugar cane when they do not grow it, so that final production – molasses, sugar and other by-products – can be divided equally between two families.

There is a particular cultural legacy in family farming that privileges reproduction of the rural unit over experimenting with more complex systems of organization. Co-operation is implicit in the farmers' way of living, but only on certain terms, as they are generally suspicious of changes to production methods. Co-operation is accepted as a means of access to the market, since the latter involves extra cost and labour, as well as specific skills. This said, the farms are now looking for alternatives in order to survive. The region is a big producer of soya, but this monoculture, as well as damaging the environment, does not suit family farming. Family farmers are finding an answer in horticulture or in raising small animals (chickens, pigs) or dairy cattle on a small scale, and in tapping into the growing demand for organic products, which command a high enough price to justify the cost of labour-intensive small-scale farming.

Conclusion

From these two diverse experiences it is possible to conclude that the possibility of organizing collective groups of producers and sellers is a real one, since this does not require large amounts of money. Half of the social enterprises in Brazil are located in rural areas, or have a rural and urban activity, as in the case of NATUAGRO. What gives significance to the associative work of these enterprises is participatory planning, co-operation and partnership, striving not only for economic viability but also for a collective project that can be called the solidarity economy. Offering finance, infrastructure and equipment is not enough if a group has not been consolidated and is not ready to face the responsibilities that such support demands.

Division and unity are tendencies in constant tension in the solidarity economy, which explains the importance of horizontal and non-hierarchical networks where the individuality of each entity is safeguarded. This is a fragile equilibrium. Harmony is guaranteed by opposition to a common enemy – for example, neoliberalism – and through shared hope in another kind of economy. Those who take part in or support the solidarity economy are expected to share certain principles such as social justice, active citizenship, solidarity and respect for nature, and to fight for an economy that distributes wealth, privileges social need instead of monopoly profit, and values the social usefulness rather than the exchange value of goods. A culture of ethical expectation circulates, along with a moral conception of the economy (Tiriba, 2001).

Alone, the social enterprises have no prospect of progressing as individual entities or of catalysing change in the socio-economic structure, but organized as networks they offer real potential for sustainable development. One of the merits of the solidarity economy movement comes from its success in creating a common identity among workers who do not know each other and who, at first sight, do not have anything in common but their struggle for survival and improvement in their life conditions. The feeling of belonging to a nationally organized group allows these workers to raise their self-esteem and to think about their future. It is necessary, in a context of extreme marginalization, for workers to feel part of a social group, proving that the great transformations come from collectivity, the identification of individuals with their peers (Castel, 2006).

The fragilities of the social enterprises stem from their lack of experience, both economic and socio-political. However, this chapter shows that strength can be found in the diversity that exists in cities and in rural areas. Most products and services necessary for local needs can, in theory, come from solidarity enterprises, if they are able to form supply chains and co-operation networks. The solidarity economy is guided by an economic rationality that is different from that which prevails in the hegemonic capitalist model. But, to be clear, it can coexist with this hegemonic model and is also conditioned by it. As a recent movement, the solidarity economy is composed of actors who largely lack technical qualifications, as well as relevant administrative, accounting and commercial experience. It requires special dedication, and patience from its members, but also 'mainstream' support. It is through external support and advocacy that nets of social relationships are established between the enterprises, that goals can be shared, questioned and reformulated. The capitalist economy cannot survive without the subsidies, services and infrastructure offered by the state. The solidarity economy, too, needs the support of public bodies and intermediaries.

Notes

1. Ministry of Labour/Secretariat of Solidarity Economy (MTE/ SENAES).
2. Part of the following account was taken from Lemes et al., 2007.

References

Abramovay, R. (2004) 'Entre Deus e o Diabo – mercados e interação humana nas ciêncas sociais', *Tempo Social – Revista de Sociologia da USP*, São Paulo.

Caillé, A. (2000) *Anthropologie du don: le tiers paradigme*, Desclée de Brouwer, Paris.

Castel, R. (2006) 'Classes sociais, desigualdades sociais, exclusão social', in C.M. Balsa et al., eds, *Conceitos e dimensões da pobreza e da exclusão social*, Ed. Unijuí, Ijuí.

Fórum Brasileiro de Economia Solidária (2008) *IV Plenária Nacional de Economia Solidária, Relatorio Final*, Brasilía.

França Filho, G.C., and J.L. Laville (2004). *Economia solidária, uma abordagem internacional*, UFRGS, Porto Alegre.

Frantz, W. (2005). *Reflexões e apontamentos sobre cooperativismo*, Ed. Unijuí, Ijuí.

Gaiger, L. (2003) *A economia solidária diante do modo de produção capitalista*, Salvador, *Caderno CRH*, 39, July–December: 181–211.

Gaiger, L. (2004) 'A Economia Solidária e o Projeto de Outra Mundialização', *DADOS – Revista de Ciências Sociais* 47(4): 799–834.

Godbout, J., and A. Caillé (1992) *L'esprit du don*, La Découverte, Paris.

Guerra, P. (2002) *Socioeconomía de la solidaridad*, Editorial Nordan-Comunidad, Montevideo.

Kraychete, G. (2006) 'Sustentabilidade dos empreendimentos da economia popular solidária', paper presented at seminar 'Economy of Popular Sectors: Sustainability and Training Strategies', www.capina.org.br/download/pub/ gkrtxtsemi.pdf.

Lechat, N. (2004) *Trajetórias intelectuais e o campo da Economia Solidária no Brasil*, doctoral thesis in Social Sciences, Universidade Estadual de Campinas, Campinas (SP).

Lechat, N., and E. Barcelos (2008) 'Autogestão: desafios políticos e metodológi- cos na incubação de empreendimentos econômicos solidários', *Rev. Katálysis* 11(1): 96–104.

Lechat, N., A. Van Der Sand and L. Juliani (2003) *Projeto PRONINC Empreender:* Implantação de uma incubadora de economia solidária na Unijuí, UNIJUÍ, Ijuí.

Lemes, F.R.M., Rasia, P.C. Vitcel and S. Marlise (2007) 'Processo educativo na formação organizacional num Empreendimento de Economia Solidária', *Anais do V Encontro Internacional de Economia Solidária, USP.*

Levesque, B., G.L. Bourque and E. Forgues (2001) *La nouvelle sociologie économique,* Ed. Desclée de Brouwer, Paris.

Mte, S. (2006) *I Conferência Nacional de Economia Solidária,* Documento final, Brasília, www.fbes.org.br.

Mte, S. (2008) *Relatório Nacional SIES, 2005/2007,* Brasília, www.mte.gov.br/ecosolidaria/sies.asp.

Nascimento, C. (2000). 'Autogestão e economia solidária', *Outros valores* 1(2), Cadernos da cidade do futuro, Florianópolis.

Sachs, I. (2004) *Desenvolvimento includente, sustentável, sustentado,* Garamond, Rio de Janeiro.

Santos, B. de S. (2001) 'Para uma Reinvenção Solidária e Participativa do Estado', in L.C.B. Pereira, et al., eds, *Sociedade e Estado em transformação,* UNESP, São Paulo.

Singer, P. (2000) Economia solidária: um modo de produção e distribuição', in P. Singer and A Souza, eds, *A economia solidária no Brasil; a autogestão como resposta ao desemprego,* Contexto, São Paolo.

Singer, P. (2002) *Introdução à Economia Solidária,* Ed. Fundação Perceu Abramo, São Paulo.

Singer, P., and A. Souza, eds (2000) *A Economia solidária no Brasil; a autogestão como resposta ao desemprego,* Contexto, São Paulo.

Thiollent, M. (1997) *Pesquisa-ação nas organizações,* Atlas, São Paulo.

Tiriba, L. (1997) 'Los trabajadores, el capitalismo y la propiedad colectiva como estrategia de supervivencia y de sociedad: rastreando el debate histórico', *Contexto e Educação* (Ijuí) 46: 7–34.

Tiriba, L. (2001) *Economia Popular e cultura do trabalho,* Ed. Unijuí, Ijuí.

9

The three pillars of the social economy:
the Quebec experience

Marguerite Mendell

Quebec: From stories to a conceptual framework

In the *Livelihood of Man* (1977), Karl Polanyi uses the term *substantivist economy* to describe the workings of all economies. It refers to processes of wealth creation that, according to Polanyi, are always embedded in cultural and institutional contexts. The social economy, as it emerges around the world, describes socially constructed economic provisioning, with its own logic embedded in social relations; or, to borrow from Julie Graham and Janelle Cornelle, it is one of the many logics of a differentiated capitalism.[1] Often, these are interpreted as pragmatic responses to so-called market and state failure to redress growing social inequality. But, as they become more numerous and more visible, the social economy is increasingly recognized as an alternative approach to economic provisioning and social organization. This is closer to the vision of a third system presented by John Pearce in this volume, which involves citizens, movements and civil society organizations as *agents* or *architects* in the design of new social arrangements, of new hybrid intermediary spaces to anchor or institutionalize this alternative approach. The risk that the social economy may also add up to numerous fragmented initiatives at the margins, often substituting for previously provided public services, must also be acknowledged, certainly in more impermeable contexts that resist the articulation of an alternative approach[2] (Amin et al., 2002).

This chapter focuses on the Quebec experience from 1998 to 2007, as a way of addressing questions relating to the place and role of the social economy in the economy. There has been and continues to be a great deal of interest in the social economy in Quebec; it is frequently regarded as a model for other regions in Canada and in many regions and countries internationally. Today, it is also considered as a counterpoise to the growing interest in social enterprise and/or social entrepreneurship in many countries that, unlike the social economy in Quebec, are often disembedded from their larger socio-economic and socio-political context. I believe that the experience of the social economy over the last ten years in Quebec allows for bold statements about its capacity to undermine the dominant paradigm. The challenges presented by the social economy to mainstream thinking through lived experiences are taken seriously.

The Quebec experience has been well documented by many researchers and policy analysts and is frequently referred to in the growing literature on the social economy internationally. With the benefit of a little over a decade, the social economy in Quebec provides important lessons that are captured in the title of this chapter. It stands on three legs: the social enterprises themselves, an enabling policy environment, and leadership. Each has contributed to the evolution, consolidation and growth of the social economy. But it is their coexistence that underwrites the agenda set by social economy actors in Quebec to construct an alternative socio-economic development model through practice. The ethnography of the social economy that this book addresses in different national contexts is essential to defining and designing the socio-economic transformation strategy in Quebec. It identifies the key actors, the enterprises, the sectors of activity involved and their impact – the jobs created, their quality/wages, and so on – and contributes to much-needed evaluation of what does and what does not work. The failures or fragile experiences must not, however, undervalue or undermine the social economy; they are challenges to be met, challenges that in many cases were expected, given numerous new sectors of activity in which the social economy is engaged, for example. The many stories, case studies of social economy enterprises that document the successes, the failures, the best practices, and so on, provide the essential narrative to evaluate the capacity of the social economy. But this critical work is insufficient on its own. The fate of the social economy is sealed if we focus only on micro case-studies, especially those in new and fragile sectors of activity. The importance of enabling conditions has also to be documented, be it policy, training, mentoring, research or networking. This has to be done in tandem with micro-ethnographies. And, finally, the role of leadership in the evolution of the social economy has to be documented. This has been acknowledged as key to the development of the social economy in Quebec and to the vital political space it currently occupies. The experience in Quebec has rested on these three pillars, each undergoing difficulties and meeting obstacles at different times, not the least of which is repositioning or re-anchoring in changing political environments.

The social economy in Quebec reflects a convergence of otherwise parallel paths over the last twenty-five years. Social movements, community-based activists and the labour movement have, throughout this period, been the architects of alternative economic strategies to reduce poverty and unemployment, and to implement new civil-society-based economic revitalization strategies. An extensive literature has grown on community-based initiatives, new investment instruments including labour solidarity funds, community land trusts, collective enterprise and so on, mark this period (Mendell et al., 2007). In many ways, the social economy in Quebec cuts across these various initiatives as it includes normative or political, juridical or structural, as well as theoretical or methodological dimensions.

The current focus on the social economy internationally has generated confusion as countries adopt their own terms and definitions. In the United States, for example, it is interpreted more narrowly, reducing the social economy almost entirely to the third sector and most recently to revenue-generating social enterprises. Within Europe, there are multiple interpretations; the broadest perhaps was the third system adopted some time ago by the European Union that situates the social economy in the larger political economy and permits a better understanding of the social economy's integration of market, non-market and non-monetary resources, much like the private and public sectors, but with clearly different objectives.³ Currently, the growing interest in and support for social enterprise internationally glosses over important culturally specific definitions. Within developing countries, reference to the solidarity economy focuses primarily on non-market activity, often closely associated with the informal sector. Within this large canvas there are many interpretations, definitions and practices. That said, these differences have enriched what we now refer to broadly as the social economy, permitting us to consider it conceptually both as a strategy for democratizing the economy and as an organizational or juridical form including co-operatives, non-profit organizations and, in many cases, private enterprises with socio-economic or 'social purpose' objectives. In English Canada the social economy also includes community economic development and the voluntary sector. The variability both within and between countries is, however, misleading. These experiences have more in common than their different nomenclature or practices reveal.

In Quebec the social economy has achieved a great deal of visibility in recent years. There are several reasons why this is interesting for researchers and policymakers, many of which are common to developments in other countries. A need to re-examine the delivery of social services is driving the policy agenda, hence the potential appeal of new forms of social service provision by social economy enterprises. Similar to the experience in numerous countries, social economy enterprises are responding to needs not met by the market or by the state. What distinguishes the Quebec story, we believe, is the clear commitment to provide *new services* that meet *new needs* or *previously unsatisfied needs*. Social economy service enterprises are not substitutes for public provision. They are not reinforcing the offloading or subcontracting of numerous public services, but quite the opposite. In Quebec, government has been and continues to be vital to the development of the social economy through public funding, enabling legislation and institutional support. It has come to accept this as critical to the capacity of the social economy to deliver. It has also come to recognize the value of working with social economy actors in designing a policy framework. This does not correspond to government offloading; it suggests a new form of government intervention. Moreover, social economy enterprises also produce goods for the market. This business model appeals to a growing number of people wishing to work collectively in many new sectors of activity that contribute to sustainable community development. The co-operative movement in Quebec has a long and successful history in numerous sectors, including finance. The Mouvement Desjardins is a leading financial institution internationally; it is rooted in Quebec society and is a mainstay of the co-operative movement. The current generation of social economy enterprises producing goods is emerging in numerous new sectors. They adopt the co-operative or not-for-profit legal form. The association with responsible consumption and important links with movements such as fair trade and the environment make the social economy business form very attractive, especially to young people.

In earlier work with my colleague Benoit Lévesque, I explored the evolving landscape of the social economy from four perspectives to reflect the hybrid nature of the social economy in Quebec. We distinguished between those social economy enterprises that respond to social and often urgent needs and those that reflect new choices or opportunities to work otherwise and in new sectors. Also, we distinguished between a predominantly non-market-based and a market-based social economy. While numerous examples can be added to those in the typology below, this classification is important to demonstrate the *multi-sectorality* of the social economy, its capacity to create wealth and employment and to meet needs for new social services. In so doing, we began the work of mapping the social economy, the sectors of activity, and their capacity to generate secure and sustainable employment.

This classification was not intended to reinforce the separation of the social and economic dimensions of the social economy often found within policy circles that pigeonhole the social economy into a social policy silo. It was an attempt to introduce the diversity of the social economy and the overlay of social and economic dimensions, even if particular enterprises and/or sectors respond to primarily social needs, while others do not. Also, several enterprises and sectors cross over the social needs/new opportunities boundaries (only two are given as examples here; see figure 9.1). The typology is helpful as

FIGURE 9.1   The social economy: a typology

Opportunities and needs / Relationship to the market	Social economy (response to social needs)	Social economy (response to new opportunities)
Non-market-based social economy (social development)	Examples: shelters for the homeless; daycare centres; collective kitchens; reintegration of school dropouts	Examples: daycare centres; perinatal centres; eco-museums;
Market-based social economy (economic development)	Examples: training businesses; re-adaptation centres; solidarity or social finance (financial products); culture	Examples: worker co-ops; recycling (environment); food (catering); culture

Source: Adapted from Lévesque and Mendell, 1999.

an ideal representation of the social economy in the Weberian sense and as a basis from which to then address the hybrid nature of many social economy enterprises and their capacities to address both needs and opportunities.

The many enterprises that make up the social economy share a common goal similar to the goals and objectives of social and solidarity economy initiatives in other countries. What distinguishes the Quebec experience, we believe, is not only its *multi-sectorality* but the innovative institutional infrastructure social economy actors have constructed to develop enabling instruments, tools and services for the social economy. It is this *integrated systemic approach* to the social economy that is key to its evolution in Quebec and to the strategic place it occupies in the political economy of the province.[4] It is key to the legitimacy and recognition of the social economy as a significant economic actor; it is key to the numerous public policies that have emerged, particularly in the last decade, to support the social economy sectorally and inter-sectorally; and it is key to *building negotiating capacity* that translates the needs of individual enterprises and regions into enabling policy, especially for more fragile enterprises and sectors.

We have learned in Quebec that an enabling environment that is not limited to accessing existing public policy tools and resources is essential for the social economy. Policy innovation for the social economy requires new *processes* of policy formation and *institutional innovation*. This means designing *intermediary inter-sectoral dialogic spaces* that represent the numerous actors involved directly in the social economy and those that share its objectives. Social economy actors must be and are the co-authors of the numerous policies that have emerged in the last decade in Quebec. The development of this political capacity is critical.

Increasingly, government has come to realize that innovative initiatives in the social economy are not necessarily designed to solve immediate problems but rather to build social and economic capacity within communities. Moreover, it is in the interest of government to develop a framework of *co-regulation* with actors.[5] This implies coordinated decentralization and linkages with different levels of government.[6] Easier access to information and knowledge needed for policy formulation increases state capacity as well. The social economy is, in many ways, spearheading what Ash Amin and Jerzy Hausner refer to as *flexible modes of governance* (Klein et al., 2009). It also means adopting a new mindset. Public funding for social services provided by social economy enterprises – homecare, daycare, for example – has to appear on the other side of the balance sheet as investment, not as expenditure. These are contracts for service: social enterprises are delivering services in the public interest. Calculating the costs and benefits derived from this reorientation does not pose a problem. The returns to such investment by government translate directly into financial savings; the multiplier effects (tax revenues from new economic activities) and externalities (social well-being) add to the argument that for government to embrace this is a good deal.

The contours of the social economy in Quebec

The social economy in Quebec has a long history; its current prominence, however, began in 1996, when the premier, Lucien Bouchard, invited community groups and social movements to participate in a Summit on the Economic and Social Future of Quebec. The Chantier de l'économie sociale was one of three *chantiers*, 'building sites' or 'task forces' assigned to propose strategies to resolve the fiscal and unemployment crisis faced by the Bouchard provincial government (1996–2001). Economic summits were not new to Quebec. *Concertation*, a term commonly used to refer to tripartite negotiations and conversations between major players in Quebec – business, government and the labour movement – is embedded in the political culture of Quebec. The state – the government of Quebec – has been engaged in economic development strategies from the Quiet Revolution in the 1960s (Mendell, 2002: 326–9, 336 n7). Almost 40 per cent of Quebec workers are unionized, placing labour in an important negotiating position, especially but not only in the public sector (Jackson and Schetagne, 2003: 6–7). What was referred to as a 'developmental state' in the literature very much characterizes Quebec from the 1960s and 1970s onwards, with the creation of numerous large state-owned enterprises (Leys and Mendell, 1992). The 'partnership state' best characterizes what is often referred to as 'Québec, Inc.' to describe the relationship between the Quebec government, labour and business from the 1980s as it established priorities for the Quebec economy and developed innovative strategies to achieve these. In this social arrangement to develop and steer the economy, the private sector is the powerful third partner, an arrangement that has characterized Quebec and has distinguished it from the rest of the country. But there was a fourth partner in 1996 for the first time: community-based organizations were at this table. Recently, the embeddedness of *concertation* within Quebec culture was tested by the current provincial government's unsuccessful drive to dismantle this process in its efforts to modernize Quebec state. The resistance came from all social actors.

Two initiatives are particularly important for positioning the social economy in Quebec today. They are part of the ethnography of the social economy in Quebec, best described as a history of institution-building and socio-economic innovation by civil society. This was particularly the case in 1983 and the creation of the Fonds de solidarité des travailleurs (Workers' Solidarity Fund) by the Fédération des travailleurs(euses) du Québec (FTQ) (Lévesque and Mendell, 1999). The Fonds de solidarité is a pension fund made up of voluntary contributions by members of the Quebec Federation of

Labour and ordinary citizens. The significance of the establishment of the Fonds, however, is the influential role assumed by the labour movement in the economic development of Quebec with this new capacity to invest in enterprises and sectors where job creation and job maintenance would be assured. The establishment of the Fonds in 1983 required both provincial and federal legislation; generous fiscal incentives were created to attract subscribers. While many focus on the impressive financial performance of this labour solidarity fund, what is interesting from our perspective is the direct engagement in economic development by the labour movement and the vital enabling role played by the state. The Confédération des syndicats nationaux (CSN), the second largest labour federation in Quebec, also established a labour solidarity fund in 1996, FondAction (Le Fonds de développement pour la coopération et l'emploi), designed to meet socio-economic objectives; it enjoys the same fiscal advantages as the Fonds de solidarité.[7]

The establishment of the Fonds de solidarité in 1983 is very important to the development of the social economy for several reasons. First of all, it was created at approximately the same time as the emergence of community economic development corporations, CDECs, in low-income neighbourhoods in Quebec. The 1980s represented a turning point for civil society. Just as the labour movement became a strategic economic actor in Quebec influencing the economic development of the province, community organizations and citizens' movements responded to the economic crisis by implementing revitalization strategies within communities hit hard by the crisis, shifting their action from social to economic intervention. This experience is also essential to situate the political place occupied by the social economy today. As is becoming clear, the 1980s set the stage for strategic repositioning of the labour movement and community actors as key players in the Quebec economy. Their direct engagement during the economic crisis was formative for the future role they would assume within local communities and at a macro-level.[8] Although civil society actors were engaged in local territorial struggles, the CDECs were the first to demonstrate the importance of multi-stakeholder collaboration to develop effective revitalization strategies. Moreover, community activists mobilized three levels of government – federal, provincial and municipal – to support the establishment of these new community-based intermediaries that would enable the private sector, the labour movement and social movements in neighbourhoods to work in partnership.[9] The CDECs became a model for the subsequent establishment of local development centres (CLDs) across the province in 1998. The value of local intermediaries was recognized; government could work more effectively with this immediate access to key actors.

The CDECs were early examples of *flexible modes of governance*, demonstrating the value of collaborative policy design. They had an important impact on the political culture and institutional innovation in Quebec, especially for the evolution of the social economy that benefits from this legacy both politically and in its clear understanding of the importance of institution-building to anchor the social economy. The legacy of the social economy rests on these experiences and on the longer and significant history of the co-operative movement in Quebec. Today, the labour movement and its solidarity funds, the co-operative movement and local development actors are part of the social economy in Quebec.[10] They collaborate through a variety of forms, including participation in governing bodies with the many other movements and sectors in the social economy. Leadership has been essential to build and consolidate these alliances and to build a social economy movement. It is not a coincidence that the leaders of the social economy today in Quebec were the architects of these earlier experiences.

Chantier de l'économie sociale: network of networks

At the Socio-economic Summit in 1996 (see Box 9.1), the Bouchard government mandated both the private sector and civil society to propose strategies to revitalize the Quebec economy. The Chantier de l'économie sociale surpassed its mandate to create 20,000 jobs in two years. Perhaps the biggest challenge was to agree on a definition of the social economy. Despite the controversy this generated in arriving at a common understanding of the social economy and fending off criticisms of the many groups that were opposed to the definition

---

BOX 9.1   The social economy definition adopted by the
Chantier de l'économie sociale

As a whole, the social economy refers to the set of activities and
organizations stemming from collective entrepreneurship, organized around the following principles and operating rules:

1. The purpose of a social economy enterprise is to serve its
   members or the community rather than to simply make
   profit.
2. It operates at arm's length from the state.
3. It promotes a democratic management process involving all
   users and/or workers through its statutes and the way it does
   business.
4. It defends the primacy of individuals and work over capital in
   the distribution of its surplus and its revenues.
5. It bases its activities on the principles of participation and individual and collective empowerment. The social economy therefore encompasses all co-operative and mutual movements and
   associations. The social economy can be developed in all sectors
   that meet the needs of the people and the community.

Source: Chantier de l'économie sociale.

---

for some time after it was adopted, it was accepted by government
and eventually by its detractors.[11]

The early work of the Chantier in 1996 resulted in the adoption of
policy measures to accommodate its recommendations. Programmes
were put in place to support emerging sectors in the social economy
such as daycare, homecare and the environment, among others. Funds
were allocated to labour-market training and business development,
and the Quebec government leveraged private-sector contributions to
create an investment fund, Réseau d'investissement social du Québec
(RISQ), to provide loan capital and technical assistance to social
economy enterprises. The two-year mandate given to the Chantier
during the Summit was broad, not tied to specific sectors of activity.
Priorities were identified by members of the Chantier. This is important, as it opened up possibilities to promote collective ownership in
numerous sectors of economic activity, enshrining the vision of the

Chantier to lay the ground for an alternative economic development strategy. I have referred to this strategy adopted by the Chantier as a *process of economic democratization* to describe a coordinated strategy of developing tools and instruments that not only provide important resources to collective enterprises, but are themselves collectively owned and democratically governed (Mendell, 2007).

In 1998 the Chantier took an important decision to become a non-profit organization, allowing it to negotiate with government on its own behalf and that of its members. Because it represented numerous sectors of activity, the limitation of negotiating with sectoral ministerial silos was clear from the outset. It is for this reason that the initial integration of the social economy into the executive committee of cabinet, a horizontal policy environment, was crucial to its development and to leverage political capacity. A special office for the social economy was then established in the Ministry of Finance and Economic Development in 2001, again a horizontal policy location that could handle the social economy. This early location of the social economy in horizontal policy settings within government was instrumental for policy formation. With the change of government in 2003, the social economy 'file' was transferred to the Ministry of Economic Development, Innovation and Trade (MDEIE) where it met a cultural barrier and numerous obstacles. Despite there being an office for the social economy within this ministry, there were many hurdles, including this ministry's responsibility for the co-operative movement, which claimed exclusive representation of the social economy, suggesting that the Chantier represented social actors at the margins of the economy. While this was a difficult moment, the embeddedness of the social economy in Quebec and the extraordinary political skills of its leadership led to an important political change. The premier of the province agreed to shift responsibility for the social economy into the more horizontal and intersectoral Ministry for Municipal and Regional Affairs. Despite these political challenges, the operations of the Chantier de l'économie sociale have been continuously funded by government, although this is always subject to renegotiation.[12]

The political role played by the Chantier has been instrumental in the development of the social economy and to its recognition as an

---

BOX 9.2   Chantier de l'économie sociale Board of Directors

- President of the Board
- President–Director General
- Sectoral representatives
    Enterprises adapted for the disabled
    Homecare
    Work integration enterprises
    Federation of co-operatives of paramedics
    Quebec association of daycare (early years) centres
    Federation of housing co-operatives
    Network of non-profit housing organizations
    Community radio association
    Micro-finance network
- Organizations supporting the social economy
    Network of worker co-operatives
    Association of technical assistance providers of Quebec
    Association of local development centres (CLDs)
    Network of Community Economic Development
        Corporations (CDECs)
- Five regional poles of the social economy across Quebec
- Labour movement
    Two large labour federations:
        Fédération des travailleurs(euses) du Québec
        Confédération des syndicats nationaux
- Community movements
    National roundtable of community development
    corporations
    Women's movement
- 'Large' (established) movements
    Quebec council on leisure
- Members (non-voting)
    Two social economy investment funds:
        RISQ (Réseau d'investissement social du Québec)
        Fiducie du Chantier de l'économie sociale
    Sectoral committee for labour market development in the
        social economy and community sector
    Community University Research Alliance on the Social
        Economy
- One independent member

Source: Chantier de l'économie sociale.

economic actor in Quebec alongside the public and private sectors. Its capacity to mobilize numerous networks contributes to its legitimacy and to its significant political role. It is not just circumstance or happenstance that gave rise to the position of strength assumed by the Chantier and to its capacity to develop a coherent and coordinated development strategy for the social economy. Its leaders are architects of institutional innovation and social change. While the social economy faces numerous difficulties, similar to those in many countries, the tools and resources developed by social economy actors and the significant political influence of the Chantier greatly increase the capacity to meet these challenges (see Box 9.2).

I have deliberately provided this detailed list to illustrate the hybrid and innovative institutional space created by the Chantier de l'économie sociale. The deliberative culture of the Chantier is unique, bringing together movements, organizations engaged in local and regional development, numerous sectors, the Chantier's divisions and partners in finance, training and labour market development and research. The last is especially important. The Chantier is a partner in an innovative research alliance with university-based researchers that contributes to an ongoing mobilization and dissemination of knowledge on the social economy. The composition of the board reflects the systemic and integrated approach that underlies the success of the social economy and the role it plays in Quebec society today.

The barriers that the social economy faces in Quebec and elsewhere are mostly institutional, such as laws and accounting norms and the absence of appropriate evaluation and measurement tools that adequately reflect the values and the value-added of collective enterprise. However, important work on social accounting and indicators is under way, and debates and discussions on legal forms have already generated new and enabling legislation for the social economy. The new economic role assumed by not-for-profit associations urgently calls for new laws to enable them to operate effectively as business entities with the ability to access investment capital, for example. Challenges for the social economy include commercialization strategies to secure markets for goods and services produced in the social economy. The Chantier has recently developed a portal that includes a detailed repertoire of all social economy enterprises in Quebec that

---

BOX 9.3   The social economy in Quebec (2002)[13]

- 7,822 enterprises (3,881 co-operative and 3,941 not-for-profit)[14]
    935 *centres de la petite enfance* (daycare)
    671 *caisses populaires* (credit unions)
    180 worker co-operatives
    103 social economy homecare enterprises
    72 worker-shareholder co-operatives (workers co-operatively acquire shares in the enterprise in which they are employed)
- Business activity excluding the *caisses populaires*
    $17.2 billion ($15.9 billion co-operatives; $1.3 billion not-for-profits)
- Business activity including the *caisses populaires*
    $102.5 billion ($101.2 billion co-operatives; $1.3 billion not-for-profits)
- Job creation in Quebec
    124,302 jobs excluding the *caisses populaires* (79,222 in co-operatives and 45,080 in not-for-profits)
    161,302 jobs including the *caisses populaires* (116,222 in co-operatives and 45,080 in not-for-profits)

Source: Chantier de l'économie sociale.

---

will create internal markets for the enterprises, a 'business to business' strategy initiated by the Chantier. Procurement policies, integrating the social economy into the movement for socially responsible consumption, labelling and fairs are among the many marketing strategies that are being explored and tested. Colleges and universities in Quebec are creating certificate and diploma programmes for new occupations and professions emerging in new sectors in the social economy. Institutional innovations such as solidarity co-operatives have expanded the co-operative model to include a broad range of stakeholders. These are only a few illustrations of the innovative capacity of the social economy in Quebec today.

Today, the social economy is considered vital to the political economy in Quebec. The data (see Box 9.3) provided by government and the co-operative sector are somewhat dated but reveal the sectoral diversity and economic capacity of the social economy. The challenge is not only to update these figures but to develop a completely new database. This work is currently under way.

The social economy in Quebec: an integrated system of social innovation

I have provided an overview of the context in which the social economy has evolved in Quebec over the last decade. I also began this chapter by stating that its success rested on three pillars: the enterprises, public policy and leadership. The Chantier has assumed an innovative leadership role, by transcending its important role to represent the numerous enterprises and sectors in the economy to construct an integrated institutional architecture including collective tools – finance, research, training, business services – developed in partnership with numerous organizations. In bringing in expertise and in developing its own, the Chantier is at the centre of an *integrated system of social innovation*. This is not only an integrated system of services and tools; the Chantier and its partners collaborate in a dynamic research environment that has increased the capacity to identify problems and potential for growth and development. The research capacity of the Chantier itself is exceptional. It has resulted in important innovations in finance and the promotion of new sectors of activity. Continuous mapping of the social economy throughout the province, exploring the potential of new sectors, identifying problem areas, development of markets – these are but a few of the areas of ongoing research undertaken by the Chantier. The development priorities of the social economy include promoting new sectors of activity, 'scaling up' existing viable enterprises and sectors, and building capacity within fragile sectors.

Capacity-generation through horizontal and vertical links

The Chantier is a horizontal network of vertically linked networks (see Figure 9.2). This structure has greatly reduced the complexity and fragmentation of many social economy experiences elsewhere. At the root of this structure is a deep commitment to democracy. While

FIGURE 9.2   Chantier de l'économie sociale

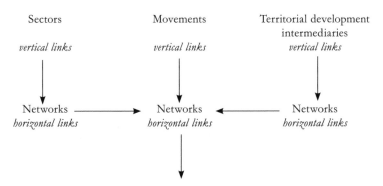

the Chantier certainly plays a powerful representative and political role, it is based in civil society, in movements and, most important, in regions throughout Quebec. The establishment of 'regional poles' was a priority for the Chantier, both to reinforce its commitment to *distributed democratic governance* by encouraging the establishment of regional 'chantiers' by local actors, and to design tools to accommodate regional specificities.

The Chantier has had an important impact on public policy over the last decade, addressing the sectoral, territorial, generic and targeted needs of the social economy.[15] This is the outcome of an ongoing conversation, a *policy dialogue*, between government and social economy actors. While the ability to negotiate with government is not new, the *process of policy design* is transforming. The numerous policies adopted over the last twenty-five years, beginning with the Fonds de solidarité and the CDECs, have been initiated and proposed by civil society. The hybrid and multi-sectoral nature of the social economy expanded this role of civil society actors in 1996 when they became the co-authors of new policies necessary to accommodate and support the strategies they were asked to develop. The last ten years of policy innovation for the social economy is best described as a *process of co-construction*. For social economy actors, the legitimacy they have developed as astute policy architects is extremely important, notwithstanding numerous hard negotiations, many outstanding issues and inadequate public support for some sectors. Government has come to realize the benefit of this process of policy formation. The Chantier is

FIGURE 9.3   Integrated systems of social innovation

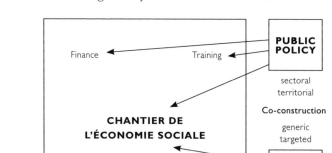

Source: Expanded from Lévesque, 2001: 7.

a powerful negotiating partner; the capacity for the social economy to speak with one voice has increased its political capacity significantly. Today, the Chantier is invited to policy dialogues on major social and economic issues in Quebec, recognizing its horizontality. Its expertise is sought on issues ranging from labour market policy to health-care reform and on annual economic budget priorities.

I have focused on context, on the successful process of institution-building that has built a social economy movement in Quebec. The strength derived from this collective engagement has increased the capacity of individual sectors to negotiate on their own behalf with the support of the Chantier, representing the social economy as a whole. In the next section, I will summarize some of the innovations and challenges faced by different sectors of the social economy with examples drawn from the homecare sector, solidarity finance and culture. I have selected research as a fourth illustration because of the important role this has played in the evolution of the social economy and in demonstrating the value of developing collective and partnership learning environments for knowledge mobilization and dissemination. This *co-construction of knowledge* is contributing to a new epistemology.

Illustrations of initiatives and innovations

One of the most important challenges for the social economy is to realize its commitment to high-quality and sustainable employment. Interestingly, despite the need to improve working conditions in several sectors (numerous part-time and precarious jobs, inadequate access to benefits, modest wages), a recent survey by the CSMO (sectoral committee on the labour market in the social economy) found that the majority of workers in the social economy are satisfied with their jobs because of the objectives and values of the enterprises in which they are working. A sector that is experiencing difficulties, however, and many challenges to improve the quality of work, is homecare.

Concerns in 1996 that the social economy would be a source of cheap labour, providing services offloaded from the public sector, were directed especially at the homecare sector. As stated above,

---

BOX 9.4   Homecare social economy enterprises

Homecare services (*aide domestique*) in the social economy:

- size of sector: $95.8 million
- 56 not-for-profit enterprises; 45 co-operatives (2006)
- more than one-third of these enterprises are not networked
- 5.6 million hours of service offered to 76,059 individuals (2005)
- employment of approximately 6,000 workers in homecare sector
- need for an additional 150,000 individuals predicted (2005–10)
- fixed $10 hourly fee for clients ($4 subsidy from government) (non-indexed; cost of these services estimated at $17 per hour)
- salaries slightly above minimum wage – have not changed in the last five years
- importance of 'relational' aspect of this work has not been recognized (this will change with the initiative by the CSMO and its partners)

Source: Jetté et al., 2008; CSMO.

the definition of the social economy adopted in 1996 clearly states that jobs in services will be *new jobs* providing *new services* to meet *new needs* of the population. Homecare services are responding to urgent and rising needs in society, especially with an ageing population. Nevertheless, this work is largely undervalued and has no professional legitimacy. Low wages and poor working conditions mirror the absence of professional status. Likewise, the quality of care is not regulated, sometimes increasing the vulnerability of the people needing these services. And while governments do recognize the need for this work, their support is inadequate and piecemeal. Recently, however, the CSMO spearheaded a successful initiative to professionalize homecare work by mobilizing the Chantier, two networks of homecare social economy enterprises, the labour movement and the Ministries of Education and Health and Social Services. This will also include training and education programmes for the sector.[16] This is yet another example of a multi-stakeholder and horizontal approach that required the active participation of at least two ministries to design an integrated strategy to address the labour-market needs of this sector.

Solidarity finance

It was clear in 1996 that financial instruments for the social economy had to be designed, with appropriate investment criteria distinct from conventional financial institutions that considered these enterprises high risk and were not able to comprehend or incorporate social returns into their calculus. The solidarity or social finance landscape has changed considerably in many parts of the world; there has been much innovation in this sector.[17] In Quebec, as in other parts of the world, the majority of financial 'products' available for the social economy are debt instruments, short- or medium-term loan capital. Paradoxically, the availability of these instruments can limit the consolidation and growth of numerous enterprises. A diversity of financial products ranging from short-term loans to forms of long-term capital is required. Given the inability of collectively owned enterprises to issue shares, the form that long-term capital investment could take had to be invented.

In 2007, the Chantier de l'économie sociale launched the Fiducie du Chantier de l'économie sociale, a $53.8 million patient capital or quasi-equity fund enabling collective enterprises to embark on long-term planning, invest in real estate and move out of a vicious cycle of debt. The new 'product' is a form of debenture, a fifteen-year investment that is only repaid at the end of the term. This is an achievement for the Chantier and for the social economy in Quebec. It is yet another example of the capacity to innovate in partnership with other actors. While the initial funding came from the federal government during a brief and important political moment,[18] and was important for leveraging additional funds, the challenge to attract other subscribers was met. Today the Fiducie is an innovative and important financial intermediary. In addition to the initial federal government grant, capitalization of the Fiducie includes sizeable investments by the two labour solidarity funds, the Fonds de solidarité ($12 million), FondAction ($8 million) and the government of Quebec ($10 million). In its short existence, the Fiducie has invested $6.2 million in nineteen projects (September 2008) and is embarking on numerous new investments.[19] It is exploring the creation of secondary markets and ultimately a solidarity finance exchange.

The role of government has been, once again, key to launching this initiative, but the impetus and the design are the work of civil society, of social economy actors who had researched innovations in financial markets elsewhere to craft a framework that suited the Quebec social economy environment. The policies adopted by the federal government, however short-lived, were extremely important to leverage the rest. For the province of Quebec, this is another example of the *co-construction of public policy*. While a direct policy instrument was not necessary to launch the Fiducie, the public investment arm of the provincial government, Investissement Québec, invested $10 million. And it could do this because part of its investment envelope is designated for the social economy. This, too, is a direct result of collaborative policy design with social economy actors. Likewise for the labour movement: as members of the board of the Chantier, the two labour solidarity funds stepped in as co-investors and partners in this important initiative.

BOX 9.5   The Fiducie du Chantier de l'économie sociale: investment products for social economy enterprises

The Chantier de l'économie sociale Trust (Fiducie) offers long-term loans repayable after fifteen years; patient capital aimed at supporting enterprises' operations and contributing to their real-estate investments.

- Amounts available: between $50,000 and $1.5 million.
  Loans are granted on the basis of financing packages in which the loan represents no more than 35 per cent of project-related costs. They are unsecured, except in the case of real-estate projects, where a subordinated debt is requested. The enterprise can repay the capital at any time.

- Investments (September 2008):

operations	$1,743,926
real estate	$4,703,409
total (19 projects)	$6,447,335

- Jobs created or consolidated: 524 (since July 2007).

- Total investment leveraged: $31,907,375.

Source: Fiducie du Chantier de l'économie sociale, 2008.

Not only has the Fiducie (see Box 9.5) responded to the need to capitalize social economy enterprises with an innovative financial product (a form of security or debenture), it has done so by building the infrastructure necessary for this type of investment activity. The need for intermediaries in the segmented market that thus far characterizes the growing social investment sector was understood in Quebec when it established a multi-stakeholder intermediary including government (federal and provincial), the labour movement and the social economy. The need to pool risk was, of course, recognized from the outset. Many of the obstacles that limit the development of the social investment market were addressed in the design of this intermediary. A coordinated strategy has avoided the 'bricolage' which tends to characterize this sector, however large the potential capital pool is within many regions and countries today.

TABLE 9.1   Investment in the social economy since 1996

Year	Amount invested ($)
1996	27,800,000
1997	20,049,998
1998	56,113,321
1999	52,312,804
2000	61,246,758
2001	82,535,643
2002	90,596,730
2003	113,127,492
2004	136,381,535
2005	114,999,693
Total	755,163,974

Source: Survey by the Research Partnership on Finance, ARUC-ES, 2006.

For the Fiducie to perform its role both on the supply side, by developing a secondary market to create a large pool of investment capital, or on the demand side, by responding to the long-term capitalization needs of enterprises, it cannot simply and passively wait for opportunities to present themselves. The Chantier's work on providing detailed information and analysis of the social economy in Quebec includes the portal to which we have referred above and also the development of an observatory, which not only maps social economy enterprises and sectors but looks at their potential as clients for the Fiducie. The development of the Fiducie thus has two arms: one reaches out to potential investors; the other to potential investees. This observatory provides useful and rich information, including a profile of the regions in which these enterprises are located. In Quebec, as elsewhere, many manufacturing industries are struggling or have disappeared. In the resource sector, forestry and fishing, mainstays of the regional economy of Quebec, have been hit very hard. In forestry, this is currently having a huge impact on the pulp and paper industry in Quebec, a large employer and source of social cohesion in regions of Quebec organized around large plants. The observatory is being designed with this in mind. What is the potential for new industries, new sectors, in the social economy? What is the current landscape? What is the investment readiness of enterprises? Which enterprises need support to be able to benefit from the capital offered by the Fiducie? Again, this is not the work of the Chantier or its regional poles alone. It requires close collaboration with the local development centres (CLDs) across Quebec, which know their communities and their needs and potential. It requires adopting the coordinated and integrated approach that characterizes the development of the social economy in Quebec.

Many solidarity finance instruments exist in Quebec, including RISQ, also established by the Chantier in 1997 (see Table 9.1). Together they have invested over $750 million in social economy enterprises from 1996 to 2006.[20] These institutions have recently recognized the need to federate and create a solidarity finance sector to increase their capacity to capitalize social economy enterprises more effectively and to raise their profile in the financial sector in Quebec.

New initiatives: the arts in Montreal

The energy to innovate, to develop tools for social economy enterprises, does not abate. This is an important and recurring theme that identifies or perhaps even distinguishes the social economy experience in Quebec. Currently the Chantier and its numerous partners are committed to consolidating social enterprises in the culture/arts sector in Montreal, a vibrant area of activity. There are currently 120 social economy enterprises with a cultural mission.[21] These enterprises are engaged in cultural mediation, placing priority on cultural democracy by increasing access to cultural activities (all forms) in communities and neighbourhoods, promoting active citizen participation in these activities, not only as spectators but as co-creators contributing to social inclusion. The numerous initiatives in Montreal are scattered across the city. There are flagship examples, such as la Tohu, a theatre dedicated to circus arts in a multi-ethnic neighbourhood in the north of the city that is playing an extraordinary role in community mobilization (Box 9.6). In addition to creating numerous jobs through

---

BOX 9.6 La Tohu

Culture at the heart of neighbourhood renewal
- a circus arts theatre opened in 2004
- a meeting-place of education, creation, production and diffusion of international circus arts
- example of green architecture; mobilizes youth as actors of sustainable development

Mission
- to turn Montreal into an international capital of circus arts
- to participate actively in the reconversion of a large quarry into an environmental complex
- contribute to the revitalization of St Michel, a low-income neighbourhood in the north of Montreal

Links with the social economy
- social inclusion
- labour market integration for the local community
- adapted training
- development of circus arts; support for artists
- additional cultural events for local community
- collective art projects to build community cohesion and solidarity

---

direct employment and through participation in work integration programmes, La Tohu is a Green building that uses innovative environmental technologies. It has become a model for sustainable community-based social economy enterprises. Other enterprises with a cultural mission include community radio and festivals for children in low-income neighbourhoods.

A current project is the development of two funds by the Chantier and its partners: (1) $1 million per year for five years to increase the capacity of cultural mediation and citizen participation in cultural activities throughout the city; and (2) a patient capital investment fund of $18 million structured along the lines of the Fiducie (no repayment until term – fifteen years) to invest in real estate for artists and cultural activities (studio space). Gentrification of several low-income neighbourhoods has forced artists out of their communities.

In a document that recommends the creation of these two funds, the Chantier and its partners emphasize the entrepreneurial nature of these initiatives that are able to self-finance 75 per cent of their activities on average while meeting social and artistic objectives. This document also outlines how new projects will develop, setting the tasks and responsibilities that draw upon the expertise of numerous partners in the analysis of projects. The proposal for this patient capital fund includes the capacity-building skills that will increase the potential of these projects to succeed. Once again, this demonstrates the partnership between local actors and the Chantier in the development of a sector.[22]

Research partnerships

As a final descriptive piece to add to this variegated ethnography of the social economy in Quebec that reinforces the importance of dialogue, of partnerships, of process, I would like to discuss the important role that an innovative research partnership, referred to earlier, has played in advancing the social economy in Quebec, in identifying its challenges and helping to propose strategies to meet them, in exploring experiences in other parts of the world and, most important, in cutting through cultural barriers between university-based researchers and practitioners.

In Quebec, the relationship between researchers and practitioners also had to be 'co-constructed'. The availability of a new Community–University Research Alliance (CURA) programme created by the federal Social Sciences and Humanities Research Council was the basis for this partnership, now a decade old. While this CURA partnership is now part of the social economy architecture in Quebec, developing it involved dialogue and time. Common objectives were not enough to erase embedded cultural differences between these two communities; this, despite long-standing relationships of trust between the participants. Many, if not most, of the researchers were already actively involved in community-based initiatives, as researchers and as activists. Still, the institutionalized partnership of the CURA was new. Today we can say that this partnership has increased the capacity for strategic interventions in the many areas of the social economy, from micro-sectoral issues to cross-cutting policy negotiations. The research clusters of the social economy (thematic and territorial) provide important documentation for analysis of the social economy, both conceptual and empirical. Researchers and practitioners collaborate on timely, urgent questions as well as on the development of tools. CURA also provides important opportunities for debate and reflection. The dialogue this has generated has been invaluable in developing a corpus of knowledge on the social economy. The broad circulation of material and the organization of numerous public events have been critical to generating a dynamic policy dialogue within Quebec and across the country.

The relationship between researchers and practitioners is solid today; together they have created an innovative environment for collective learning that is both interdisciplinary and participatory. Action research is not new. However, constructing an institutional environment that demonstrates the value of integrated research and interactive learning is challenging conventional approaches to education, research and pedagogy. The CURAs transcend institutional boundaries in new and innovative ways. A growing number of students are involved either indirectly through an increase in university courses and programmes on community economic development and the social economy or directly as interns or research assistants in a variety of projects. In Quebec, more and more young people have embraced the social economy as an alternative democratically based economic development model committed to social justice and equity. The underlying principles of the social economy speak to young people alienated by a predominantly market-driven ideology.

In many ways, the research alliance in Quebec is an additional component in what we may call the *strategic mobilization* that has characterized the evolution of the social economy in Quebec. This is truly the leitmotif of our story. The development of concrete tools and instruments – finance, training, enterprise development, research – runs parallel to the ongoing commitment to mobilization and alliance-building locally, regionally and nationally. The presence of the social economy in the policy arena is the outcome of this dynamic process, as is the successful mobilization of financial and political resources. But there were no short cuts; this took time.

Conclusion

In Quebec the social economy has moved beyond situated initiatives to design an integrated multi-sectoral and inter-spatial *network of networks* of civil society actors empowered to influence policy at municipal, provincial and federal levels of government. The capacity to speak with one voice, to have an interlocutor that negotiates on behalf of the many sectors, movements and territorial development intermediaries, distinguishes this experience from others. In other words, this was and continues to be a political project. The social economy in Quebec is rooted in radical politics and citizen-based initiatives that have shifted from opposition to constructing an alternative democratic development strategy. The Chantier is a complex and reticular organization committed to distributed governance. It has designed an innovative *dialogic space*. Institutionalization of the social economy in Quebec, therefore, describes the processes instituted by the Chantier itself. Is this experience transferable? I believe so. The alliances and leadership at the core of the social economy in Quebec provide important lessons. In other words, the social economy has first to *reach in* and build a movement whose collective goals transcend those of its individual member organizations and groups. *Reaching out* is more difficult, given different political contexts, but, as we have demonstrated, governing institutions are more permeable today in many parts of the world, given their universal failure to address poverty and social exclusion. We increasingly hear and read about the need for horizontality within government and for multi-stakeholder policy sites for so-called complex problems. These opportunities must be seized. What is perhaps unique in Quebec is the strategic capacity of social economy actors to capture this political moment and transform formal governance institutions by creating and consolidating alternative institutional arrangements in which they play a key role.

Notes

1. See Julie Graham and Janelle Cornwell's chapter in this volume.
2. In their book *Placing the Social Economy* (2002), Ash Amin et al. distinguish between different social economy experiences in the UK, demonstrating the importance of enabling or pre-existing socio-economic, demographic and institutional conditions, including leadership capacity. The possibility of

drafting a systemic approach for the social economy is context-dependent, as they point out. We have to ask how porous these contexts are so as not to be trapped in scenarios of impossibility if the above preconditions do not yet exist.

3. This corresponds with the concept of the plural economy developed by Jean-Louis Laville (1996).

4. This does not imply that the social economy is not vulnerable to changing governments and new priorities. It does mean, however, that the embeddedness of the social economy in Quebec makes it more difficult for governments to introduce radically new policies that would negatively affect the social economy. This explains the extensive investment made by social economy actors in maintaining a high level of visibility and demonstrating the positive outcome for government of maintaining an open dialogue.

5. The reference to co-regulation is useful because it is both inter-sectoral (horizontal) and spatial (territorial) (Fung and Wright, 2003; Giugni et al., 1998; Sirianni and Friedland, 2001; Bradford, 2005).

6. In the USA, examples of linkages and decentralization are 'comprehensive community development strategies; in Canada there is reference to 'place-based' strategies.

7. Unlike the Fonds de solidarité, FondAction invests in enterprises with social and environmental objectives and, therefore, in the social economy. The Fonds de solidarité has supported the social economy through its membership on the board of the Chantier de l'économie sociale and through some of its subsidiary funds (Mendell et al., 2003). Today, it is an investor in a quasi-equity social economy investment fund, la Fiducie, designed and developed by the Chantier de l'économie sociale. Fondaction is also an investor in la Fiducie.

8. The Fonds de solidarité created local funds to support community-based initiatives; FondAction followed suit in the 1990s. That a coordinated strategy, including the need for financial instruments, was essential at the local level was well understood by the labour movement. Its role in the macro-economy of Quebec was expected, given its resources and economic power.

9. In Quebec, citizens' movements were mobilized and active; their initiatives of the 1970s have been institutionalized and form a large part of the social service landscape in Quebec. Community health clinics became the model for province-wide local community clinics; community legal clinics were the basis for province-wide legal aid, and parent-controlled non-profit daycare is the foundation for universal daycare in Quebec.

10. This collaboration has not always been easy or evident. At different times, the social economy could best be described as a 'tension field'. Early on, the women's movement rejected the very principles underlying the social economy; today they are partners. The established co-operative movement in Quebec, which has adopted a largely corporatist stance, poses challenges for social economy actors, as it does in many countries.

11. Quebec is not alone in this experience. Definitional wrangling has characterized the social economy in many regions and countries around the

world. As stated earlier, this is a contested term, hence the nomenclature to describe this activity varies.

12. The government of Quebec provided $250,000 per year to the Chantier to cover its operating costs for 1996–98. Between 1998 and 2003, the amount varied between $325,000 and $450,000 per year. In 2004 the government assured financing of $450,000 per year for three years. It not only renewed this commitment but has increased funding to $650,000 for the next three years.

13. I note that there is ongoing work to update and improve data collection for the social economy. This includes the Chantier portal that will provide both quantitative and qualitative information about social economy enterprises.

14. I identify only a few of the large sectors of activity in the economy. In fact, social economy enterprises exist in approximately twenty sectors of activity including communications, culture, housing, media, tourism, the environment (recycling), forestry and agriculture. They also include consumer co-operatives in the education sector, for example. Recently, a very large consumer co-operative was created by the daycare network to act as a single purchaser for over 900 early childcare centres. It is important to note the multi-sectorality of the social economy to dispel the image that it is exclusively in the service sector. Moreover, where it exists in services, these are not being provided by the market or by the public sector, as we have pointed out. Finally, the data presented exclude the very large agricultural and financial co-operatives. This information is included, however, when we wish to give a global picture of not-for-profit organizations and co-operatives in Quebec.

15. The first two are self-explanatory. Generic policies include finance, enterprise support programmes and initiatives, labour-market policies, research. Targeted policies refer to specific communities: youth, cultural minorities, aboriginal communities, the disabled.

16. This project to professionalize the work of homecare providers is the second recent example of the social economy to codify work that had no prior classification. With the increased number of jobs in social economy enterprises engaged in recycling activities, the classification *valoriste* was designated to codify this *métier* (trade) and provide occupational training in secondary educational institutions. This legitimation of work is key to the capacity of the social economy not only to name new occupations, trades and professions, but to demonstrate their value.

17. We have done numerous studies on solidarity finance and what we call development capital in Quebec to document the evolution of this innovative financial sector (Chantier de l'économie sociale, 2006). We have also begun to document these innovations in other countries to develop a better understanding of the new instruments that have emerged and their capacity to respond to the financial needs of social economy enterprises (Mendell and Nogales, 2008).

18. In 2004 the former Liberal government at the federal level launched a social economy initiative. It turned to the Chantier for advice on determining

206 The social economy

priorities. Capitalization of enterprises was top on the list, followed by funding for capacity-building and research. The federal government announced a commitment of $132 million towards this initiative, of which $100 million would be allocated to capitalization. Quebec was awarded $30 million for this purpose. When the government fell, the Conservative government withdrew these commitments. However, funds already allocated were left in place, though reduced. The initial $30 million was reduced to $22.8 million for Quebec.

19. This investment, in many sectors of activity, will leverage an additional $31.2 million, permitting the consolidation and creation of over 500 jobs.
20. The research alliance produced this information, which was provided by solidarity financial actors in Quebec. It was prepared for the Social Economy Summit in 2006 to celebrate the tenth anniversary of the 1996 summit that established the Chantier de l'économie sociale. For the numerous local development intermediaries (CLDs) that exist throughout the province and have financial investment tools for the social economy, the data came from the ministry, MDEIE (Quebec). For 2004–05, we consulted the annual reports of these CLDs.
21. There are over 500 social economy enterprises in the city of Montreal in numerous sectors of activity.
22. Partners: Association culturelle du Sud-Ouest (ACSO); six community economic development corporations (CDECs) across Montreal; and the Comité de l'économie sociale de l'Ile de Montréal (CESIM, a division of the provincial conference of elected representatives (CRE) in the regions (Montreal).

References

Amin, A., A. Cameron and R. Hudson (2002) *Placing the Social Economy*, Routledge, New York.
Bradford, N. (2005). 'Place-based public policy: Towards a new urban and community agenda', Canadian Policy Research Network, Ottawa.
Dalton, G. (1969) 'Theoretical issues in economic anthropology', *Current Anthropology* 10(1): 63–102.
Fung, A., and E.O. Wright (2003) *Deepening Democracy: Institutional Innovations in Empowered Deliberative Democracy*, Verso, London.
Giugni, M.G., D. McAdam and C. Tilly (1998) *From Contention to Democracy*, Rowman & Littlefield, Lanham MD.
Jackson, A., and S. Schetagne (2003) 'Solidarity forever? An analysis of changes in union density', Research Paper No. 25, Canadian Labour Congress, Ottawa, http://canadian-labour.ca/updir/solforeverEn.pdf.
Jetté, C., P. Leclerc and Y. Vaillancourt (2008) 'Social economy and home care services in Quebec: Towards new institutional arrangements', paper presented to the Association of Non-profit and Social Economy Research (ANSER), University of British Columbia, Vancouver, June.
Klein, J.-L., D.G. Tremblay and D.R. Bussières (2009) 'Social economy-based

local initiatives and social innovation: A Montreal case study', *International Journal of Technology Management*.

Laville, J.-L. (1996) 'Economie et solidarité: linéaments d'une problèmatique', in *Réconcilier l'économique et le social. L'économie plurielle*, OECD, Paris.

Lévesque, B. (2001) 'Système québécois d'innovation en économie sociale', *Rapport annuel de l'ARUC-ÉS*.

Leys, C., and M. Mendell (1992) 'Capitalism, socialism, culture and social movements', in M. Mendell and C. Leys, eds, *Culture and Social Change*, Black Rose Books, Montreal.

Mendell, M. (2002) 'The social economy in Quebec: Discourses and strategies', in A.B. Bakan and E. MacDonald, eds, *Critical Political Studies: Debates and Dialogues from the Left*, McGill-Queen's University Press, Montreal.

Mendell, M. (2003) 'Karl Polanyi (1886–1964)', in *Biographical Dictionary of Social and Cultural Anthropology*, ed. A. Vered, Routledge, New York.

Mendell, M. (2007) 'Karl Polanyi and instituted processes of economic democratization', in M. Harvey, R. Ramologan and S. Randles, eds, *Polanyian Perspectives on Embedded Economic Processes: Development and Transformation*, Manchester University Press, Manchester.

Mendell, M., and B. Lévesque (1999) 'L'économie social au Québec: éléments théoriques at empiriques pour le débat e la recherche', *Lien social et politiques* 41: 105–18.

Mendell, M., and R. Nogales (2008) 'Social enterprises in OECD Member Countries: What are the financial streams?', in *The New Frontiers of Social Enterprises*, OECD, Paris.

Mendell, M., J.-L. Laville and B. Lévesque (2007) 'The social economy: Diverse approaches and practices in Europe and Canada', in *The Social Economy: Building Inclusive Economies*, OECD, Paris.

Mendell, M., B. Lévesque and R. Rouzier (2003) 'New forms of financing social economy enterprises and organizations in Québec', in *The Non-Profit Sector in the 21st Century: A Stakeholder for Economy and Society*, OECD, Paris.

Polanyi, K. (1977) *The Livelihood of Man*, Academic Press, New York.

Polanyi, K., C.M. Arensberg and H.W. Pearson (eds) (1957) *Trade and Market in the Early Empires: Economies in History and Theory*, Free Press and Falcon Wing's Press, Glencoe IL.

Sirianni, C., and L. Friedland (2001) *Civic Innovation in America: Community Empowerment, Public Policy and the Movement for Civic Renewal*, University of California Press, Berkeley.

10

Social economy and development
in Poland

Jerzy Hausner

The social economy[1] can be seen as that sector of the economy which helps to streamline the state and market. Even if we were sceptically to judge the market and state, by their very nature, as inefficient and unreliable, it would still be possible to argue that they could be made less inefficient and less unreliable, with the social economy and social entrepreneurship assisting in this process. Social entrepreneurship could be seen to create additional development space, if filled by well-prepared and competent actors. In recognizing such actors, wise public authorities would not want to subordinate them, or indeed even to use them to crowd out the private sector. Wise public authorities would not want to behave in a doctrinaire or utopian fashion, fearing the market and then creating something top-down and calling it social entrepreneurship.

Even if this seems a logical assumption, the question remains how to apply it in particular local contexts, especially in the post-communist countries, more precisely in a country such as Poland, where, on the one hand, the Communist period interrupted the natural development of social economy and, on the other, the conditions for the development of social economy do not exist to a sufficient degree if at all. This chapter examines the cultural and institutional legacies affecting the potential of the social economy in Poland, and goes on, in the second half, to outline a comprehensive set of policy interventions that would strengthen the Polish social economy and its contribution to economy and society.

General and historical background

In Poland there exists a long and successful tradition of social economy, linked in particular to the development of mutual societies in the nineteenth century and various types of co-operative in the twentieth century. As Frączak (2006) notes, in 1914 in the Polish lands there were 3,745 co-operatives with 1,458,562 members, whose total shares were valued at 162.7 million gold francs and whose savings deposits were worth almost a billion gold francs.

This tradition was radically interrupted by the Communist period. But today it is not possible simply to reactivate the legacy of the social economy. The organizations that survived have a completely different organizational culture now and a modified 'genetic' code.

According to Leś and Jeliazkova (2007: 192), the negative impact of the Communist period on social economy institutions can be traced to three forces. The first is a distortion of the notions of philanthropy, charity, pluralism, mutuality, self-help and voluntary work, which acquired a pejorative meaning. The second is a dramatic reduction in the type and size of social economy organizations: in most regions, they were limited to only one allowable type of association and quasi-cooperative sector. The third aspect is the nationalization and incorporation of some civil society organizations into the state infrastructure.

Forced co-operatives and participation resulted in a proliferation of quasi-social economy organizations that were effectively tools of the state and were utilized and manipulated accordingly, thereby impacting negatively upon social capital. On the other hand, it is also the case that powerful cultural and historical factors impact upon civic involvement today. This is shown by Herbst's (2006) research on the geography of the social economy in Poland.[2] Data at the level of municipalities reveal a much higher degree of civic involvement in associations and commercial activity in the west of Poland compared

FIGURE 10.1 Number of associations and foundations per capita in Polish regions (not including cities)

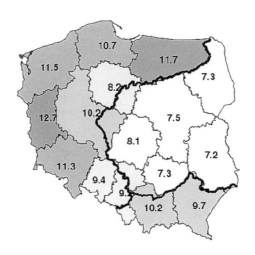

Source: Herbst, 2006.

to the east, demarcated by a sharp line that runs along the borders of the former Prussian, Austrian and Russian partitions of Poland in the eighteenth century (see Figure 10.1).

Herbst emphasizes, however, that this picture of civic involvement in associations is also influenced by 'harder' differences than culture, such as differences in the settlement density of municipalities located in the former Prussian, Austrian and Russian partitions, as well as differences in the size of those municipalities and their populations. The varying intensity of economic activity and civic involvement in associations is influenced by both 'culture' and 'structure' – in other words, by the environment in which that activity takes place. Therefore, in order to explain current differences, we need to look at the factors that have determined the development of the Polish lands since the Middle Ages.

In his excellent commentary on the historical background to Poland's division into two distinct geographical areas (West/East), Gorzelak (2002) notes the impact of processes of 'long duration'. From the Middle Ages the western part of today's Poland was more

FIGURE 10.2   Organizations performing business activity per capita in Polish regions (mean scores for local communities, estimated on the basis of REGON business register analysis)

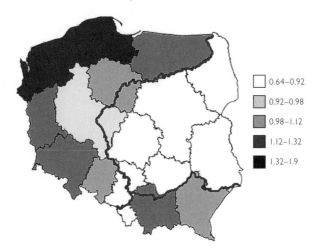

☐	0.64–0.92
☐	0.92–0.98
☐	0.98–1.12
☐	1.12–1.32
■	1.32–1.9

Source: Herbst, 2006.

developed than the eastern part (for instance, the Romanesque style in architecture was not to be found east of the Vistula river). This division was deepened by the Partitions, whose borders are visible, socially and economically, to this day. After 1990, eastern Poland, whose potential remains largely pre-industrial, paid a lower price for the structural changes that took place during the 1990–92 period, but equally, after 1992, it proved to be much less capable of meeting the challenges of an open, competitive, knowledge-based economy. The current regression of some regions in eastern Poland is to a large extent the result of this structural underdevelopment and the inability of regions in eastern Poland, as well as rural regions of central Poland, to meet the challenges of a modern open economy.

Various types of capital are needed to trigger development at the regional level – financial, ecological, human and social. And, when available, local development seems strongly dependent on regional social ties and governance networks, marked by reciprocity, mutual dependence, joint activity and local government. The basis of effective regional coordination networks seems, above all, trust and openness to partnership. The importance of these factors in the Polish context is best seen in areas that were formerly home to state collective farms. Here we can see the importance of social ties and the impact that social capital has on the quality of the labour market and entrepreneurship. Most problematic are towns and regions that suffered forced industrialization (classic industrial complexes from the Communist period) before the Second World War during a period of authoritarian rule in the 1930s. In all places where industry was forcibly developed by state imposition there is social atomization and a lack of social capital, with communities far less able to cope with current problems, including unemployment. It is no accident that in south-eastern Poland local government is more efficient at the commune level. If we compare the two agricultural regions of Warmia-Mazury and Podkarpacie we clearly see that local government and local administration function much better in Podkarpacie (Swianiewicz et al., 2000).

In this context, Frączak (2006) makes the insightful observation that Polish experiences during the period of Partitions reveal the insignificance of the legal form of a given activity. It wasn't law that determined the different ways in which people acted, but the social conditions of the day. For exactly this reason, in Poland today the social economy encounters the most difficult conditions in precisely the places where it is most needed – in eastern Poland. The vast majority of areas with accumulated barriers to development are found in eastern and central parts of Poland: the eastern border regions, the former Central Industrial Region, and areas on the periphery of large towns in regions of eastern Poland (Wilkin, 2005).

Placing the social economy

How should we define the social economy in terms of its usefulness or function? The danger is to be too minimalist or too maximalist. For example, Sałustowicz's (2006: 23–41) widely discussed proposal seems to me to be too wide, too maximalist for an economy such as the Polish one. Sałustowicz identifies five functions for the social economy:

1. From the perspective of employment policy and the labour market, the social economy is expected to deliver new jobs, particularly for marginalized people or those threatened with marginalization. It is also expected to deliver services in the area of professional training and to facilitate transfer into the so-called first labour market.
2. From the perspective of social policy, the social economy is expected to deliver social services for individuals or communities, especially in areas where neither the private nor the public sector is able to satisfy growing social needs.
3. From the perspective of social integration, the task set for the social economy is to increase social capital.
4. From the perspective of democratization, the social economy is expected to bring individuals and social groups into the political decision-making process.
5. From the perspective of social change, the social economy is meant to be the place where an alternative social and economic system is created.

I have my doubts about the fourth and, particularly, the fifth functions. But perhaps it is enough to agree the first three, which define how and where social economy organizations operate, so that policy support can be delivered. This would create space for open discussion on the political and alternative economic credentials of the social economy – an issue of conflicting opinion – without hampering policy action.

The social economy develops in a space delineated by, among other factors, the market economy (the private sector) and the state (the public sector). However, this space is formed not independently but as a consequence of the relations between the two sectors. The relations between social economy and the private sector, for example, can develop according to one of three rules: competition, coexistence or complementarity. I believe that the best conditions for the development of the social economy are provided by complementarity, which opens the way for exchange and co-operation. As regards relations between the social economy and the public sector, the possibilities range from hostility and indifference, to clientelism and partnership.

It seems clear to me that only partnership creates good conditions for social economy organizations to develop. Clientelism means, on the one hand, that these organizations are treated instrumentally, and, on the other, that they become dependent on state authorities. Consequently, though they may have access to material resources, they will not be able to fulfil their mission creatively. Social economy organizations should co-operate with state institutions and take advantage of public support, but it is important that such co-operation does not deprive them of autonomy or of the possibility to manage their own resources and be innovative.

In order to define the place of the social economy, it is also important to define the relations between the social economy and the NGO sector. The two are not synonymous. Not all NGOs conduct commercial activity and not all social economy institutions are NGOs. The matter becomes even more complicated if we consider the notion of 'social enterprise' or 'social entrepreneurship'. Social enterprises can be formed only within the space of the social economy, while the latter cannot exist without the activities of the NGO sector. Of course, the NGO sector could be called the 'third' sector, and the social economy sector the 'fourth' sector, but this would hide the symbiotic relationship needed if they are to function at all. This becomes all the more important if, as Izdebski (2007) stresses, NGOs are prevented by legislation from undertaking independent commercial activity. The distinction, therefore, should not imply separation but interdependence: one that combines the social mission of NGOs with the commercial activity of social enterprises.

The general relations between the three sectors (institutional systems) of modern societies are complicated, dynamic and uneven. The weakest element is without doubt the third sector, which, in particular, must be careful not to become dominated by, or subordinated to, the public or private sectors. NGOs, in supporting the social economy, could redress this imbalance. NGOs and the social economy need each other: the social economy allows civic organizations to remain free of the state and its pathologies, while civic organizations enable social enterprises to remain free of the market and its pathologies. In turn, NGOs, in order to fulfil their statutory aims, especially the provision of social services, must co-operate with the public administration. They need this co-operation also to secure public funds to finance their activities. Equally, if they only perform tasks commissioned from them by the public administration, they lose their independence and become the assistant – not to say the instrument – of the state in the conduct of its public policy.

With these differences and overlaps in mind, how might the social economy flourish as an independent but collaborative partner in the modern economy? I would list the following 'macro-systemic' conditions as central:

- the presence of a significant degree of social capital, including trust and reciprocity;
- development of an organizational culture among stakeholders;
- diverse forms of institutionalized partnership;
- the accessibility of social audit instruments and experience in applying such audits;
- observance of the rule of subsidiarity and its practical, operational implementation;
- the development of varied forms of governance, including multi-level governance.

These conditions create space for the development of the social economy, including social entrepreneurship. Does this mean that, in their absence, the social economy cannot develop? I do not believe so. On the contrary, the social economy will develop in every social space. One would have to abolish society, reciprocity and solidarity for the social economy not to develop at all. However, the nature of this social space will strongly determine how the sector is organized and how it operates. The scale of the social economy and its organizational forms are strongly dependent upon the social space in which they develop. Under favourable conditions, the social economy develops innovatively and naturally; if such conditions are absent, the development will be limited in scale, or it will degenerate, losing autonomy and dynamism. And this is the fundamental problem facing the social economy in Poland and in other post-Communist countries. The above macro-social conditions exist only to a limited degree.

The social economy in Poland

Two indicators of the weak contextual conditions for the social economy in Poland are low levels of generated trust (Figure 10.3) and low NGO membership (Figure 10.4).

Generally, the level of social capital in Poland is very low, as is the level of civic participation and involvement. The structures of state and society are built on hierarchical principles, threatening a systematic return to centralist tendencies. Vast numbers of people are dependent on the state and expect the state to intervene directly in their lives. At the same time, they do not trust the state, just as

FIGURE 10.3   Percentage of individuals (aged 18+) who trust other people

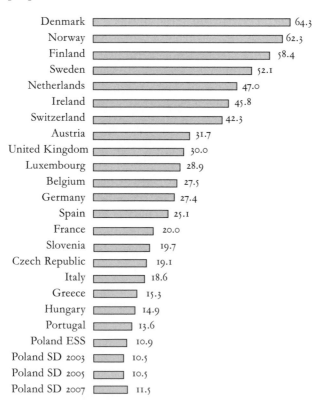

Source: For all countries, including Poland, European Social Survey (ESS, 2002); for Poland, Polish Social Survey (PSS) 'Social Diagnosis' 2003–07.

they do not trust each other. The state acknowledges NGOs but treats them instrumentally and politicizes them. Subsidiarity remains nipped in the bud.

Despite this, social economy organizations are taking first steps to conduct economic activity in the new Poland. Rymsza (2006: 9) notes, however, that such organizations do not like taking risks, as demonstrated by their conservative attitude to investing their money. In 2003, only 3.5 per cent of organizations invested resources in economic activity, and a minuscule proportion – only 0.8 per cent – attempted to increase their capital by purchasing shares, bonds or

FIGURE 10.4 Average number of organizations to which respondents (aged 18+) belong

Sweden	2.6
Denmark	2.5
Norway	2.4
Netherlands	2.3
Austria	2.1
Luxembourg	2.0
Belgium	1.6
Ireland	1.6
Finland	1.6
United Kingdom	1.6
Germany	1.6
Israel	1.3
France	1.0
Slovenia	0.9
Spain	0.7
Italy	0.6
Portugal	0.5
Greece	0.4
Hungary	0.4
Poland ESS	0.3
Poland SD 2003	0.14
Poland SD 2005	0.15
Poland SD 2007	0.2

Source: For all countries, including Poland, European Social Survey (ESS, 2002); for Poland, Polish Social Survey (PSS) 'Social Diagnosis' 2003–07.

other securities. According to Zagrodzka (2006: 7), in 2004, 16 per cent of NGOs conducted economic activity; in 2006 the figure had fallen to only 8 per cent.

Many social economy organizations focus on the problems of social exclusion and unemployment. This is understandable given that they are among the most pressing social issues in Poland today. However, as Gosk (2006) notes, in Poland around 30,000 people leave prison each year, only 10 per cent of people with mental health problems receive some sort of social care or occupational therapy, while 400,000 people suffering from schizophrenia or other mental disorders receive no help at all; and the number of homeless people is estimated at 30,000 to 80,000. Yet 77 per cent of NGOs specializing in employment issues focus on training for the unemployed. This trend is also noted by Herbst (2006: 25), who states that the majority of organizations resembling social enterprises are concerned with providing education and training. In 2004, only 2.2 per cent of NGOs hired unemployed people under public works projects, while 1.6 per cent hired disabled people within the framework of so-called assisted employment. Generally, the proportion of disabled people employed by the NGO sector in Poland is almost half that in the public or private sector.

Data on the various forms of social economy organizations registered in Poland are presented in Table 10.1. Social economy organizations in Poland are only now beginning to conduct commercial activity. Not all of the organizations included in Table 10.1 conduct commercial activity, and still fewer conduct such activity continuously. It is estimated that 40 per cent of professional and economic organizations are involved in commercial and paid activity – approximately 1,500–2,000 organizations; in the case of NGOs, this figure is almost 20 per cent, or 8–9,000 organizations (Wygnański, 2008). However, if we adopt stricter criteria of independent entrepreneurship and apply them consistently, it turns out that barely 5 per cent of all organizations meet the criteria to be considered social enterprises, which means that the estimated number of such organizations in Poland is approximately 2,000. In addition, applying a measure of independent welfare activity, the number of social enterprises fulfilling their social function is, at most, likely to be 1,500.

TABLE 10.1   Basic data on social economy organizations in Poland

Type of organization	No. of organizations registered	No. of employees	No. of members
'Traditional' social economy			
Associations and foundations	63,000	120,000	9–10,000,000
Self-governing economic organizations	5,500	33,000	1,100,000
Co-operatives	12,800	440,000	6,000,000
of which disabled persons' co-operatives	350	55,000	30,000
Mutual insurance societies	9	500	–
Other mutual organizations	880	–	–
'New' social economy			
Social co-operatives	60	400	500
Vocational training centres	35	1,700	–
Social integration centres and clubs	35	500	–
Total	*c.* 83,000	*c.* 600,000	*c.* 17,000,000

Source: Wygnański, 2008: 23.

More generally, co-operation between the NGO sector and local government is not high. Local authorities treat NGOs more as petitioners than as partners. According to Jachimowicz (2006: 17–18), this is due to:

- The huge disproportion in resources between local authorities and NGOs: NGOs are constantly trying to make ends meet; they don't have financial, material or human resources, and are unable to take advantage of their trump cards, namely the activism of their leaders, the work of their voluntary staff, their direct contact with people in need, their knowledge of social problems.
- The inability of NGOs to obtain funds other than from local authorities, which means that they are dependent on a single source

of financing and liable to become subordinated to public authorities, whilst being perceived by these authorities as petitioners for money.

- The fact that NGOs do not co-operate with one another and do not create their own representative bodies that could promote their interests.
- The creation of co-operation programmes without the participation of NGOs, due to their weak bargaining power.

Frączak (2006: 11) summarizes the most important problems facing the social economy in Poland today:

> attempts to base the activities of NGOs on their members (voluntary work, subscriptions) have not been successful. This is due to the gradual decline in civic involvement and the huge supply of various types of public resources, which, although they often involve complicated procedures and modification of mission statements, are basically a much surer and potentially more rewarding method of securing funds than methods based on public trust and civic involvement. Therefore, to some degree the sector has become more 'etatist'; in other words, it has become increasingly similar, also in institutional terms, to the public administration. Presently, various attempts are being made to 'commercialize' the sector; in other words, to search for an economic dimension to civic activities. However, there remains little chance that NGOs will forgo the relatively stable – albeit tedious – procedures for obtaining EU funds in favour of risky activities on the open market.

My own research confirms the above, based on a series of studies.[3] This research has led me to conclude that the social economy can be characterized in the following way:

1. Organizations that can be considered social enterprises are basically emanations of NGOs. In most cases, without NGOs they would not have been established in the first place and would not be able to operate.
2. The main objective of the enterprises is to combat social exclusion and reintegrate excluded people.
3. The enterprises are only partially oriented towards providing public (and social) services. This mainly stems from the fact that, although local authorities help them and often provide them with

sufficient resources, they do not consider them as alternative providers of services.

4. Social enterprises obtain the majority of their funds from the public sector. So far they have tended to avoid taking risks and being verified by the market.

5. Activities are only loosely market-based. In most cases, the private sector is involved as a sponsor, not business partner.

6. The main barriers to the development of social enterprises are: the accumulation of negative social and economic factors in rural and weakly urbanized areas; the lack of public trust towards initiatives undertaken by social enterprises; the inertia of local communities; the perception that social enterprises are organizations operating in areas of social exclusion and thus offer low-quality goods and services; the lack of public trust towards creating local partnerships and an unwillingness to co-operate in order to achieve common goals; the lack of co-operation between social enterprises.

7. Another factor hampering the development of social enterprises is inadequate legal regulation.

Supporting the social economy

So, in this situation, what can be done to support the development of the social economy? There is no easy answer to this question, but in general terms it would be necessary to set in motion a whole range of measures, whose purpose would be to involve various organizations (local government, regional and local associations, the civil service, NGOs, universities, think-tanks, private companies, business associations, the media) in specific social economy-oriented undertakings, and consequently to create a social movement around the social economy facing upwards, towards central state structures, and downwards, towards local communities. Ultimately, the goal would be to stimulate measures, both from the top and from the bottom, that could help forge social ties and a culture of reciprocity and subsidiarity.

The binding force of such a movement would have to be an institutionalized partnership involving diverse actors and taking place at various territorial levels of the state. Such partnership implies joint influence whilst maintaining a careful balance between co-operation and autonomy; it implies mutual respect, equal participation in the decision-making process, joint responsibility and transparency (Brinkerhoff, 2006). Malena (1995) identifies partnership as: common goals and values; mutual trust, respect and equality; joint responsibility; transparency; mutual understanding of the political, economic and cultural context and of institutional constraints; and long-term involvement in joint work.

Guided by such conviction, in 2007 I publicly proposed a scheme to treat the social economy as a 'development category',[4] so that systematic effort could be put into elaborating the concept as:

- an analytical category – allowing the situation to be defined;
- a strategic thinking category – triggering the imagination and allowing a vision of development to be formulated;
- a planning category – allowing the action plan to be prepared;
- a management category – allowing formal, legal and organizational conditions to be created to enable the planned measures to be undertaken and institutionalized.

If properly elaborated the development category can create a readiness and capacity for action. Linking the above categories within an axiomatic and practical framework can allow both a programme and its actors to emerge. A comprehensive and multi-pronged approach is needed to sustain a viable and independent social economy in Poland.

To develop the social economy as an analytical category, it is important to:

- develop and adopt, for the purpose of public statistics, an operating definition of the social economy;
- define the dimensions of the social economy, its potential, and its role in solving key social problems;
- maintain a record of social economy organizations;
- launch research projects and create centres for social economy research;
- develop criteria and indicators for assessing the effectiveness and performance of social economy organizations.

To develop the social economy as a strategic category, attention should focus on:

- disseminating knowledge on the subject of the social economy;
- including the social economy in university curricula;
- developing postgraduate studies on the social economy;
- organizing a national debate on the problems of the social economy;
- identifying the development functions of the social economy;
- formulating national and regional strategies for promoting and developing the social economy.

In order to develop the social economy as a planning category, policies should seek to:

- determine the instruments for promoting and developing the social economy;
- develop and launch operational support programmes;
- create a system for monitoring the state of the sector and evaluating practice in accordance with the principles of evidence-based policy;
- establish a National Social Economy Observatory.

Finally, to develop the social economy as a governance category, a priority should be to:

- establish an optimum legal environment;
- create a financial infrastructure and set of financial instruments;
- implement a mechanism of targeted public procurement;
- establish a social economy web portal, and develop mechanisms and instruments for using the Internet to market and contract the services of social economy organizations;
- develop professional consultancy services for social economy organizations;
- train a professional body of public organizers, entrepreneurs and managers;
- develop an organizational culture, create a list of best practices, and disseminate action blueprints;
- create an accreditation and auditing system for social economy organizations;

- create regional social economy agreements operating on the basis of public–social–private partnerships.

The issue of financing social economy organizations requires more delicacy. The observations made earlier show that public resources can lead to negative consequences for social entrepreneurship, such as clientelism, reliance on public financing, loss of initiative, risk avoidance, evasion of responsibility, corrupt practices and unfair competition. We frequently witness in Poland situations in which public resources are in reality used to prop up organizations rather than to achieve social goals.

These observations force two considerations: first, what should be the rules for financing the social economy from public funds; second, how should they be implemented in practice? So far as rules are concerned, a general principle should be that public finances must not be the sole source of funding. Regarding implementation, what is important is not only how much money is given and to whom, but how it is given. Six possible courses of action for public authorities who want to finance social enterprises might be suggested:

1. The establishment of regulations to enable private companies to finance social entrepreneurship and to encourage them to do so. Private companies could allocate 1 per cent of their corporate income tax to a social enterprise in the same way that private individuals can allocate 1 per cent of their personal tax to a public benefit organization. There is no reason why parliament could not legislate for private companies to allocate 1 per cent of their tax to some form of social entrepreneurship.

2. Public financing of social entrepreneurship within a system of public–private–social partnership. It is important in this instance that the state establishes the appropriate regulations and provides resources as capital for guarantee and loan funds. At the same time, the public authorities should not directly control the funds. If they are to be effective, the funds must be professionally managed – in the same way that private financial instruments are managed. Their purpose is to loan, not to distribute, money.

3. Indirect support for social entrepreneurship and innovation. As in the case of market-based entrepreneurship, founding capital is

essential for social entrepreneurship; perhaps even more so, since it is harder to launch a social enterprise even though the capital requirements are lower. In this instance, a safe instrument – one that also gives public control – could be that of global grants. Of assistance in establishing global grants could be a Civic Initiatives Fund, whose purpose is to reward public innovation, new initiatives and new solutions, by providing money and checking through public control whether the desired effects are being achieved.

4. Specific fiscal privileges. These privileges must not eliminate risk, but should compensate social enterprises for undertaking tasks which the market is unwilling to perform because they are not sufficiently profitable and which the state is unable to perform effectively. Social enterprises undertake tasks that reintegrate excluded people, and this should attract compensation for any reduced efficiency and because such reintegration reduces the claim on direct public financing. The stream of existing social transfers should be channelled towards social enterprises that reintegrate excluded people.

5. Direct and conditional financing of projects that must take into account such aspects as: the relevance of the project, whether the social enterprise is being established on the basis of local partnership, as well as co-financing and sustainability. When providing this type of financing, it is important to ensure that well-intended plans do not merely culminate in a one-off measure but actually have development potential.

6. Competitive contracting of specific services, following proper understanding and application of the constitutional principle of subsidiarity.

These six methods are not mutually exclusive. However, they must be regulated in such a way that anyone who decides to launch a social enterprise will know that in order to obtain public funds certain requirements will need to be fulfilled. The six methods also have something else in common: financing is provided not because an organization exists, but in order to help it earn money. The public financing of any social economy project, for example a social enterprise, must establish whether it will in time generate revenue and become self-financing. In accordance with this principle, direct public financing should only be made available for a limited period of time. One option is for financing to reduce gradually, such that the enterprise is encouraged and mobilized to become independent.

While social enterprises should be allowed to access public funds, this should not spawn dependency. The state should regulate social entrepreneurship in such a way that the avoidance of direct public financing is possible and even likely. This will only occur when public authorities perceive social entrepreneurship as an important and essential partner and actor of socio-economic development. In Poland, at present, public resources tend to hinder, rather than to help, social entrepreneurship.

Social economy institutions may prove especially useful in developing services – whose success depends on changing the attitudes and behaviours of small communities where local ties and identification are strong. One important field is environmental services, including waste collection and management. In this instance, overcoming long-held habits is of fundamental importance, and cannot easily be achieved through persuasion or sanctions. The list of environmental services that could be offered by social economy organizations might include, for instance, the creation and protection of green space or the use of local renewable energy sources.

This focus may prove to be promising in the rural areas, which cover a vast part of Poland. In Europe, rural development is becoming increasingly distanced from commercial agricultural activity, moving in the direction of 'multifunctional development'. As Wilkin (2005) points out, this involves, in particular, the non-market function of agriculture connected with preserving the natural environment, protecting the cultural landscape of the countryside, and recognizing the importance of agriculture for rural communities. This development philosophy is favoured by the European Union, which lends its support through major structural resources.

The deliberate orientation of the social economy towards the creation of local systems of social services is much needed in Poland at the present time. It would accelerate the development of the social economy, including in parts of the country where it is currently absent. If oriented in this way, social economy organizations and institutions will be able to maintain their social character, bolstered by their local roots and links to local communities. It would avoid the growing danger of NGOs becoming more commercial and oligarchic, acting in the interests of their employees and transforming the third sector into a corporatist lobbying structure.

In the legislative sphere, the most pressing issue is to design and pass an act on social enterprises. Current regulations do not provide the appropriate conditions and incentives for such organizations. Analysis of the various legal forms of social economy in Poland (Hausner et al., 2007) shows that the status of social enterprises is poorly regulated in Polish legislation. It is possible but difficult to set up and run such enterprises. The reason is that although parliament has allowed social organizations and local governments to pursue commercial activity, it has consistently sought to limit this activity so that it doesn't take on the characteristics of a regular business. Legislators seem to have adhered to the motto 'Social economy, yes; social enterprises, no.' In this way, legislators have in practice made it impossible for the social economy to achieve its fundamental goal, namely to tackle social exclusion by helping people get training and jobs. A good example of this thinking is the absence in Poland of regulations on the activities of non-profit or not-for-profit organizations (Izdebski and Małek, 2005), which means, in practice, that socially beneficial activity cannot be conducted in the form of an enterprise. Instead, it has to be squeezed into the activity of associations or foundations, or possibly carried out by public institutions in the form of social integration and vocational development centres, or in the form of a municipal enterprise, which is of little use in achieving social goals.

The issue of separating statutory activities – social mission and commercial activity – is one of the most important and most difficult problems associated with introducing regulations on social entrepreneurship. The legislation is complicated as it relates to various branches of law: labour law, welfare, the activities of NGOs, commercial activity, public finances, taxation, and so on. What would aid the development of social entrepreneurship is if all 'local partnerships' were accorded some form of common legal status connected with the projects they undertake.

The implementation of the action plan outlined above will not only help social economy organizations but will also strengthen the macro-conditions for activities to take place. It will, in time, facilitate the growth of social capital, the creation of horizontal partnerships for the benefit of the social economy (with participation from both public and private civic organizations), and the creation of new governance networks and institutionally complex delivery systems.

However, there is also a serious danger that in Poland the development of the social economy will be imposed from above by the government in its quest to find solutions to help absorb huge EU funds. Instead of being a bottom-up response to pressing social problems, the social economy could become an opportunist venture that will probably waste resources or fail to contribute to authentic forms of social economy. The fundamental barrier to the development of the social economy in Poland is cultural, not economic, in nature. There is a syndrome of studied hopelessness, which took shape during the Communist period and which is now being prolonged by an embedded welfare expectation. Its main features are the expectation that the state should provide every-thing, accompanied by a lack of belief in oneself, an unwillingness to undergo training and raise qualifications, passivity and social isolation. For people and groups with this kind of mentality, social development is seen to be unprofitable and risky.

Conclusion

In Poland and in post-Communist countries generally, of key impor-tance is the establishment of a social movement that can act as an engine of the social economy. I am opposed to treating the social economy as a systemic alternative to the market economy or the democratic state. The purpose of stimulating the social economy should be to test innovative economic or remedial solutions on a 'safe' scale – particularly on a local scale – to solve social problems more effectively and indirectly contribute to a more efficient state and economy. As Anheier (2002) notes in reference to the third sector, the social economy broadens the potential means of solving the problems of modern societies.

The particular systemic advantage of the social economy may be that its solutions can lead to complex goods delivery systems whose logic goes beyond the framework of classical public goods theory. It is precisely the creation of such complex systems that will determine the development trajectory and future of the social economy. Such systems enable the production–consumption dichotomy to be overcome and enable social economy organizations to avoid becoming subordinated to public administration. And, as Borzaga and Santuari (2003) emphasize, this means that social economy organizations can offer new services or new means of providing traditional services. The creation of multisectoral and multilevel systems of goods delivery will affect how the market economy, state, civil society and households function. One effect might be to render the social economy a practical means of tackling many social problems at a local level, thereby disturbing legacies of hierarchical governance.

Notes

1. I assume that the social economy is a sector of the economy in which organizations are oriented towards public benefit, and that the profits they make serve a public purpose. Their mission is a consequence of autonomous management, democratic decision-making and local ties – and is protected by those arrangements.

2. The article is part of the EQUAL project's report *In Search of the Polish Model of Social Economy*, which provided a point of reference for a three-year research project aimed at determining the conditionings for developing the social economy in Poland. It is based on secondary data, mainly from the Polish Business Register (REGON) and the Database of the Non-Profit Organizations run by the Klon/Jawor Association. The basic aim of the analysis was to depict the spatial distribution of different types of institutions which at that time were recognized as prospective fields of social entrepreneurship development in Poland: associations and foundations (approx. 65,000 entities), with particular focus on those engaging in serious business activity (approx. 9,000), different types of co-operatives (approx. 12,000), business and vocational organizations (approx. 5,500) and much less numerous institutions of the 'new social economy', established as a response to the popularity of the social economy concept (e.g. social co-operatives). The maps and findings presented in the article ought to be treated as representations of the 'geography of births' of the analysed institutions, rather than representations of their actual spatial spread.

3. The research, conducted in 2006, covered fifty social enterprises in the Małopolska region. Using a questionnaire and interviews, the research looked at three aspects of how enterprises operate: axiology, praxiology

and public consent. In the axiological dimension, the research concerned the area of operation of social enterprises, the goals of their activities, and the social added value they created; in the praxiological dimension, the research concerned financial aspects of the activities of social enterprises, their human resources and the management of those resources; and in the dimension of public consent, the research concerned public participation in the activities of social enterprises, the forms and trajectories of co-operation between social enterprises and other institutions, and the relations of social enterprises with the social environment. In a subsequent stage of the research, following a multilevel analysis, key factors governing the development of social enterprises were identified (see Hausner et al., 2007).

4. I put forward this proposal a year after leaving the Cabinet. It took the form of an expert study carried out within the framework of a major project entitled 'In Search of a Polish Model of Social Economy', financed by the EQUAL programme.

References

Anheier, H.K. (2002) 'The Third Sector in Europe: Five theses', London School of Economics Working Papers, Department of Economics.

Anheier, H.K., and S. Martens (2003) 'International and European perspectives on the non profit sector: Data, theory, statistics', in *The Non-profit Sector in a Changing Economy*, OECD, Paris.

Borzaga, C., and A. Santuari (2003) 'New trends in the non-profit sector in Europe: The emergence of social entrepreneurship', in *The Non-profit Sector in a Changing Economy*, OECD, Paris.

Brinkerhoff, J.M. (2006) 'Defining partnership between the government sector and non-profit organizations', in *The Third Sector for Advanced Students. Modern Theories of the Third Sector – A Collection of Essays* (in Polish), Stowarzyszenie Klon/Jawor, Warsaw.

Frączak, P. (2006) 'An outline of the history of Polish social economy' (in Polish), Annex to *In Search of a Polish Model of Social Economy*, report, FISE, Warsaw.

Gorzelak, G. (2002) 'The chances of Polish regions in an integrated Europe' (in Polish), *Studia Regionalne i Lokalne* 2–3: 55–73.

Gosk, I. (2006) 'Social economy as a labour market actor' (in Polish). Annex to *In Search of a Polish Model of Social Economy*, report, FISE, Warsaw.

Hausner, J., N. Laurisz and S. Mazur (2007) 'The concept of social enterprises' (in Polish), in Jerzy Hausner, ed., *Managing Social Economy Institutions, Course Book*, Małopolska School of Public Administration, Krakow University of Economics, Krakow.

Herbst, J. (2006) 'The geography of Polish social economy' (in Polish), Annex to *In Search of a Polish Model of Social Economy*, report, FISE, Warsaw.

Izdebski, H. (2007) 'Social cooperatives and non-governmental organizations – expected consequences of the law on social cooperatives' (in Polish), *Trzeci Sektor* 7: 7–13.

Izdebski, H., and M. Małek (2005) 'Legal forms of undertaking and conducting activities for the purpose of achieving socially beneficial goals outside the public finance sector' (in Polish), study commissioned by the Academy for the Development of Philanthropy in Poland, Warsaw.

Jachimowicz, A. (2006) 'Local government and non-governmental organizations – partners in the development of social economy?' (in Polish), Annex to *In Search of a Polish Model of Social Economy*, report, FISE, Warsaw.

Leś, E., and M. Jeliazkova (2007) 'The social economy in central, east and southeast Europe', in A. Noya and E. Clarence, eds, *The Social Economy: Building Inclusive Economies*, OECD, Paris.

Malena, C. (1995) 'Relations between Northern and Southern non-governmental development organizations', *Canadian Journal of Development Studies* 16(9): 7–29.

Rymsza, A. (2006) 'Barriers to the development of social entrepreneurship in Poland in light of the organizational culture of the third sector' (in Polish), Annex to *In Search of a Polish Model of Social Economy*, report, FISE, Warsaw.

Sałustowicz, P. (2006) 'The notion and functions of social economy', in P. Sałustowicz and H. Guzowska, eds, *Social Economy and Social Hopelessness – Prospects and Barriers* (in Polish), Office of the Polish Ombudsman, Warsaw.

Swianiewicz P., W. Dziemianowicz and M. Mackiewicz (2000) *The Institutional Effectiveness of the Local Government Administration in Poland* (in Polish), Institute for Market Economy Research, Warsaw–Gdansk.

Wilkin, J. (2005) 'Occupational, social and ownership transformations in rural areas' (in Polish), expert study for the Government Centre for Strategic Studies, mimeo.

Wygnański, J.J. (2008) *The Commercialization of Non-governmental Organizations: Possibility or Necessity?* (in Polish), Stowarzyszenie Klon/Jawor, Warsaw.

Zagrodzka, T. (2006) 'Managing finances in non-governmental organizations – new challenges' (in Polish), Annex to *In Search of a Polish Model of Social Economy*, report, FISE, Warsaw.

II

Supporting the social and solidarity economy in the European Union

Jean-Louis Laville

Personal services are one field in which demand is growing quickly in response to major social and demographic developments, chief among these being higher rates of female employment, changes in family structures and population ageing. The proportion of single-person households in Europe, similarly, is on the increase. This trend goes hand in hand with a growth in single-parent families. These are the underlying trends which are generating a growing need for personal services for the elderly and disabled, and for childcare services. For instance, the Childcare Network has estimated that providing services for an additional 10 per cent of young children could generate some 415,000 new jobs (or 625,000 if the knock-on effect on other sectors is included). Other major changes, such as growing urbanization in Europe, the reduction in working time, higher levels of education and increased concern for the environment, are creating a demand for urban, cultural, leisure and environmental services, and all of these could be the source of new jobs. The White Paper that sets out the European Community's thinking for the twenty-first century (European Commission, 1993) puts the stress on dealing with new needs and tapping new sources of employment: 'Many needs are still waiting to be satisfied. They correspond to changes in lifestyles, the

BOX 11.1   The European Commission's new services typology

- *Everyday services*
  domestic services
  childcare
  new information and communication technologies
  help for young people in difficulty, and integration
- *Quality of life services*
  housing security
  local public transport
  rehabilitation of urban public areas
  local shops
  energy
- *Cultural and leisure services*
  tourism
  audiovisual
  cultural heritage
  local cultural development
  sport
- *Environmental services*
  waste management
  water management
  protection and maintenance of natural areas
  regulation and control of pollution, and associated
  installations

Source: European Commission, 1995.

transformation of family structures, the increase in the number of working women, and the new aspirations of the elderly and of very old people. They also stem from the need to repair damage to the environment and to renovate the most disadvantaged urban areas.' It affirms that 'some three million new jobs could be created in the Community, covering local services, improvements in the quality of life and environmental protection' (European Commission, 1993: 20).

To take a more detailed look at this question, the European Commission conducted a survey which led, eventually, in 1995, to a Commission working document entitled *Local Development and*

Employment Initiatives. This document confirmed the importance of these new activities and the originality of successful approaches. The result was a typology of nineteen types of service in four main sectors of activity covering the new needs. This chapter, based on research in four countries (Germany, France, Italy, the United Kingdom) on about two dozen successful social enterprises which have been running for at least three years and meet important local needs in novel ways, seeks to go in more detail into how such initiatives arise and how they can be consolidated. These case studies cover a wide range of service areas.

New services, new needs, new modes

The new services are not only a reflection of the growing importance of services in a tertiary economy. There is general agreement that the new jobs in the future will come mainly from the service sector (European Commission, 1996: 8), that the services that local initiatives and others covered in this book describe are best characterized as 'relational services' – that is, services based on direct interaction between the service provider and user. Such services are clearly distinct from standard services such as banking, insurance, telecommunications and public administration, which deal with codifiable information and are therefore of an industrial nature (see Baumol, 1967). At a time when industry and standardizable services – the bedrock of expansion up to and including the 1970s – are having to cope with international competition and major changes in information-handling technologies, preventing them from maintaining the capacity to generate employment as they have done in the past, local initiatives may offer a way of creating activities and new jobs in the relational services.

The collective dimension of services

Some of the new EU and similar social economy initiatives are concerned with *collective services*, in the traditional sense of the term, particularly in response to environmental problems, such as improved management of natural resources or the quality of life in problem areas.

A typical example are the Régies de quartier in France, which take on people from such areas and are 'owned' in part by housing associations and local authorities in order to provide caretaking or security services, or to manage the physical and natural environment.

Alongside these collective services, other initiatives provide services that meet individual needs but are also of benefit to the local community as a whole; in this sense, we might reasonably describe them as *socially useful* or *quasi-collective services*. The fact that such services are publicly regulated shows that the anticipated benefits are expected not just to accrue to private consumers, but also to tackle broader issues of social justice or collective externalities.

An obvious example of a blurring of the distinction between individual and collective services is that of childcare provision. Here, various authorities become involved in the funding of childcare provision for reasons of equity, so as to make the service accessible to as many people as possible, and to carry out quality checks. They may also intervene to generalize positive externalities for society in general, for example by facilitating the greater availability of women in the labour market or by enhacing the educational role of childcare facilities. The same goes for other personal services. For instance, initiatives providing housing for AIDS victims cannot be seen as just a service to individuals because they also pose the question of what place such people have in our society. The people behind these initiatives are carers who want to find alternative solutions to hospitalization for persons excluded from the family environment. By the same token, home-help services for the elderly generate positive externalities for society, by offering alternatives to hospitalization and preventing health expenditure on the elderly.

Another type of quasi-collective role fulfilled by the new initiatives recognized by the EU, but now for workers rather than consumers, concerns employment integration. Although the initiatives seek to integrate individuals into work, they also internalize the social costs that firms generally externalize, along with ensuring that occupational integration objectives go hand in hand with service provision proper. The originality of the initiatives lies in refusing to recruit people because they belong to 'target groups'; job integration is seen as the by-product of servicing a social need.

The democratic dimension

Local initiatives focusing on both the individual and the collective aspects of service provision blur the dividing line between the economic and the social. Key actors feel strongly that democracy cannot be achieved solely by making social adjustments to the market mechanism. For them, democratic relationships need to be embedded within economic initiatives, especially when market and state dynamics are unable to provide work for the active population as a whole. Accordingly the actors often see the initiatives as a means of extending democracy at the local level through the economy rather than the other way round. Such a goal is seen to be achieved, for example, by the role of the initiatives in internalizing social or environmental costs which tend to be externalized by other businesses. The local initiatives take responsibility for functions such as the occupational integration of disadvantaged people and the long-term unemployed, as well as for long-term development strategies for maintaining the local heritage and protecting the environment. The democratic goal is also considered to be attained by complying with such principles as occupational equality between men and women or accessibility to the goods and services produced.

The new initiatives are more than simply a source of jobs. They belong to a development model which embraces social cohesion and active citizenship. The initiatives belong to the 'social' or 'solidarity' economy, and, for this, share common traits.

Founding the local social economy

One of these traits relates to how the initiatives arise. A striking aspect of local service initiatives as opposed to other forms of business creation is their ability to gain backing from a social support network shaped by similar concerns and reflecting their democratic dimension.

Social support networks

Local initiatives are able to rally partners from different backgrounds. In some cases these are the *potential users of the services*, who identify a demand and seek to respond to it. In one case, for example, a group of young people decided to open a café with live music, Le Gueulard, in response to a need they felt personally (see Box 11.2).

BOX 11.2   The founders of Le Gueulard (France)

Le Gueulard was the brainchild in the 1980s of fifteen young people from disadvantaged districts of Nilvange, a town of 8,000 inhabitants in the region of Thionville in Lorraine, who met regularly in cafés. At the time, the group complained that there was nowhere to go where people could express themselves and feel at home: 'We couldn't find anywhere around here where everyone felt at home and which gave us a good image, while performing a certain cultural function. So we said: why not set one up ourselves?'

The social ethos of the establishment stemmed above all from the 'humanist' ideal (to use their own words) of its founders, promoting tolerance, open-mindedness, a listening environment, activity and social interaction. Tolerance and acceptance of differences both by a conventional and reserved population and by the institutions have developed as Le Gueulard itself has promoted these values.

At the time the project was created, 1984, the founders all had long hair, and they feel now that this gave them a bad image in the town at the very time when they felt a need for integration through a social and cultural life that they could structure themselves. It was against this background that Le Gueulard came into being.

The mayor of Nilvange played an important mediating role with the institutions: 'They all had long hair. Inevitably that made the place a den of iniquity in the eyes of the police and they raided it on many occasions ... it took all a great deal of effort to intercede and tell them that wasn't the way to go about things; the fact that they had long hair did not necessarily make them drug addicts, and so on and so forth. In the end, we sorted it out but there were a lot of teething problems at the start, particularly as they were also getting a bad press in the other cafés, which focused on this aspect.'

It was the mayor and the local council who pleaded the cause of the music café to a local population that was initially very hostile. In fact, the public was won over so completely that the planning officer has become a member of the town council.

In other cases *professionals* act as intermediaries and identify social demands which have not yet been catered for in order to bring about the creation of new initiatives. Such professionals may be local public officials, individuals directly involved in the sector in which the service has been developed, or intermediaries helping new organizations to get off the ground. There are also *mixed groups of users and professionals*: a gap may be identified as a result of contact between individuals who have encountered certain needs in their daily lives and professionals aware of particular problem areas.

Other ventures arise out of *shared awareness of a problem perceived as urgent and requiring action*. Despite the diverse backgrounds of the people involved, they have a common experience that has made them 'demand side stakeholders' (see Ben Ner and Van Hoomissen, 1991). This enables the support groups to generate real ideas for services, because their starting point is the perception that there are no suitable answers to the problems they are encountering. In this, the new venture differs from standard approaches shaped solely by market or social needs analysis. The clear message is that public authorities wishing to support local initiatives must concentrate more on promoting the emergence of such 'demand side stakeholders' than on researching unsatisfied needs.

Local orientation is an integral factor, because the appearance of such stakeholders involves proximity in two senses: objective proximity in the geographical sense, and subjective proximity shaped by the relational dimension of the service. Action depends on the creation of a local forum for dialogue based on interactive exchange which enables supply to be matched with demand without imposing stereotyped answers on the needs that are identified. This helps to reorient service provision towards the joint construction of supply and demand in which users play a key role, through their own direct initiative, through the intervention of professionals aware of unsatisfied demand, or through partners concerned about the issue in question.

Social and civic entrepreneurs

While the social network is an active component of local initiatives, the impetus provided by entrepreneurs is essential for their success. However, their motivation is not purely material. While entrepreneurs obviously desire a return on investment, they also seem keen on developing new ways of 'living together' through their shared concern for a common good. A feature of such entrepreneurs is their desire to enhance democracy at local level through economic activity. They are known as 'social and civic entrepreneurs' because their economic activity is shaped by a model of society-serving economy. For example, although the director of Kinderbüro (Box 11.3) says that the initiative has a commercial nature, the route she has taken

---

BOX 11.3   The founder of Kinderbüro (Germany)

The whole concept of Kinderbüro rests on the knowledge, professional track record, campaigning spirit, personality and reputation of its founder Gisela Erler, and in particular her strong feelings about the situation of women.

Gisela Erler is a trained sociologist and worked in this capacity for twenty years at the Deutschen Jungen Institute in Munich. Her research there concentrated on the family and working women. In 1987 she published the *Müttermanifeste*, which had a strong impact among her peers, in the press and among the political parties.

Her ecological awareness led her to become active in the Green Party, which set up a whole range of working parties on the status of women, reconciling work and family life, and so on, in the 1980s. She reports that, in practice, the Greens had very conventional ideas about the role of women. Just as progress was being made, German unification and the deteriorating economic situation meant that nothing was done to resolve women's work–family dilemma. There were other priorities to worry about.

Her German and American background, and various visits to the United States, together with her acute perception of the situation of women, drew the founder of Kinderbüro into the ranks of the enterprise creators, with a number of aims:

- helping women to reconcile work and family;
- creating jobs to develop outside of Kinderbüro;
- changing the relationship between private enterprise and the state;
- improving the professional skills of the people recruited and putting the relationship between families and staff on a more professional footing.

shows how important her own ideas about the role of women have been in getting the project off the ground.

Project partnerships

The links between support networks and entrepreneurs vary among different initiatives. The entrepreneur may mobilize the network, just as the network may lead to the emergence of the entrepreneur. These two interlinked components should always be considered as such. However, they should not be confused with the third, and just as indispensable, component, which is local partnership. The hypothesis that can be put forward from an observation of local support systems is that there is a risk of partnership becoming an end in itself rather than a means to an end. Partnerships are supposed to break down barriers that hinder public action, in particular by improving coordination between state and local authorities. Faced with operational difficulties, partnerships can become dominated by an inter-institutional logic which, rather than mobilizing local society, can swell the ranks of social engineers whose powers of expertise lie in their knowledge of administrative circles, resources and procedures. The paradox of local partnership in such a context is that its initial concern to shift decision-making closer to the 'grassroots' can end up with problems being tackled in a technical way by forums monopolized by specialists.

To ensure that target groups remain genuinely and actively involved, public authorities must place themselves in a situation where they can listen to and enter into a dialogue with the society that they claim to serve. It is by finding the right balance between *respecting the autonomy of the project* and *providing a supportive partnership* that local initiatives can work best. Such awareness can yield innovative institutional changes, including new laws recognizing the originality of operating methods (see Box 11.4 for the law on social co-operatives in Italy).

Sometimes laws are given substance by innovations originating in the community at large. One example is Exodus. In 1975, Law 354 establishing alternative penalties for prisoners was passed in Italy. At the end of 1986, the judge responsible for overseeing the terms and conditions of prisoners' sentences and the charity Catholic Aid noted that there was a legal framework making it possible to deploy

BOX 11.4   Legal recognition of social welfare co-operatives (Italy)

The operating principles of social co-operatives were recognized and legitimized by Law 381 of 8 November 1991. Since 1981 such co-operatives had been calling for a national law in keeping with the specific nature of this type of co-operative. Labour co-operatives are in principle intended to provide their workers with ownership of a production resource, whereas social solidarity co-operatives mobilize a broader and more heterogeneous social base.

The contribution of the 1991 law, which was debated for almost ten years before being passed, was to recognize the goals of such enterprises, defined not to maximize the interests of their partners but to look for 'the human advancement and social integration of citizens as a way of serving the general interests of the community'. This law thus establishes the principle, reserved in the past for associations, of social solidarity, putting founding principles of the co-operative movement on an institutional footing.

Source: Law of 8 November 1991, No. 381, 'Regulation of social welfare co-operatives'; definition in Article 1.

alternative penalties for people in prison, but that there were no specific schemes to implement these alternative penalties. They asked Brescia's consortium of social co-operatives (Sol. Co. Brescia) to come up with a project: Exodus was launched at the end of 1987.

From local initiatives to social and solidarity economy

Although the new local initiatives share common features at their origins, their types of economic institutionalization can vary. Poised between for-profit markets and public-sector objectives of general interest are social enterprises with hybrid mixes of resource and institutional form (see Figure 11.1; also Borzaga and Defourny, 2000; Nyssens, 2006).

FIGURE 11.1   Local initiatives: from emergence to institutionalization

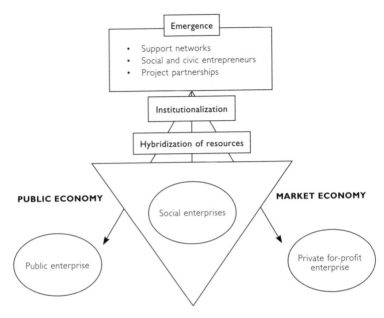

A distinctive type of institutionalization is now appearing through local initiatives, involving a hybrid mixture of commercial, non-commercial and non-monetary resources. This is not just a temporary means of operation associated with the establishment of an initiative, but one increasingly becoming a permanent method of balanced management.

This institutional arrangement comes with different denominations in different countries (e.g. social co-operatives, self-help groups, community businesses, etc.). However, across the varying national contexts two common aspects are shared. First the initiatives share an *entrepreneurial dynamism* in the sense that the production of goods or services is carried out by a group relying on self-financing, assistance from the public authorities, and mobilization of non-monetary resources (voluntary workers, voluntary contributions). Second, they share *a social, environmental or cultural objective* in the sense that the activity is aimed not at increasing profit for its own sake, but at providing a service to stakeholders, with profit reinvested for this purpose.

La Feuille d'Érable: An example of social and solidarity economy

La Feuille d'Érable in Rennes, France, demonstrates the partnership innovations that can facilitate new activities committed to the social and solidarity economy. La Feuille d'Érable's economic operation in waste paper is built largely on an agreement signed in 1988 to maintain and develop the waste paper/cardboard recovery and recycling industries, which are of national importance. Then, France imported 50 per cent of its requirements for paper, cardboard and papermaking pulp. The city of Rennes agreement involves the various stakeholders and trades in the waste paper/cardboard recovery and recycling industry. It accepts that self-financing of enterprises through the sale of recovered materials is an illusion which must be set aside if the recycling industry is to be supported. It was through its ability to mobilize public resources that La Feuille d'Érable was able to continue its activity. Non-commercial resources amount to almost 50 per cent of its operating budget. New national regulations allowing the removal of household waste by third-party ventures ensured that La Feuille d'Érable was able to rely on public contracts, which have ensured its survival.

The public support allows La Feuille d'Érable both to survive and to deliver its social and solidarity commitments. The support comes in the form of price guarantees for an agreed volume of waste paper collected by the social enterprise, which enables it to have stable resources that ensure the continuity of its activity. Under the agreement the enterprise recovers 2,300 tonnes of waste paper/cardboard from a population of 200,000, guaranteeing a turnover of €161,000 per year. La Feuille d'Érable was the first venture to benefit from such a contract in a city. The scheme is now replicated in 300 communes or groups of communes in France.

Such financial cushioning is not an obstacle to core social economy principles. Quite the contrary. The enterprise continues to rely on and attract voluntary help. For example, La Feuille d'Érable enjoys the voluntary, unprejudiced involvement of its project managers. Though now less important than when the venture was launched, this input is still crucial for the continuation of the project. It also relies on civic volunteers, who organize events and awareness-raising events on recycled paper in schools. It would be impossible to carry out such activities without them. It is through such actions that the non-commercial aspects of the enterprise's original objectives are achieved, namely the promotion and distribution of recycled paper and raising public awareness of the problems of wastage, recovery and recycling. Finally, La Feuille d'Érable relies on the participation of users. Such participation is difficult to measure, but is vital for the economic operation of the service: local collection could not take place without a process of selective sorting at source. User involvement helps to increase waste recovery and efficiency. It is estimated to have reduced costs by 50 per cent.

Policy recommendations

Public support for the social and solidarity economy still lacks clarity on the prime function of this sector, specifically its relationships to social measures against unemployment. From the 1980s, different states in Europe have come to recognize the role of local initiatives in this sector, but only as a vehicle for reintegrating the most disadvantaged into work. Strongly conditioned by social measures to combat unemployment, the initiatives found themselves forced into the rationale of the employment programmes being implemented, losing sight of their original aims (see Box 11.5). Once they fall into this trap, the local initiatives are redirected from the objective of exploring new means by which tomorrow's activities and jobs can be created towards becoming a palliative potentially legitimating deteriorating working conditions and wages.

Turning to more practical concerns, the obstacles most frequently encountered by ventures in the social and solidarity economy affect all stages of the initiative, from the original idea to start-up and operation. *In the initial phase*, when putting together the idea of the project, promoters are obliged to 'prove themselves' in order to obtain funding. This introduces automatic selection, even in schemes most open to innovation. The initial screening process eliminates many projects that are highly motivated but unfamiliar with the institutional channels of financing. This bias especially affects disadvantaged communities, which, instead of being assisted in putting together their projects, are systematically discouraged

BOX 11.5 The significance and limitations of social policy unemployment programmes

To counter increasing unemployment through active employment policy, and in the light of the evident limitations of training and recruitment subsidies, various social policy measures directed towards employment have been developed in Europe. Based on new forms of work combining productive activity and social integration measures, these take their inspiration from a simple observation. On the one hand, there remain a number of unsatisfied needs, and, on the other, a large number of people remain unemployed. It would therefore appear logical to promote job creation in activities responding to the latent demand.

One limitation of this linkage relates to the replacement of qualitative with quantitative targets, under the pressure of the sheer volume of unemployment that needs tackling. Support becomes a question of numbers. However strong the understanding at the beginning of the programmes that the jobs created will not substitute regular jobs in the private or public sector, or effortlessly facilitate reintegration, its significance is gradually eroded.

The social programmes then serve a second permanent labour market, one in which the unemployed continue to be found only temporary work. In this situation, in many ways unprecedented, a restrictive definition of the initiatives leads to their assimilation into a particular type of social programme. Rather than being considered on their own terms, they are treated as an amalgam of social measures and new activities. The outcome is reciprocal frustration – the representatives of local communities and the public sector who encourage activities in this field are disappointed with the results obtained, while the promoters complain of lack of support. The consequence is the proliferation of temporary, menial work, against the central principles of the social and solidarity economy.

because their ideas are deemed unrealistic according to standard administrative criteria.

In such unfavourable conditions, the only projects to get through are those whose promoters are well versed in the ins and outs of administrative procedures, those supported by local worthies, or those which enjoy the services of local development actors (provided by the social institutions, local authorities, etc.). Opportunities are far from equal.

In the start-up phase of projects there is a need for recognition of the intangible investment needed for projects to succeed. Projects cannot simply be thrown together, and the construction process is made more complex by the multiplicity of environments faced: socio-cultural (users, self-help networks, etc.), commercial (for market resources), institutional and political/administrative (for non-market resources). Traditional structures for supporting business creation fail to recognize the multidimensional nature of social and solidarity economy projects. There is therefore a need for methods attentive to the whole creation process, making available specialist help as and when required. Without this kind of support, any absence of professional expertise can increase distrust among local authorities, who perceive the project as an added social expense or meriting only casual, one-off support with no follow-up. The fragile status of promoters and staff means that projects face constant problems of continuity, sometimes solved by recourse to standard employment and social integration measures, deflecting the project from its original social rationale. Furthermore, initial investment costs and the need to set up an operating budget raise problems which are often practically insurmountable without the input of the project creators' own resources.

During the operational phase the main danger lies in funders adhering strictly to standard practices and controls. Current structures provide little room for manoeuvre to initiate new contracts as needs develop, with enterprises confined to activities originally proposed, unless they are prepared to battle for the occasional funds earmarked for innovation. Such funds, however, which are available in most financing institutions, tend to be non-renewable and fail to unlock funding from other budget headings.

On the basis of these observations, eight proposals can be made, in concluding this chapter, to help remedy the most crucial problems. They mainly concern operating methods, which need to be adapted to local circumstances.

1. Financing intangible investment

To prevent the problem of too many projects being submitted, thus forcing ventures to lower wage costs as a means of financing and putting together activities without adequate planning, policy priority should be given to financing the intangible investment on which the quality of future services will depend. Public authorities could, for example, undertake to finance projects which aim to create sustainable jobs and contribute to strengthening social cohesion, as long as project promoters agree to work with an advisory structure to assist them in formalizing their project. To compensate for the failure of available funds to keep up with investment needs, which explains a good measure of failure and high turnover of projects, provision should be made for a one-year *grant for project construction*.

2. Training for project promoters

Training for people developing local initiatives in the social and solidarity economy should be encouraged and seen as distinct from training for business creation, which fails to take into account the factors at play in the emergence of such initiatives, such as the wide variety of ways in which institutions become involved. The organization of training specific to local initiatives is even more crucial in view of the fact that project promoters are forced to rely on voluntary input, which clearly generates selection biases. This is why *paid training* should be given to project promoters who have already completed the first stage, to provide them with a recognized period to get all activities under way.

3. Engineering for project start-up

Another recurring difficulty relates to financing management work because of the length of time needed to win the confidence of partners and clients and the wide variety of resources needed to negotiate with various partners. Various ways are found to get around this problem, including: underpayment of directors, giving priority to the volume of output at the expense of quality, recourse to state employment reintegration measures to recruit the first employees. All such responses have a negative impact because they give credence to the belief that local initiatives consist of badly paid and menial tasks shoddily thrown together into a project. Two types of start-up aid could be used to prevent this: a programme of *aid to help create management and supervisory positions* within the initiatives, or a programme of *aid to secure an operating budget*.

Such intervention would help to reduce the wage burden, which is a crucial factor at start-up, without forcing the project initiators to resort to official unemployment measures and the restrictions they come with. It is essential to ensure that start-up funding is freed from policies targeting specific populations. Ventures need to be able to select according to the skills required and not the availability of particular agents under government aid programmes without considering the nature of the activity concerned.

4. Support to increase the professional status of jobs created

Since training for employees should be closely adapted to the work done, *access to continuing training funds* must be increased. For homecare services in particular, training, monitoring and exchange of experience on work carried out, and psychological support are all factors in improving the quality of the service. Payment, which at present is discretionary and linked to external training leading to qualifications, must be made general and also extended to support continuing internal training.

It is also important to *establish recognized means of formalizing the content of training* developed in initiatives, which in some cases could act as a 'prototype'. Public authorities could then properly support measures to upgrade the professional status of jobs, since such measures would be born out of experience. What is needed is assistance that can respond to the demands arising from collective reflection between ventures in similar activities, and the sharing of similar aspirations to upgrade the professional status of jobs.

5. Assistance for volunteers

While reliance on voluntary input due to lack of resources must be avoided, genuinely voluntary contributions should be encouraged. There are two ways in which public authorities could help: *financing voluntary service measures developed and implemented* by social economy federations and networks; and working with the competent authorities to establish a *general system to cover the risks* to which volunteer workers can be exposed, and to recognize rights associated with voluntary work, such as recognition of experience acquired through working with voluntary associations.

The way to avoid working on a cost-cutting, semi-official, basis in the social economy is to find a way of combining paid work with statutory guarantees for voluntary work, the value of which must be recognized in a society in which free time is increasing and in which there is a need to re-establish community ties.

6. Support for intermediaries

The capacity of local social economy initiatives to grow hinges to a large extent on the strength of second-level organizations such as consortia, networks or national committees which combine support and representation functions with other functions: such as *support, research, external communication*, and *internal communication*. Public support for these second-level institutions is of prime importance.

7. Building up a promotional environment

These measures depend upon a move to transform the political and administrative system into a real system for encouraging initiatives. The best approach is local, to ensure adequate responsiveness. A first change needed is in the way local authorities operate: social economy initiatives cannot be treated merely as an aspect of social policy, but *social economy advisers* should be appointed within departments dealing with economic affairs, employment and vocational training.

The advisers could draw up *multi-annual agreements* specifying the financial contributions expected from the various partners, measured against clear targets. This would mean that local initiatives would no longer need to waste their energy on permanently renegotiating funding arrangements, and concentrate instead on developing services and relations with users and clients. The agreements could also act as a form of quality assurance. A comprehensive report would be submitted annually to parties to the agreement, and the public authorities would be empowered to undertake any form of evaluation deemed necessary to decide on the renewal or amendment of a multi-annual agreement.

It is also important, in the interests of equality, for the public authorities to have teams of *developers* capable of helping local ventures to turn ideas into real projects. Such agents could receive training on a sectoral or regional basis or through volunteer advisory structures to increase their capacity for action in the field.

8. *Developmental public policies*

Finally, real policy support for the social economy must be of a developmental nature and include an element of trial and error. Progressive adjustments are only possible if there is a monitoring and evaluation body capable of giving real-time support, monitoring outcomes and proposing changes from time to time. Essentially, public policy decisions in this area, where activities are closely linked to the community, should not be purely technical and administrative, but open to democratic discussion.

Policy support, thus, has to establish *social dialogue on a local basis*, bringing together social partners, local politicians and representatives of associations. The aim should be to open up a whole new field of negotiation on the problems of local social cohesion and employment that can lead to real mobilization. This would mean tying existing

---

BOX 11.6   From network to public policies: France's solidarity economy

In France, enterprises identifying themselves with the social and solidarity economy launched an appeal in 1995 for recognition. These included the Comité national de liaison des Régies de quartier. In 1997 the networks were involved in a new appeal for policy recognition. They called upon the government to open the way for a right to initiative in this area, to support professionalization of jobs and networking of initiatives, set up regional funds for the development of local initiatives, and promote local social dialogue. In 2002, a national secretariat was established inside government for two years, and from 2004 several hundreds of elected public officers have been in charge of stimulating the social and solidarity economy at the local and regional levels, implementing innovative public policies in this field.

BOX 11.7 Collective agreement covering workers in Italian social co-operatives

Since 1 April 1992, the status of employees in social co-operatives has been governed by a collective agreement. The agreement was signed by various co-operative movements – the General Social Cooperative Association, the National Association of Service Co-operatives (LEGA), FEDER Solidarietà – and by the trade-union movements – the General Confederation of Italian Workers (CGIL), the Italian Confederation of Workers' Unions (CISL), the Union of Italian Workers (UIL).

The agreement's aim is to organize relations between the various partners (private and public) and to identify and approve the economic integration of disadvantaged persons. To ensure that local issues can be adequately dealt with, provision has been made in the agreement for joint committees within each province. The main functions of these committees are to ensure that the collective agreement is properly applied and to verify the support procedures and integration process for the disadvantaged groups.

---

funds in the areas of social assistance, enterprise support, job creation and training into new negotiation arrangements. Negotiation could take the form of local concertation bodies bringing together employers, trade unions and association representatives. *Innovative public policies* are needed (see Boxes 11.6 and 11.7).

This could include financially supporting *transnational information and co-operation networks* so that a public culture of legitimacy around the social and solidarity economy can grow and so that actors and activists in different contexts can learn from each other and strengthen the global role and standing of this important sector of the economy. This book is one contribution in this direction.

References

Baumol, W.J. (1967) 'Macroeconomics of unbalanced growth: The anatomy of urban crisis', *American Economic Review* 58(3): 896–7.

Ben, A., and T. Van Hoomissen (1991) 'Non-profit organisations in the mixed economy', *Annals of Public and Cooperative Economy* 4: 519–49.

Borzaga, C., and J. Defourny, eds (2000). *The Emergence of Social Enterprise in Europe*, Routledge, London.

European Commission (1993) *Growth, Competitiveness, Employment: The Challenges and Way Forward into the 21st Century*, Luxembourg.

European Commission (1995) *Local Development and Employment Initiatives: Investigation in the European Union*, Brussels.

European Community (1996) *First Report on Local Development and Employment Initiative: Lessons for Territorial and Local Employment Pacts*, Commission working document, Brussels.

Laville, J.-L., and M. Nyssens (2001) *Les services sociaux entre associations. État et marché*, La Découverte, Paris.

Nyssens, M., ed. (2006) *Social Enterprise: At the Crossroads of Market, Public Policies and Civil Society*, Routledge, London.

Notes on contributors

María Sol Arroyo is an anthropologist with a Master's degree in social economy. In recent years, she has worked on the relationship between local economy and social economy. She has worked as a researcher at Trabajando por la Economía Social, a civic organization that promotes the social economy, and she also advises Argentine NGOs on issues of institutional growth and development.

Ash Amin is Professor of Geography and Executive Director of the Institute of Advanced Study at Durham University. He is a Fellow of the British Academy. He has advised OECD's Territorial Development Unit as, most recently, external expert on the OECD's study of Cape Town, 2008. He has written or edited fifteen books and a hundred articles and book chapters, served many international boards of social science journals, and held numerous research council and EU grants. His research interests include work on the dynamics of the social economy in the UK, urban and regional development, the politics of spatial and social equity, and various dimensions of social theory.

Carlo Borzaga is Professor in the Department of Economics at the University of Trento, where he teaches Political Economics and Labour Economics. He is president of the European Research Institute on

Co-operative and Social Enterprises, managing editor of the journal *Economic Analysis* and a member of the Italian Associations of Labour Economists (AIEL) and the European Research Network EMES (Emergence of Social Enterprises). He has written extensively on non-profit organizations, social enterprises and labour economics.

Jenny Cameron is Associate Professor in the Discipline of Geography and Environmental Studies at the University of Newcastle (Australia). She has worked with local and state governments and community agencies on participatory action research projects to initiate social enterprises. Her innovative work on using an assets- or strengths-based community development approach to foster economic diversity has been applied internationally in contexts that include the Philippines and Indonesia.

José Luis Coraggio is Full Researcher of the Instituto del Conurbano de la Universidad Nacional de General Sarmiento and Academic Director of the Master's Program in Social Economy. He coordinates the Latin American Research Network on Social and Solidarity Economy (RILESS) and has extensive experience in research, teaching and economic policy advising in Argentina, Mexico, Nicaragua and Ecuador. His current research is on the social economy, local development and social policies. He has written or edited more than 140 papers and 26 books.

Janelle Cornwell is a Ph.D. candidate in geography at the University of Massachusetts Amherst, working under the supervision of Professor Julie Graham. Her primary research interests include worker-owned co-operatives and other non-capitalist economic organizations and activities. She is currently conducting ethnographic research for her dissertation on community enterprises in the Pioneer Valley of Massachusetts.

The Community Economies Collective Kioloa is a writing group that was formed in December 2007 to reflect upon and write up the experience of social enterprise developments in which group members have been involved. The group included NGO representatives from the Philippines: May-an Villalba and Benilda Flores-Rom, executive directors of Unlad Kabayan Migrant Services Foundation Inc., and Maureen Balaba and Joy Miralles-Apag, founding members of Bohol Initiatives for Migration and Community Development. It also included academic members of an Australian Research Council and AusAID-funded action research project: chief investigators Professor Katherine Gibson and Dr Deirdre McKay, Department of Human Geography, Research School of Pacific and Asian Studies at the Australian National University; and ANU graduate scholars Amanda Cahill (Human Geography) and Jayne Curnow (Anthropology). Others included in the collective were ANU graduate scholars in Human Geography, Michelle Carnegie, Ann Hill and Gerda Roelvink. The collective jointly wrote up accounts of each social enterprise for a variety of popular, academic and policy audiences, and **Katherine Gibson** has reworked these into the current chapter.

Sara Depedri is research fellow in the Department of Economics at the University of Trento. She received her Ph.D. in Law and Economics at the University of Siena with a thesis on working relationships, incentives and contractual flexibility. Her current research focuses on motivations and worker satisfaction, especially in social co-operatives and non-profit organizations.

Julie Graham is Professor of Economic Geography at the University of Massachusetts Amherst. Under the pen name J.K. Gibson-Graham, she has co-authored with Katherine Gibson many books and articles challenging the usual vision of capitalism as the dominant or only viable form of economy. Over the past fifteen years she has been engaged in research, activism and teaching related to diverse development pathways and community economies, including the economy of generosity that is fuelled by gifts of labour, goods and money and the social economy comprising social and community enterprises, not-for-profits, co-operatives and other community-oriented organizations. Her most recent book with Katherine Gibson, *A Postcapitalist Politics*, focuses on building community economies in the face of globalization. The book draws upon their ongoing action research and examples from around the world of communities that are constructing their own economic institutions, enlarging the commons, and (re-)creating themselves as subjects who can desire, construct and inhabit 'other worlds'.

Jerzy Hausner holds the Chair of Public Economy and Administration at the Cracow University of Economics. He has been active in government since the end of Communism: from 1994 to 1996 he served as Director-General of the Prime Minister's Office; in 1997 he was appointed Undersecretary of State at the Prime Minister's Chancery and Government Commissioner for Social Security Reform; from 2001 to 2005 he was Minister of Labour and Social Policy, and then Minister of Economy, Labour and Social Policy and Minister of Economy and Labour; from 2003 to 2005 he was the Deputy Prime Minister. His research focuses on the interaction of economy and politics (political economy, public economy and public administration). He has authored 250 publications, including 51 books and monographs, 58 journal articles and 46 chapters in books.

Jean-Louis Laville is Professor at the Conservatoire National des Arts et Métiers (CNAM, Paris), Chair of Service Relations and Co-director of the Laboratoire Interdisciplinaire pour la Sociologie Economique (LISE UMR 6209), CNAM–CNRS. His work is in the field of economic sociology, in which he has written extensively about the alternative and social economies, through both theoretical and empirical inquiries. He is one of Europe's leading voices on the social economy, having led many large research projects in France and the EU. He is on the international editorial board of five journals.

Noëlle Lechat is Professor in the Social Sciences Department of UNIJUÍ, in Brazil. She has worked on the landless workers' movement and many other topics relating to the solidarity economy, gender, ethnicity, unemployment and social movements in Brazil. In 2005 and 2007 she coordinated a large project mapping solidarity economy enterprises in the Northwest Region of RS. She is actively involved in the solidarity economy, through her involvement in the Permanent Seminary of Popular Education, her coordination of an extension course in Solidarity Economy and the Incubator of Solidarity Economy of UNIJUÍ, and her contribution to helping create the Forum of Solidarity Economy of the Northwest Region of RS. She has contributed to a recent book, *The Other Economy*, in addition to writing many other publications on the solidarity economy.

Marguerite Mendell is Vice Principal and Associate Professor at the School of Community and Public Affairs and Director of the Karl Polanyi Institute of Political Economy, Concordia University, Montreal. She is a member of the editorial committee of the journal *Economie et Solidarité*, and member of the advisory board of *Studies in Political Economy*. Her current research concentrates on the areas of community economic development, alternative investment strategies, financial institutions and the social economy in Quebec, economic democracy and governance, and the life and work of Karl Polanyi. She is a member of the board of directors, Chantier de l'économie social, and former president of the Montreal Community Loan Association. She has published in both English and French on the social economy, local development, alternative investment strategies, economic democracy, and on the work of Karl Polanyi, especially as it relates to contemporary democratic economic development strategies.

John Pearce has worked in community development for more than forty years. He currently runs his own consulting organization (Community Enterprise Consultancy and Research) and was formerly Chief Executive of Strathclyde Community Business. He is a director of CBS (Community Business Scotland) Network and of the Social Audit Network and has been an executive committee member of COMMACT (Commonwealth Association for Local Action and Development). In recent years he has focused on developing a social accounting and audit process suitable for social economy organizations and is a SAN-approved social auditor. He has facilitated social accounting throughout the UK and in India, New Zealand and Australia.

Index

160; national census 2005–7, 161;
National Conference of Solidarity
Economies 2006, 165; National
Service of Rural Learning
(SENAR), 171; Science and
Technology Ministry (FINEP),
163; social enterprise research, 18;
southern rural, 14; third sector
activism, 159
Brotherhood of St Laurence, 95

Callon, M., 9
Cameron, Jenny, 7, 18
Campaign for Community Values,
USA, 44
Canada, 15, 19; English, 179; Executive
Services Office, 125; Social
Sciences and Humanities Research
Council, 201; *see also* Quebec
capacity-building, 132, 201
capitalism: asset-stripping, 139; crises
of, 12; critics of, 3; production-line
characteristics, 146, 150; property-
rights regime, 140–41
CARE, Canada Fund for Local
Initiatives, 124
Cáritas, 171
Catholic Aid, 240
CDECs (community economic
development corporations)
Quebec, 184–5, 192
Central de Trabajadores Argentinos,
153
Centro Agricola, Massachusetts, 40;
'incubator', 49; NR, enterprises
housed, 39
CERES Community Environment
Park, Melbourne, 94
Chantier de l'économie sociale,
Quebec, 186–7, 195, 203; Board of
Directors, 188; cultural mediation
fund, 200; deliberative culture, 189;
expertise, 193; Fiducie, 196–9;
research capacity, 191
charities, 27
childcare provision, 235; Childcare
Network, 232; self-organized
crèches, 4, 8
China, 124
Christian Aid, 124

civic involvement: factors, 210, 220;
marginalized people, 129
Clark, A., 69, 71
clientelism(s), 214, 224, UK, 28, 31
Coin Street Community Builders,
29–30
collective ownership, 186–7
collective services, 234; quasi-, 235
Colon, Hilda, 55
Comité national de liaison des Régies
de quartier, 250
communication tools, 136
community: activism recuperation, 30;
benefit checks needed, 23; cultural
mobilization, 199; 'economics', 38,
48, 62; grassroots activism, 94;
intentional building, 44; land
trusts, 178; leadership issue, 55;
organizations' local legacies, 17
community business movement,
Scotland, 6
Community Economics Collective, 7,
18
community enterprises: as activism,
113; economic experimentation, 93,
107, 128; researcher (CER), 129, 133;
self-organized, 96; state support,
95; success criteria, 105–6; surplus
production purposes, 101; UK
reclassification, 29; *see also* social
economy; social enterprises
Community Partnering Project, 136
Community Renewal Programme,
Australia, 104–5
Community–University Research
Alliance (CURA), Quebec, 201–2
complementarity, with private sector,
213
concertation: bodies, 251; history of,
183
Confédération des syndicats nationaux
(CSN), Quebec, 184
Confederation of Workers' Unions
(CSIL), Italy, 251
confidence, generation of, 136
continuity: continuum concept, 28;
problems of, 246
co-operatives: autonomy, 160;
exchange activities, 10; farmer,
169; financial, 180; forced, 209;